The
Golf Mystic

Shifting the Paradigm

Gary Battersby

The
Golf Mystic

Published in the United States of America by Golf Mystic Publishers.

3909 Indian River Dr., Cocoa, Florida 32926

954-868-5545

www.golfmystic.net

ISBN 978-0-615-33079-2

Editor: Donna Dawson, CPE

Printed in USA

GB

To my parents,
who sacrificed their time and worked tirelessly to provide
six children opportunities that they never had.

Acknowledgments

Many thanks to all my friends who took the time to read the manuscript and make helpful suggestions, especially Kay Erlanson, who got me started; Kaysie Usher and Tristan Boyd, who took on the tedious task of transferring my handwritten notes to computer; Len Golub, who enlisted Nancy Popick in the first edit; Sari Mathes for her editing and insightful creative suggestions; Kim Martin for formatting the book; Harold Wine for his encouragement and support; Terry Miller for his candid observations, suggestions, and last push to finish the manuscript; and lastly my loving wife, Ali, for her unending support in this project and all areas of my life.

Foreword
by Bob Toski

When Gary asked me to write the foreword to *The Golf Mystic*, I readily agreed. Little did I know what a challenging task I had accepted. I had not yet read the work. As I began reading the manuscript and reached deeper into it, I soon realized I was hardly prepared to write it. However, after taking the time to absorb all the material Gary presents and some long thought, I felt that I could acknowledge the tremendous insight and philosophical thinking described in this book about golf, the golf swing, and life. Indeed, Gary is reaching out with a message about his ongoing journey in life through golf.

I know one cannot standardize the art of teaching the golf swing, but this book gives some serious thought on how to improve the teaching and learning of this great game. I hope and believe this work will create a much-needed paradigm shift in golf instruction. *The Golf Mystic* will captivate you. I found the conversations throughout the book wonderfully intriguing, as they related to golf and life. I consider this book an immense achievement. It is hard to imagine the time and effort it took to produce this unique work for both learning and reading pleasure.

For me, there are not enough words to describe the beauty of Gary's writing. One should read it more than once to grasp the depth of thought and insight. My thanks, congratulations, and sincere best wishes to Gary for writing *The Golf Mystic*.

3/17/2011

CONTENTS

Introduction 1

Part One

1.   Reminiscing 7
2.   The First Day: Joe's Story 29
3   The Lesson Begins 39
4   Awareness: Feel or Analysis 57
5   Just Fly the Plane 67
6   A New Day 81
7   The Physics—and the Feeling 87
8   If the Club Is OK, the Swing Is OK! 91
9   The Grip 113
10   Defining Moments 119
11   Beginning Players: Aiming 131
12   True Fundamentals 139
13   Ditch Digging 143
14   Fishing 155
15   Why Golfers Slice 167
16   My Swing— and My Brain 185
17   Swing Styles 195
18   The Curl Again 203
19   Arcs and Swing Length 213

Part Two

20   Larry Finds His Path and Walt Feels the Energy 219
21   Judy: A New Golfer Gets a Grip 235
22   Wally: Slimming Down the Fat Shot 247
23   Freddie: Curing the Shanks 255
24   Personality Types 259

25   Tommy: The Kid's Alright 271

26   Back to Pompano 281

27   Robert: I Hate My Swing 293

28   Woo: Can He Trust the Twirl? 307

29   John: The Power of Visualization 317

30   Reflecting on My Future 327

31   Dinner 337

32   My Last Night 347

INTRODUCTION

T his story had to be written. That belief is based on my experience of a life in golf. I began caddying at the age of eight, first at Grosse Isle Country Club in Michigan, then at the Sharon Golf Club in Ohio, and finally at Congressional CC in Potomac, Maryland. I caddied for the best players and observed as many talented golfers as I could.

As time passed, I began working at these courses in every capacity. I cleaned clubs, worked the range, and washed dishes for parties. I was on the golf maintenance crew, where I began working at the bottom rung of the ladder. With my brother Alan, I weeded flower beds, tees, and greens.

We had the good fortune at these clubs to have fine skilled leaders with integrity, leaders who had great patience with our lack of experience. As time went on Alan left golf, but I stayed. I learned to maintain machinery and grow healthy turf. At the same time I took advantage of the employee privileges that allowed me to practice my game.

Years later, with the help of several friends and my partner, Bob Toski, I developed the first Golf Learning Center in the United States at Broward College in Coconut Creek, Florida. We started from scratch and did almost everything ourselves. We had to clear the land; shape the tees, greens, and bunkers; dig irrigation; grow turf; and plant trees. All the while my mind was preoccupied with developing better ways to teach and communicate about the golf swing. I kept practicing and teaching. My teaching continues to evolve, but now taking center stage in my work are the many relationships that have developed because of this great game. I treasure these friendships beyond measure.

Over the years, there has hardly been a moment when golf was not on my mind and in my heart. This game, and the golf swing itself, has brought

1

intrigue, wonder, sorrow, and joy to my life. In recent years, however, I have disagreed with the direction in which the game has been heading, especially golf swing instruction. I am skeptical about some of those who have been chosen to lead the game. I believe the majority of golfers deserve better than they are getting. Thus, the need to write this book.

Rather than writing a typical golf instruction book, I wanted to create something unique in style and content. Because I have witnessed such struggle and frustration at every level, I also wanted to provide the tools needed for golfers to improve. And I hope to entertain the reader a little along the way.

I would love everyone to know that within them they hold unique potential and that there is a way to draw it out without spending a fortune and a lifetime on the practice tee! The goal of this book is to encourage golfers to begin thinking usefully on their own and trusting their instincts so they can ultimately enjoy the game like never before. My method begins with developing enough awareness and confidence to feel safe and carefree with one's swing. It culminates when a golfer looks forward to getting out on the course and playing the game to their potential.

I believe golf mirrors life in the emotions, the learning, the sport of it, and the relationships it fosters. In keeping with those ideas, this narrative provides a window into the heart and mind of a golfer who has lost his way, both in his professional life and his personal relationships. During his journey, the golfer begins to transform, with the help of a seasoned mentor who had experienced similar struggles. He provides strategies that awaken and free our golfer from his self-created failure. But ultimately, deep and profound change is always a choice, and the decision is in the hands of the decider.

Freedom and peace of mind are probably two of the most sought-after quality of life goals. Golf has the potential to elicit great feelings of freedom. We play the game outdoors all over the world on beautiful natural terrain. This is one of the most appealing aspects of the game. Whether we're walking nine holes at the local 'muni' after work or playing for a national championship, golf has the potential to provide limitless feelings of freedom, achievement, sorrow, gratitude, struggle, and joy. Every emotion conceivable will manifest itself at one time or another if you play the game long enough.

Golf encompasses so much of what makes us human and so much of what makes life worthwhile. We must not lose this perspective, no matter why we play the game. I hope that in reading this story you catch a glimpse of yourself and learn something. If readers can smile, chuckle, or shake their heads in amusement, I have in some small way been successful.

PART ONE

1
REMINISCING

Curled under the blankets, trying to stay warm, I anxiously waited for the alarm to go off. I had given up trying to sleep hours before. Every ten minutes or so, my eyes would open and squint at the red numbers on the clock radio, willing them to tell me it was five AM I had an early flight to catch.

It had been bitter cold, the kind of brutal New England winter when your feet dread the morning floor and the shower can't steam up fast enough. I was happy to be getting away from the dark days and grimy slush for even a little while. I pushed myself out of bed. The smiling TV weatherwoman was forecasting a Nor'easter, but her sadistic grin held no power over me. I would soon be in the tropical land of Bermuda grass, sand, and sunshine. In no time, I was dressed, packed, and waiting by the front window for my ride. Before long, the cabbie pulled up and flashed his lights. I locked up and was on my way.

The cabbie was obviously an expatriate from an equatorial country: heat wafted through the partition as we headed for the airport. Fifteen minutes later, he handed over my bags and took my money with fingerless gloves, hustling back into his four-wheeled furnace before either of us could utter a thank you.

I checked my luggage and went through the usual security rigmarole. I grabbed a *Boston Herald* and stood on yet another line to board.

Eventually, I was on the plane and belted into my seat. But we sat for a good thirty minutes with no movement. A flight attendant finally explained that we were waiting for de-icing. I wondered if the plane was going to get off the ground before the storm hit. I turned to the sports section, but my attention wandered.

This journey was essential—it was when I would either realize my quest or abandon it. Claire had accused me of running away from her and from reality. I hadn't been able to make her understand that this trip wasn't about fleeing because I hadn't been able to make it clear to her, or myself, exactly what I was pursuing.

Could I find him? Would he agree to work with me? Would I be able to learn from him? Could he change my golf teaching philosophy and help me find my groove? Would my dream come true or was I in search of the Holy Golf Grail?

A family of four occupied the three seats directly in front of me. Nice, I thought, a winter vacation in sunny Florida, family-style. However, the two boys were chattering at high pitch, squawking for their parents' permission to order Cokes. I shuddered to think how they'd sound after a dose of caffeine. It was barely breakfast time and they were already marching their dirty little boots up the backs of the seats in front of them. It amazes me when parents think their little darlings are the entertainment crew and that when the kids are performing, the parents are off duty. Dad let his seatback down and cracked my kneecaps.

Beside me, in the aisle seat, was a middle-aged woman who seemed to think she owned the whole row, including the entire overhead compartment. One of her bulging carry-on bags wouldn't fit in the compartment, so she crammed it under the seat—in front of me. Patience was never my strong point. "This is the last time I fly," I muttered, not caring if my neighbors heard the irritation in my voice.

But I knew it probably wasn't being crammed, sardine-style, into the middle seat in coach, these people, or the tedious airline procedures that were the real sources of my frustration. Confusion and negativity had dominated my emotional weather for more than a season. God knows there was a lesson for me here. The few mortals who remained in my life had advised me that my state of mind needed adjusting. Besides my golf game being in the gutter, my relationship with Claire had just ended.

Claire. She was beautiful, clichés be damned, both inside and out. She was smart. No, she was wise. She had the kind of common wisdom that you'd expect from someone older, someone who had had a lot of experience riding life's roller coaster. She was a serious woman in every sense of the word.

Wearing one of my old flannels, she could pass for a teenager, but in a dress, Claire defined 'woman.' Big hazel eyes, high cheekbones, golden skin, and hair the color of chestnuts in autumn. But gorgeous as she was, Claire didn't seem to know it.

Claire, my most difficult student. Serious and literal, she took her lack of golf skill in stride. Her lessons began as a Christmas gift from her fiancé, meant to convince her she wouldn't become a golf widow after the wedding. Jason accompanied her to her lessons, although his ability on the golf course was exceptional. He wanted immediate results, but Claire seemed hopeless. She'd roll her eyes and toss her bangs to the side with every missed shot, tension ricocheting between her and Jason.

I tried to make light of it, to break the tension, but Jason's interest in Claire diminished with her lack of progress. By Easter, there wasn't much to mask his derision and her disdain. At a Mothers' Day outing with Jason's parents, Claire handled herself with dignity when Jason's mother, a matronly golf queen, deadpanned that he shouldn't want her for a caddy, much less a wife. Jason apparently agreed. By Memorial Day, she was coming for her lessons alone.

It took a while, but when I finally got up the nerve to ask her out for coffee after a lesson, we followed up Starbuck's with burgers at a local dive. I took her to a comedy film festival for our first real date, and by Labor Day, we were an item.

Claire was a little older than me, but that only seemed to make her more fragile. Jason, among others, had eroded her trust. And she had seen things as a nurse, and later as a social worker, that had opened her eyes to the darker side of human nature. She wore a serious demeanor like battle armor. If my mission was to make her laugh, hers was to make an adult of me. She indulged my taste for the Three Stooges, Fletch, and Britcoms, while I humored her by sitting through *Gone with the Wind* and countless Cary Grant movies. We both loved romantic comedies, but saved them for the rain.

We learned to cook together and mastered the art of the perfect burger. That was at the beginning, when everything was perfect. Then, with my game spiraling downward, my golf practice consumed my time. She complained that I was emotionally unavailable, whatever that meant, and it caught me completely off guard. I got defensive. Didn't she understand that I was making a last-ditch effort to get my career on track? She couldn't seem to accept the time and commitment my career required, just as I was surprised to hear that our relationship needed more of those same things.

I thought she would be the one, but the timing was obviously off. She wanted serious commitment, while I was content to enjoy the pre-honeymoon of our getting to know each other better while I dealt with the really important stuff in my world, like my golf game. Yeah, I was head over heels for Claire, but I figured she should just know how I felt and trust we'd have a future together. Somehow it all fell apart before I could tell her.

Sitting there on the runway, reminiscing, I knew I needed to be more positive if I was going to get anything of value from the next few days. I felt broken and depressed about practically everything in my life, especially how things had ended with Claire. Somehow, contemplating how this trip had come together, I managed to lie back in my seat and close my eyes. I fell into a semi-conscious state.

My mind drifted over the whirlwind of events this past weekend—the golf summit in New Orleans, back to Boston for an overnight, catching this flight to Ft. Lauderdale, and all the little coincidences that had led me to this seat on this plane.

My teaching had provided me with a decent income. I was a popular instructor and many golfers sought me out. My reputation, built on a great eye for finding flaws in a golf swing, was something I prided myself on. It made me feel good, and I had made a career of it. But deep down I felt something was missing. Lately I had been dissatisfied with the direction my career was taking. The depth of my boredom was quite evident when I'd recently found myself watching the clock during lessons, wishing they would end. My teaching had become listless.

It was embarrassing for me, a teaching golf pro, to admit I really wasn't interested in my students' problems, at least not as much as my own. To be completely honest, I didn't believe I was good at teaching or at playing the game. I had pretended for a long time, concealing these sentiments, until I could no longer bear the feeling of being an imposter. I had to either get out of the game completely or change the course I was following.

What became painfully obvious, though, was that hard as I tried, I could not change on my own. I had tried all kinds of ways to get interested again, to bolster my confidence, but nothing seemed to last. Just when I'd think I was making progress, reality would set in and I'd be back at square one.

Then one day I was checking out the program for the National Golf Teachers Symposium, a sort of summit meeting of the so-called best golf teachers in America. This year it was in New Orleans. Though I had decided to boycott these events just a year earlier, this one was different: I had long before accepted an invitation to speak at the symposium. But there was a problem now. Me. I just wasn't into it. Sure, I could go through the motions of giving a presentation, but I was unlikely to get anything out of the other sessions.

On top of that, these meetings usually become major social events. I'm not a great socializer to begin with; after Claire, I was feeling pretty anti-social. Partying did not appeal to me. I would be better off not attending. I had more serious matters to tend to. I needed to break my golf roadblock. My instruction was stale and going nowhere fast, but I didn't know how to stop it.

But then something changed my mind. Just as I was about to pick up the phone and cancel my appearance, my eyes had fallen on the list of speakers. Just below my name was another that caught my eye—and piqued my curiosity: Joe Burlington.

Burlington had a sort of mystical allure in golf circles. If he were in politics, he would be considered a fringe element. He was deliberately and proudly different. He wasn't cast in the mainstream golf teacher mold. Some people derisively called him a rebel; others held him as a guru. I was surprised he was speaking at the summit at all. I knew Burlington's approach to teaching was radically different from mine and fundamentally different from everything popular in golf, from the traditional school to the currently accepted state of the art. But maybe a dose of Joe Burlington's far-fetched, off-the-wall philosophy was exactly what I needed.

I had heard bits of gossip about him over the years from other pros, but Burlington's name did not really come up very often. He had almost disappeared some ten years before; as far as I knew, he wasn't even teaching anymore. Despite his unorthodox style, I had heard some wonderful things about his teaching. I guess one could say Joe Burlington was a bit of a golfing legend. Talk was that he had a gift—he could always get the most from the least. Curious golf teachers from all over would come to watch him work. Some became fans, others critics.

Burlington's communication skills and ability to flight a golf ball were uncontested, but it was the way he used his various interests and hobbies to engage his students' learning that was controversial. Teachers who had worked with him praised him to the heavens. They said you had to experience Joe Burlington personally to have any idea of how special he was. "There isn't a teacher alive with more talent, awareness, and compassion than Joe Burlington," one of my golf teaching heroes told me. Burlington's critics found his offbeat persona entertaining fodder for jokes.

If I could arrange to meet him at the summit and discuss my problems with him, maybe he could give me a strategy that would extricate me from some of my problems. I figured his would at least be a different approach, and I needed *something* to shock me out of my inertia.

I was going to the symposium after all. I would take the opportunity to seek him out, with the hope that he could turn my game around, give me some magic. The sudden clarity of my decision surprised me. It was not a decision based on logic. It was born of desperation—in my mind, Burlington was my eleventh-hour effort before I threw in the golf towel for good. I would be totally honest with him and hold nothing back—no more masks, no more pretending. I'd just let it all hang out and see what came of it.

I had arrived in New Orleans the night before the summit and planned to attend Joe's talk, which was right after mine. I thought I'd introduce myself backstage and take it from there.

I had presented my session rather robotically, just going through the motions, and answered questions on autopilot. Nothing I said was new, but thankfully my talk seemed well received. I was distracted by my real reason for being there.

Anxious to get to a good seat for Burlington's session, I had hurried from the hall where I had given my talk. I made my way quickly around the oval building to the larger theater where Burlington was to speak. I arrived early—the doors hadn't opened yet. I took a seat outside and waited. The sign near the door read,

Speaker: Joe Burlington,
Topic: The Future of Golf Instruction

Interesting title, I thought. A few other pros were gathering around the entrance. When the locks turned and the doors creaked open, I raced inside to get a seat close to the stage. Within minutes, many people had filed into the hall.

The stage was set with only a solitary chair and a small table holding a glass of water. The simplicity contrasted with the atmosphere of most golf seminars. Normally stages were filled with chalkboards, props, electronic devices, and video screens. Presenters were essentially selling the latest gadgets—all the newest instruction accessories and devices. Burlington's setup seemed bare and incomplete.

I was psyched for Joe's arrival. The packed hall was noisy—everyone was chattering in anticipation of what the enigmatic golfer would have to say. The lights finally dimmed and the room fell silent. Onto the stage strode Joe Burlington. Tall and slender, but with a sinewy, muscular build, he had a crop of reddish-brown hair and a coppery tone to his face. The Florida sun had taken its toll. Burlington had distinctive features: high cheekbones, a prominent jaw, and deep lines across his forehead. His arms were long and well-defined, his hands massive. He wore a yellow knit shirt, khaki slacks, and moccasins with no socks. Joe Burlington definitely did not dress the part of a typical golf pro. He appeared confident. The audience began to applaud with what seemed a warm greeting. When the noise quieted, he had walked slowly to the front of the stage, looked into the audience, and begun.

"Thank you all for coming. I am delighted to have been invited to share with you tonight. I'm Joe Burlington, and it's been a long while since I've done anything like this." He paused, squinted up at the spotlights, and continued. "Well, let's get right to it. I'm here to talk about the future of golf instruction. The popularity of the game is flourishing throughout the world. Golfing has grown up." His voice boomed.

"Tonight I'd like to limit the discussion to how we approach instruction of swinging the club as it relates to the multitude of people who we now serve, our students. Secondly, it behooves us, as golf professionals, to examine the direction our teaching is headed, don't you think? I'd like to ask everyone to think about these questions for a minute."

Burlington paused and then fired his ammo. "Why did we all choose this profession? Are our instruction techniques really working? Are we making a positive impact or are we confusing our students? Are we actually moving in a better direction? Are we really serving our public well?"

He took a moment to let his audience absorb his buckshot questions. Immediately there seemed to be growing discomfort in the room. The air had changed. No one expected this stinging demand for self-examination. We were all used to feel-good, ego-stroking seminars that praised our efforts—pep rallies for the status quo. The pro sitting next to me had muttered, "Who does he think he is?"

But my God, we all should know these questions need to be asked. Agreeing with Joe Burlington appeared put me deep in the minority, though. The pros had been waiting for the jokes and small talk that usually warm up the audience; they weren't ready for Burlington's serious questions and obvious passion.

A pro near the front had raised his hand, and Joe sat down on the chair and gave him the floor. "Since we already seem to be getting deep into teaching philosophy, Mr. Burlington, what do you consider the most important aspect of learning a golf swing? What do you think is essential?" I had recognized this pro, but couldn't put a name to his face. He didn't look happy. I thought it was possible he was trying to trip Burlington up.

Burlington had been silent for a moment, then stood up. The whispering stopped; the hall was still. He had walked along the front of the stage, looking up to the lights again, and as he turned his eyes back downward, he stopped directly in front of the pro who had spoken and offered a pleasant smile. "A very good question. To really get down to the bare bones, the essentials, as you say, the only thing a golfer needs to do is create an environment of swing motion for release."

The pro had pursed his lips, but his eyes registered comprehension. He smiled back at Burlington with a nod of approval. Wow, I thought, Joe's answer immediately disarmed that pro. Whether the pro had meant to provoke an argument or not, Burlington had just described the essence of the whole golf swing in a single sentence. He had delivered, wrapped with a bow, what I considered the golf swing's Holy Grail.

But the pro hadn't finished with Burlington. "Could you clarify release?" He stressed each syllable of the last word as if they were separate words.

Without hesitation, Burlington had responded, "Release of the club's energy into the ball to the desired target."

"Then what do you mean by an environment of swing motion?"

"An environment of swing motion is a particular swing rhythm and path pattern that provides for the release. The key is that they are repeatable and, in my view, completely compatible with momentum and centrifugal force."

The front rows had remained quiet. Many of us had never heard such a complete, yet succinct, explanation of the essence of the swing. A few pros in the back, though, had begun to murmur among themselves. They didn't seem to want to be questioned.

"Any more questions before I continue?" Burlington had asked. No one moved. Then Burlington had asked another question. "Why is it that with all the advanced technology, instruction gadgets, video analysis, and special clubs, today's golfers, on average, are poorer players than they were years ago? Have any of you ever wondered?"

It was as if Burlington had bent down, put his hand upon my crown, screwed open my head, and snatched the thoughts right out of my mind. The audience had begun buzzing, but not from curiosity like I was. An undercurrent of displeasure and derision had become apparent in the whispers. Burlington waited and began again only after giving that part of the audience time to load and take aim.

"You see," he'd continued, "one problem is that we're losing creativity in our approach. We've signed on to one cookie-cutter way to impart our experience and it's in direct conflict with the way individuals learn. I believe we really must get on the wavelength of our students, meet them at the point where they are in their development, and then just nudge them in the best direction. As we teach, it's important to awaken students and show them how to use their tools of awareness."

Another pro in front had raised his hand. Joe graciously paused and acknowledged him. "Question?"

"I just wanted to know if your program gives students a roadmap to help them get where they're going."

Burlington had contemplated the question. Speaking in a low voice, almost to himself, he said, "How can I put this? Socrates said that our job as teachers is to help sharpen our students' sense of direction so that when they really get going and are on their own, they can travel without a map. Fellas," he'd said, "and ladies, the truth is that the most successful learning experience will leave the student confident and with no need for a coach anymore. Yes," he'd mused, "really, the goal for us as instructors is to become obsolete."

I could tell folks were really getting uncomfortable now. Over the rumbling, I had heard some comments. The consensus was that this philosophy would put us all out of work.

Burlington had continued. "From all I've heard recently, we're headed in the direction of trying to clone golfers, make them all the same, and teach them all the same. With the new technology and all, we have deluded ourselves into believing that there's no room for uniqueness." He had put his foot on the chair and leaned into the audience. "You see, I diametrically oppose that point of view. Each person is unique. It is our job to enter each student's own world and view it from their perspective. And then use all of a student's individual strengths to help him improve. I have found that if you approach instruction this way, it is likely that you will reduce inner and outer conflict. The student's mind and body will be more receptive. You will find that his or her potential will emerge and, more importantly, it will be sustainable.

"And just maybe, all these gadgets and theories are not really helping. Maybe they're just confusing the issue. I believe we need to completely revamp our approach."

A pro in the front row spoke up. "And what do you propose?"

Burlington hadn't answered immediately. He'd nodded slowly before speaking. "I believe we need a complete paradigm shift."

"What does that mean?" the pro had asked.

Burlington had walked back and forth across the front of the stage, pondering. Then he came to a dead stop and pivoted toward the audience. He smiled as though he had just had an a-ha moment. He spread his arms wide. "The whole creates the parts; in other words, the behavior of the parts of a swing comes from knowing the whole swing."[1] He brought his hands together, matching his words. "That's it. That's the paradigm shift." Judging by the satisfied look on his face, he seemed to think he was getting somewhere.

Little did he know the agenda of the majority. I really hadn't understood his answer. A paradigm shift? How could the whole create the parts?

As Burlington took a sip of water, I had heard some snickering. To my surprise, I heard the doors at the back of the room open. More people started to stand up. The doors slammed shut, then opened again. The exodus had begun. To my right, one of the young teachers had looked at me and asked under his breath, "Who the hell is this guy?" I didn't respond. "What success has he had?" he mocked, louder. "If we're teaching for the right reasons, we should become obsolete? Paradigm shift—is he nuts?"

Burlington had heard the end of the pro's comment as he moved across the stage toward us. Playfully, he asked the guy to elaborate. Without hesitation, the pro reiterated his opinion. "Mr. Burlington, with all due respect, we don't need to be told how to teach or even be told to look at what the future might bring. We're already successful. We've gone from the caddy shack to five-star hotels and teaching on television."

Burlington had nodded in agreement about the change in status of golf pros over the past thirty years. But I knew that wasn't his point. Burlington went back and sat down, facing us, his elbows on the table. Waiting in silence, he sipped his water and peered first at the young pro and then into the remaining audience. As he'd scanned the room from back to front, he'd seemed to be taking in what was left of the audience. He'd seemed to be looking deeply into each of us with a look of sadness, but no trace of anger. He was clearly not intimidated.

He had answered the young pro quietly. "One should be careful how one defines success." His voice increased in volume as he continued. "Taking a hard, honest look forces us to examine and evaluate. It gives us an opportunity to improve our present condition. It's OK to disagree with me. When I'm finished, I will gladly answer any more questions you may have."

But then another pro had begun speaking without waiting to be called upon. Courtesy was no longer part of this gathering. "Can't you be more specific with this paradigm shift thing? I could never teach without my video camera!"

Burlington had fired away, describing three more major differences in his approach. "Since you're using video, I assume you believe in parts, position, and analysis." The pro had nodded. "When it comes to developing a swing, I believe in wholes, patterns, and feel. We are on opposite sides of the spectrum. That doesn't make me right and you wrong, we are just very different. So a discussion is in order, wouldn't you say?" The pro sat down and turned his face away. Negative emotions were running high.

Very few of us were still there to listen. Even Burlington's logic and conciliatory tone couldn't create a positive atmosphere. More of the remaining people had filed out. Burlington, to my surprise, had raised his hands as if to say, OK, I tried. I thought, no, don't stop now, but there was just too much resistance. The hall had gone from standing room only to being less than half full. I was sure he felt disrespected; it would be difficult to misinterpret the almost hostile energy.

He had started to apologize to those still sitting quietly. "Maybe some folks aren't ready for..." but his voice trailed off. Then he placed the glass of water back on the table and left the stage. The hall had emptied in seconds. I had heard the remarks of some of the younger fellows: "Who *is* this guy?" "What a waste of time!"

Even so, there were a few in the crowd who seemed to be thinking along my line. They had walked out more slowly. I shook my head. I thought I could really use some of Burlington's experience. I had gone into the game for something more than material gain, not just to raise my standard of living. I wanted to help others improve their game and I wanted to be an example of what he was talking about. I wanted to be able to *do* what I taught, too. I sat there stunned and disappointed. I already admired Joe Burlington. His message was clear and he was fearless in speaking his mind: Be creative, be different, be effective, and seek true success. I really needed to meet him. I urgently had to talk with him. Maybe this is *the* guy.

I couldn't believe what I had just witnessed. What was I to do? I couldn't just sit there and watch what seemed like my last hope vanish. I needed to make my move if I was ever going to meet Joe Burlington.

I had rushed backstage and asked a stagehand where Burlington had gone. He nodded toward an exit at the end of the hall. I was almost at a full run as I slammed the crossbar of the emergency exit with both hands. My heart was pounding. I felt like the walls of my chest couldn't contain the pressure building up within me.

Adrenaline surging through my arteries, I knew I could catch him, but which way to go? One thought kept cycling through my brain: This is your chance, there is no other chance; this is your chance, there is no other chance. I'd let my instincts take over and turned left down St. Louis Street, toward the hotel district of the French quarter.

There were people everywhere. As I'd moved steadily forward, weaving my way through the crowd, I'd scanned both sides of the street. There! Just half a block ahead of me I thought I caught sight of him. Tall; yellow shirt, khakis, moccasins. There couldn't be two of them. He was getting into a cab.

I'd screamed out his name but my voice was drowned out by the noise of the street. He did pause and look around, as though he had felt something, but then ducked into the cab and was gone. I'd tried to yell again but the air escaping my lungs arrived on my lips voiceless.

Relax, I commanded myself, take a deep breath, get ahold of yourself. He's gone, but he's not dead. I just need to get to South Florida. But I don't have my clubs and my flight back to Boston leaves in a couple of hours.

I'd figured I could get back to Boston, collect my stuff, and catch an early flight to Ft. Lauderdale. I could probably look Burlington up on the Internet, give him a call, and arrange a one-on-one. I knew he had taught at a driving range on a college campus at one time. How many of those could there be? All I really had to do was make sure I was on that plane in plenty of time. I walked back to my hotel, collected my stuff, and checked out. Soon I was on my way to the airport.

After checking in, I still had plenty of time before the flight, so I'd gotten out my laptop and tried Googling "Joe Burlington, South Florida." The search came up empty. I should have known—he's not on the Internet. He's from a completely different time and place and has a whole different way of thinking. Probably doesn't even own a computer. I'd have to try to reach him when I got there.

The flight to Boston had gone smoothly. Before I left the airport, I'd booked the first flight out to Ft. Lauderdale the next morning.

I still had some big problems: I had no appointment with Burlington and no place to stay. But my mind had gone into high gear. When I got home, I'd called my friends the Pedersens, who ran a little bed and breakfast on the beach in Pompano. Claire and I used to stay there whenever we visited South

Florida. Mrs. Pedersen explained that they really weren't open for the season yet and wouldn't be there, but if I didn't mind self-service I was welcome. She cheerfully said she'd give us our usual room. She couldn't know Claire and I had broken up and it was too complicated to tell her now.

Plan B was working. I'd go down to Florida and ask around. Someone had to have heard of Joe Burlington at one of the local munis. Was this magical thinking? Had I lost touch with reality? Claire had accused me of impulsive, compulsive, and every other pulsive behavior they dissect in therapy. I would call her when I knew she would be out, leave a message about my plan, and that's that. I didn't want to be talked out of it. This was my chance; there was no other chance.

That thought became my mantra and volleyed back and forth in my mind with the doubts. What if he wouldn't see me or didn't have time? Could I pull this off? This is my chance; there is no other chance.

Just then a tap on my shoulder from the flight attendant awakened me from my daze: We would be landing in Ft. Lauderdale soon and could I please raise my seatback, etcetera. I couldn't believe I'd been in a semi-conscious dream-state of recollection through the whole flight.

The captain announced that it was sunny and fifty degrees warmer than the Boston winter I had left. I rented a car and made my way north on I-95.

The B&B was nice—a typical Florida two-story home from the sixties, white brick with yellow trim, a tile roof, and a wrap-around porch. It always amazed me how bright things were in Florida at this time of year. There is so much color and life, while up north, everything is gray and barren. I strode up the front walk and found the keys under the planter, just as Mrs. Pedersen had said, and let myself in. The front room opened up to a beautiful view of the dunes and the ocean just beyond. It was as blue as the sky, with hints of deeper turquoise. Visions of Claire and I on the beach washed through my mind, leaving me with an empty feeling in my gut and an ache in my chest. I couldn't accept that she wasn't in my life anymore.

I found a note on the kitchen table welcoming me and giving me a few details about the house. I took my bag up to my room and unpacked. I wanted to be ready to get going early in the morning. The room had two dormers overlooking the ocean.

I opened the windows and let the sea sounds lull me back to another time. I thought of calling Claire, but didn't know what to say. Memories intruded— us sharing this spot, walking the beach, swimming in the sea, and making love in between. The warm twilight breeze made me miss her.

Determined to block those thoughts, I lay down on the bed and went through a mental checklist of my plans for tomorrow. I decided to skip dinner and fell asleep early.

I got up later than I had intended, showered, got dressed and walked down to my favorite local diner. It was owned and operated by a guy named Lou, a former commercial fisherman turned sport fishing guide turned short-order cook.

Lou was a down-to-earth guy and I always enjoyed shooting the breeze with him. He had been through life's school of hard knocks, working most of his life on the water, and he looked it too. We had gotten to know each other fairly well with my annual visits and had become good friends. He always had hot coffee, great bacon, and fresh bread from the bakery next door.

I picked up a newspaper and headed inside. Lou wasn't here today— probably fishing, I guessed. I opened the paper to the sports page, where there were ads for golf courses. Pompano Beach Municipal was a short ride up Federal Highway.

At the course, I found the parking lot full. Must be a tournament today. I parked, got my clubs out of the trunk, and headed to the practice putting green. The first tee was full, with about ten golf carts lined up. There were several guys putting. The course was adjacent to Pompano Airport and I watched small planes practicing touch and goes. It was refreshing not to see houses or condos, just thirty-six holes and a clubhouse. Even though the condition looked a little rough, the course had character.

I put down my bag next to the green and got out my putter and three balls to get a feel for the Bermuda grass. At the far side of the green I noticed three guys having a match. I tried a few putts, waited till they finished, and went over to them. "Excuse me, I'm not from around here and I'm trying to locate a local pro. Was wondering if any of you knew of him."

"What's his name?"

"Joe Burlington."

They looked at me funny, and all three answered in unison. "Joe Burlington." The oldest-looking one took over for the group and offered, "He's already teed off. Probably on the third hole by now. Sometimes he plays in our weekly skins game. Usually wins too. If you wait around maybe you can catch him. Are you a golf pro?"

"Why, yes."

"We have room for one more. Do you want to play with us?" the spokesman asked.

"Well, I don't know. I've just arrived from Boston and haven't played since last fall. I'm not sure you would want me today."

"Come on, you can't hurt us. We'll even pick up your greens fee."

"No, really, I was just looking to speak to Mr. Burlington."

"Well, you can't speak to him now, so why not join us and I'll introduce you after the round. He'll be at the bar having a cold beer; you won't miss him."

I gave them a shrug and decided it was fated. "OK. When do we tee off?"

"In a couple minutes."

"I need to hit some practice balls."

"No time for that now, brogie. Just do like Joe; he never warms up. Besides, it's just skins. If you can make a few birdies or an eagle, we'll have a great day. And maybe take some of Joe's money."

I wasn't comfortable with this arrangement, but went to the side of the green to get my clubs and headed for the first tee. Tim, the spokesman, introduced me to Jake and Will. "Geoff," I replied, to introduce myself. Soon our turn came and they nodded me the honor; they were going to play from the regular tees; I had to play back. The first hole was a short par four so I drew my three wood from the bag, made a couple of practice swings, and slammed it down the middle. Not bad for not warming up.

The three older guys teed off, all with their own peculiar style, but nailed the balls a good distance down the middle. Everyone had a short iron to the green. They each, without hesitation, landed their shots on the green not too far from the hole. When I reached my ball, I needed only a short wedge. I hate these half shots. I took a couple practice swings and proceeded to fat the shot into the front bunker. My reaction was to slam the toe of the club into the ground in disgust. I pulled hard and got the club out of the turf and slammed it into my bag.

Great. Here we go again. I was angry and embarrassed. In front of three amateurs, with an easy shot like that I couldn't even hit the green. I called myself stupid and muttered my displeasure all the way to the greenside bunker. The three of them pretended not to watch out of standard golfer's courtesy. But I knew what they were thinking: What kind of pro is this? Having not lost my turn I took my wedge into the bunker. Great, a buried lie. I closed the face and took a wicked lash at it. The ball came out and scooted across the green. I was still away, took my putter and holed it from thirty feet.

The guys applauded, but I could hardly smile considering the way I had played the hole. What a lousy par. The embarrassing half wedge on the first hole lingered in my mind for several holes, taking its toll on my whole game.

We continued to play at a good pace through the first nine holes. Once a player was out of the hole, he would just pick up. As we made the turn my mind was getting cluttered. Which swing would I use to just get through the day and save face? I was inconsistent throughout that first nine, which was what frustrated me so about this game. I never knew what was going to happen. I tried to avoid my driver, too. After a couple of blocks sailed out of play to the right on the front nine, I knew my driver and I were definitely not friends today. I managed to scramble for a couple more pars on the front nine, but never scored a birdie. I knew these guys thought they'd wasted their money with me on their skins team but at least we weren't waiting on every shot. That would have been the last straw for me.

On the eleventh hole, Tim approached me. We were stalled by two groups waiting to play a long par three over water. He could tell I was frustrated. I had taken a seat on the bench next to the tee. "So you're here to see Joe Burlington?"

"Yes." I shook my head, looking down at my three iron. "Well, I don't actually have an appointment—I was hoping to get one. I came down here on a whim, just hoping to get some time with him. I saw him in New Orleans speaking at the teaching summit."

"Oh, we heard about that. Some spectacle, I understand."

"Yes—I've never seen anything quite like it." I paused and then asked, "How well do you know Joe Burlington?"

"Quite well, but mostly as an observer. I've watched him teach a lot over the years. His whole demeanor fascinates me, but that's just me."

"Have you ever had a lesson from Joe?"

"Well, yes."

"Do you still work with him?"

"No."

"Why not?" I asked, a little surprised by Tim's answer.

"Don't get me wrong: I don't take lessons from anyone anymore 'cause I don't need 'em."

"What do you mean?"

"I learned what I had to watching him give lessons to others and taking that one lesson myself. Joe doesn't believe in giving a person a lot of lessons. Once you know yourself and your swing, you just keep working on the principles he teaches."

"What did he do for you? Or for the people you've seen him give lessons to?"

"Let's see...how can I put this? He gets everyone to find the patterns of the club, and then has you identify how it feels, and then you are off on your own. He really gets you to know yourself. Knocks out all the conflict."

"How did he help you with your swing?"

"Before Joe, I had worked with a lot of teachers; they all thought I had a chronic problem not shifting my lower body in my swing."

"You didn't?"

"Well, I did, and I didn't."

"What do you mean?"

"I tried with all my other teachers to shift," Tim explained. "It was obvious that I needed to, and video showed it clearly. But every time I tried to shift, everything would go haywire. My swing would become completely discombobulated. I was at my wits' end, and even though I'd heard he was rather eccentric, I decided to give him a call."

"What did Joe do?"

"You might not believe it, but he really didn't do anything with my swing directly, except for teaching me his release trigger, which he calls 'the curl.'" I pretended like I'd heard of it and motioned for Tim to continue. "Well, he pulled out one of his foam Pathfinders, pieces of foam that could be bent any way to help a golfer see and adjust his swing path or any impact dynamic. The foam tubes replaced the old three-foot two-by-fours teachers used to use." I still used the wood and my students feared it—golfers could really wrench their hands if they hit the wood with a club as it approached impact.

Tim continued. "Joe explained that the foam provides a visual boundary so the golfer wouldn't swing the club outside the target line. He said when these flexible boundaries are set on the ground, the mind unconsciously takes care of the path and the golfer can singularly focus on the timing of the release, the angle of attack, and the curl, as Joe put it. I had never heard of the release referred to that way and was intrigued. So Joe set the Pathfinder up about twelve inches behind the ball and looped it up a couple inches above the ground. Then he had me place the club on the ground behind the foam instead of behind the ball. He asked me to make a swing from there but on the way down, I was to swing the club over the foam and let the club impact the ball. I was skeptical at first, and hesitated, but I did as he instructed. I missed the ball completely on my first attempt as the club passed over the foam and the ball, but I noticed that without trying I did the 'Gary Player walkthrough.' I mean, my feet and legs shifted well forward to get the club over the foam without me even trying!

"I waited for more direction, but Joe stood there silently nodding for me to swing again. I made another swing and barely contacted the ball, but I knew he was onto something because I shifted like never before. I looked back at him again as he waited without speaking. So I tried a third time. I swung the club over the foam and into the ball. To my amazement the club struck the ball solidly on the downward side of the arc. My feet, legs, and whole lower body had shifted to get the club over the foam again. I even took a divot in front of where the ball lay and I hadn't taken a proper divot in years. What impressed me most was that he never told me how to do it. It just happened naturally when the club swung over the foam.

"It took about five minutes, then he spent five more minutes on my release and I haven't seen him since, except here at the golf course. Geoff, the sophistication and elegance of his strategy is masked by its simplicity. He always asks me how I'm doing, and I can honestly say, once I got the picture of the club's pattern, I've never had a problem shifting again. Go figure."

Just then, Jake turned to me and said, "Geoff, you're up."

I was excited by Tim's story. It took me completely out of the self-created funk I'd experienced since the first hole. I walked up to the tee and launched my three iron ten yards over the green directly over the flag. It was the most solid shot I'd hit all day. New hope was liberating me, and my golf swing seemed to get easier with each successive shot. Exhilarated, I played the final eight holes in four under. The guys were impressed, but I knew that most of my success was the result of the optimism planted by the story of Tim's lesson with Joe.

After we finished the round, they invited me to play again later in the week. Jake even wanted a lesson from me after seeing my play on the back nine. I guess he figured I just needed a nine-hole warm up, never suspecting the real reason for my late-game success. Tim and I walked together to the bar outside the clubhouse, where we turned in our score card. I looked up at the skins board. So far Burlington had three skins but my four birdies on the back nine negated two of them. It made for an easy introduction to Joe.

Tim grabbed my arm and directed me to the far side of the bar, where Joe seemed to be admiring what was left of the head on his amber Labatt Blue. He was sprinkling salt in the glass and watching the granules descend to the bottom as bubbles ascended, giving life to the beer and more of a head on top—an old Irish trick. There were several golfers milling around chatting about their rounds and how close they'd come to getting a skin; after all, they were worth about $150 each. Typical of golfers—I'd done it many times myself—they were lamenting what could have been. Joe was just sitting there listening.

Burlington turned as he sensed our approach. Tim reached for Joe's extended hand and said, "Joe, this is Geoff Mallory. He's from Boston. He's just foiled two of your skins on the back nine, but he wanted to meet you, and I agreed to do the honors." Joe reached for my hand and smiled.

"Nice play, Geoff. Pleased to meet you. What brings you to South Florida?"

"You," I blurted out.

"Oh, really?"

"Yes." I stammered a little, then continued. "I was in New Orleans two days ago when you gave your presentation. I've been chasing you since you left the stage."

He looked at me somewhat perplexed. "Chasing me?"

"What you were saying really intrigued me." I hesitated, but he simply waited. "I was wondering if I could speak to you about working on my golf."

He sat still and silent for a moment. Had I caught him off guard? With the break in conversation, things seemed awkward. He repeated, "You were in New Orleans? Nice town."

I repeated my request and his expression signaled understanding. It was a strange moment. He looked over at the scoreboard. "Judging from the way you played on the back nine, it doesn't seem to me that I could be of help to you."

"You don't know the half of it. I'm a teaching pro too, and I know I could really use your help." That was as politely as I could put it without sounding desperate.

"Well, what kind of help do you need?"

I hesitated, not expecting the question. "I need any kind of help you can give me."

Burlington paused for a moment. "Let me think about what I have going on." He counted to himself on his fingers. Then he looked up at me and said, "You can come out tomorrow. How long are you in town for?"

"A few days."

"I could work with you on your game and if you like, you can observe some lessons I'll be giving this week." I didn't know how to thank him. He changed gears as he downed the rest of his beer. "Listen, I'd be happy to chat, but right now I have to run. There are a few things I need to do at the golf center, since I took most of the day off to play in our little skins game. You can get directions to my place from Tim. Meet me there tomorrow, nine AM sharp."

I couldn't believe it had really been that easy. Joe left, but Tim invited me to stay for a late lunch. I was hungry. We all ordered cheeseburgers and fries at the outdoor bar under the tent, where there was a charcoal grill. I picked up the tab with my winnings and listened to their stories about Joe Burlington.

Tim, Jake, and Will had all worked with the enigmatic pro, but Jake was the only one who couldn't seem to sign onto his approach. "He was just too strange for me," he said.

Tim interrupted, "You never gave him a chance, Jake, with your attitude and all your techniques." Apparently, Jake, besides taking a lot of lessons from a lot of pros, had tried all kinds of techniques that overpopulated the monthly magazines and the golf channel.

Before we left, I got the phone numbers of my newfound friends. I was feeling proud of the way I finished the round and they were serious about playing again later in the week. I felt a twinge of self-doubt at the invitation. What if I couldn't continue playing the way I'd left off on the back nine today? After playing well, I was already feeling insecure.

Would Burlington be able to help?

2

THE FIRST DAY: JOE'S STORY

The morning came quickly. I hadn't slept soundly; I was too excited. I grabbed a quick breakfast and dashed off to the golf center. I didn't know what to expect.

As I got closer, I thought maybe I'd made a wrong turn, but was certain I'd followed Tim's directions exactly. This was clearly not the nicest part of town; I was more than a little surprised. Years earlier, I had attended a teaching summit at the palatial Boca Raton Hotel, dubbed the Pink Palace, just up the road. It was only a few miles away, but it seemed Burlington's Golf Center would be light years from the Palace—in appearance, at least.

The golf center seemed to be an afterthought, tacked onto a local college. It had no parking lot of its own, so I parked on the street. As I approached the long wooden ramp leading to the pro shop, memories of the caddy days of my youth hit me. The Burlington Golf Center building resembled an old caddy shack from where I grew up in Boston.

The shop attendant was a pleasant little guy in an old Yankees jersey. He paused in his work filling the club-cleaning buckets with fresh water when he saw me. "Good morning, I'm Jim. What can I do for you?"

"I'm here to see Joe Burlington. I have a 9 o'clock appointment."

Jim nodded. "He's down at the maintenance barn." I followed him into the pro shop. "I'll buzz him." He pushed the call button on the squawk box, but there was no answer. He tried again. "He never answers this thing," the Yankees fan muttered, shaking his head in frustration. "I don't even know why we have one. You'd better go down there yourself." He pointed toward a barn about 300 yards away. I grabbed my clubs and headed in that direction.

My mind was racing. I was having serious second thoughts. Was coming here a big mistake? This place wasn't what I'd expected at all. Claire was right: My impulsiveness had gotten the best of me again. Part of me wanted to turn around then and there, but something made me keep going.

Nearing the fence that surrounded the maintenance area, I came close to stepping on a big yellow dog that looked exactly like Marmaduke of comic book fame. The dog lay motionless, except for one eye, which he opened to take a good long look at me. He let out a big sigh and resumed his slumber. I guess he figured I was no threat.

I passed through the gates into a yard filled with all kinds of turf equipment and several vintage golf carts. I moved through the white pines that surrounded a wooden workshop of about twenty by thirty feet, its doors wide open. I stopped just inside the doors on a rather uneven concrete floor covered with pine needles blown in by the wind. I looked for Joe. Or any sign of life.

I scanned the room. One side contained a table saw, stone grinder, drill press, and air compressor. Several tables were loaded with various tools and golf course maintenance supplies. Looking up into the rafters, I saw old golf clubs, boxes of shafts and grips, a ladder, and what appeared to be green foam tubes with orange ends sticking out of boxes. On the other side of the room was a stackable washer/dryer, a microwave, and a small refrigerator. It looked like someone both worked and lived in here. Still, there was no sign of life inside.

My doubts were growing fast. My gaze fell to the floor toward the back of the building. There *was* somebody there. A utility vehicle was jacked up a few inches above the floor, and a pair of legs peeked out from under it.

I called out tentatively. "Joe?"

He slid out from under the machine. "Good morning. Geoff?" His hands were darkened by dirt and grease from the old machine he was working on.

"Yes. Jim tried to call you on the squawk box, but...."

"Yes, I know. I hate that thing," he chuckled, "especially when I'm in the middle of something. I was just about to adjust the rollers and sharpen the reels on the cutting units, but first we need to get them up on that table over there." I noticed he had included me in this task. He pointed across the room. "I figured Jim would send you down here. We use those reels for the main practice tee. They're beginning to tear the grass instead of giving it a clean cut. I need to balance them out, too. I figured I had some time before you arrived so I got started."

He got up off his roller, grabbed an old towel to wipe some of the dirt off his hands, and pointed at the reels on the floor. "These are heavy." I stood there, still somewhat dumbfounded, until he asked, "Would you mind putting down your clubs and giving me a hand with this reel? We need to get it up on the table so I can adjust it. It'll only take five minutes."

I felt it was a little presumptuous of him to ask, but I put down my bag and went over to help him. The reel was indeed heavy and awkward. We got it up on the table and he propped it up so the front roller was in the air. Then he picked up what was clearly a homemade tool and slid it back and forth along the rollers. It was tight on one end and slid too easily on the other. He quietly said, "There, you see? This is not even." Burlington began loosening bolts on each side of the rollers. He pried on the adjusters until the steel bar was equal in tension on both ends and the middle.

"Just one more thing and we can get started. Let's lift this reel down onto the floor." He skidded one of the reels along the floor to the triplex and angled it in place to reconnect to the mower. Then, grease gun in hand, he lubed the tee mower. There must have been a hundred grease fittings on that machine and he had to crawl on his knees on the concrete floor to get at some of them, but his overalls were already filthy. While he performed that task, he explained the importance of lubricating all the joints.

I was beginning to get impatient. It looked like Joe Burlington was more into golf course maintenance than golf instruction. Didn't he remember why I was here? I wasn't interested in this stuff. I was accustomed to being treated like a true pro and my ego was protesting. Maybe this *was* a big mistake. If things continued this way, there was no way I was going to spend a week of precious vacation time with a man who looked like a turf mechanic! But judging from his score yesterday, I knew he could play golf. Could he teach? But what could I do—tell him I had a new shirt on and I didn't want to get dirty? Burlington, in contrast, was filthy and sweating from his work but apparently didn't care how he appeared.

I stood there in his shop, looking down at him working under the mower. I argued with myself: Don't be so quick to judge; see what happens next. Take it easy for once in your life. I forced myself to shut down my initial judgments for the moment and declared a temporary ceasefire. I tried to convince myself to stick with this commitment. Claire had accused me of lack of commitment, not just with her, but even with the small stuff of life. Her exact words were that I couldn't even commit to a frozen dinner or an ice cream flavor. Looking over my current situation and how much I'd invested in it, I decided at least to go through with the first day as planned.

While I pondered, Burlington was putting another cutting unit back on the mower. As he called out for different wrenches, like a surgical nurse I automatically assisted him; I don't know why. I watched as he adjusted the cutting unit and turned a few nuts to secure the reel to the machine. His hands worked quickly and with ease, his experience obvious. I got some grease on my hands from handling the tools, but it wasn't much, and watching Burlington work was hypnotic. Burlington seemed very keen on preventive maintenance. He was smiling and humming and really seemed to enjoy this work. I was still a little miffed at the reception, but curious about what might come next.

"Well, that's it for now," he suddenly exclaimed, and got up from under the mower. He stood up, took off his cap, wiped the sweat from his brow, and walked to the sink outside the building. Soaping up, he bent and grabbed a fistful of loose sand from the ground to help scrub the grease off his hands. Drying with a shop towel, he said, "Now—let's begin again. Good morning!"

This time, looking me straight in the eyes, Joe Burlington shook my hand with a sure grip. As I looked at him, I could tell he had spent a lot of time outdoors—his skin was weathered and his hands were rough. He looked more in his element here; I noticed again his strong jaw, youthful eyes, and full head of auburn hair, streaked where the sun had bleached it.

As we shook hands, I could feel him studying me. I could sense something different. Joe Burlington radiated an energy—a force—one that I can only describe as an inner strength emanating outward, something I had never felt before. Powerful, yet peaceful and friendly, not intimidating at all. I sensed a strong compassion—so strong I could almost see it.

Our conversation began again benignly—small talk at first. We exchanged the pleasantries scripted for first lessons. As I shifted my focus away from my first impressions of the place and Burlington's maintenance work, I could tell he was decidedly different. He had a presence, something special, but I couldn't put my finger on it just yet. And I couldn't merge this new image with my first impressions. Had I reacted prematurely and with prejudice? I figured I would find out soon enough.

Burlington interrupted my second-guessing. "You can go on ahead, Geoff. I need to change into more comfortable clothes." He pointed me in the direction of his practice area just around the corner from the shop. "I'll join you in a few minutes." As I walked out, I heard him call after me, "You can warm up if you like."

Burlington came around the corner with "Marmaduke" (whose real name, I learned, was Otter) at his heels about ten minutes later. Just like the summit, he wore a plain yellow shirt, khaki trousers, and moccasins without socks. This guy didn't look like he was about to give a golf lesson. But it occurred to me that it might be refreshing to work with someone who wasn't from the celebrity golf pro mold. I had hit a few shots to warm up, but then decided it would be more productive if we could talk before I showed him my swing. He came up next to me and said, "Let's get started." We stood on a small square of closely cropped Bermuda grass. He motioned for the dog to join us. Otter yawned, reluctantly got up, and waddled over. He sniffed the spot on arrival, laid down right behind us, and closed his eyes. It seemed like only a few seconds passed before we could hear Otter's rhythmic snoring.

We sat down on the chairs that stood off to the side and Burlington said, "Well, you've come a long distance. I hope I can help you make it worth your while, eh?"

"I think you can from what I've heard about your reputation."

"I wouldn't put too much stock in someone else's say-so if I were you, Geoff." What did he mean by that? I had given him a compliment and he had volleyed it right back at me, not gingerly either, but spiking it over the net.

I intercepted. "I notice you have a Canadian accent of sorts. Do you come from Canada?"

"No, but my father was from Ontario and his family was from Ireland. I think that's where I got my love of links courses, from the Irish ancestors. Those courses are so naturally beautiful, they prove nature's elegance, don't they?" He looked at me and I nodded in agreement. "But to answer your question, I was born in Michigan. I'm a Midwesterner. My habit of saying 'eh' comes from years ago, when I taught in Canada. I adapt the language based on how I feel and what I need to say. Invariably, the meaning is clear, even if the words are incoherent. I believe communication is about meaning, not structure. Like golf swings—it's not form, it's function, eh?" He looking directly at me and lifted his brows. I could tell he was wondering if I'd picked up on his neatly packaged morsel of golf and life philosophy.

There was a long pause. Burlington didn't help to push it along much—he didn't seem like one to engage in trivial talk. Silence between sentences didn't seem to bother him, but I felt awkward and pressured to keep the conversation going. "Did you grow up in Michigan?" It was all I could think to ask.

"No, not really. We moved around a lot growing up. Dad always provided for us, but he lived simply, working daily and playing golf a couple afternoons a week during season. He started us playing golf. As I think back on it, he had a pretty good swing himself." Burlington smiled, enjoying the memory.

" 'Us'?" I questioned.

"There were six of us—a real handful for my mother—and we each have dramatically different personalities. My mother, well, she was whatever she needed to be—a homemaker, a hairstylist, sang on the radio. I think I got my diversity from her. She was not a golfer when she and my father met, but as soon as she touched a club you could tell she had a natural knack for it."

"Where did your mother come from?" I asked.

"Mom's family immigrated from Italy. She was Italian to the core. Family, family, family. Her whole focus was on raising us kids. She gave up all other activities in her life to concentrate on us not going astray." Burlington had no reservations about sharing his past.

I didn't want to pry, but I did want to know more about him, and I felt that these were perfectly normal questions. "Did you begin your golf career in Michigan?"

"Yes. Like many older golf professionals, I began as a caddy. But, because of my dad's work, we never lived in one place too long. It was hard once we got into high school. You make new friends and miss the old ones. We'd have to find new jobs and adjust to a new town just when the old one was becoming comfortable and familiar. But I really got into playing golf and teaching when we moved to the hills and horse country of Ohio, where my brothers and I worked at a club in Sharon Center. "

"How old were you?"

"I was just fourteen." This time he didn't crack a smile.

"You mean you began teaching at fourteen?" I asked, incredulous.

"Well, in a sense I did. Club members, and even the golf pros, would ask me my opinion about their swings and I would just tell them what I thought. The surprising thing was that I felt very comfortable doing this. They trusted me. I really don't know why, except they knew I was pretty good for my age and I practiced a whole lot. I was very consistent with my swing and my shots. They used to admire my balance." He laughed, remembering with delight.

"I was...diminutive for my age," Burlington went on animatedly, "so I was somewhat disadvantaged when I competed within my age group. I knew at a very young age that I wanted to work in golf and be outdoors. That is what really attracted me to the game. The golf swing itself just fascinated me, and it still does. I studied hard and watched all the best players on television. I did go to a few matches and tournaments in Akron. Yeah, I was fascinated by Hogan, Nelson, and Snead, but I was too young to go in person. Except for Snead; I saw him play up close." He added, "I did study film of them all practicing, though.

"We—my brothers and I—always worked at the golf course. As employees, our privileges and playing time were quite limited. We got into the habit of practicing our swings and that, as you know, can be a two-edged sword. We could practice however much we wanted. We were fortunate that there were two exceptional pros where we worked in our teens, and they encouraged us to work on our games as much as possible. These pros were highly skilled players and understood what it took to get good. I tried to emulate their examples—you know, pass it on to kids the way they did to my brothers and me. Anyway, I practiced a lot and loved it. I wanted badly to have the best swing and play the finest golf game I could."

"What happened to get you into golf full time? I asked. "Did you go into college on scholarship?"

"No, I did not have a scholarship," Burlington said. "They were hard to come by, but I did qualify as a walk-on at university—only to be told that I couldn't play," he smiled wryly. "I didn't beat the scholarship players by enough strokes. C'est la vie! I got over it eventually and it was a good lesson in life for me: It's not always fair."

"You competed a lot?"

"Yes, and I had reasonable success as a junior golfer. But then things turned sour. I mean, my whole golf game turned inside out. I got steadily worse even though I knew what I wanted to achieve and had access to the best instruction."

"Did you take a lot of lessons?"

"No, Geoff, I don't believe in taking a lot of lessons. I had spent approximately eight days taking lessons from one man. I didn't need more than that. Since then, I have been working on mastering what he taught me forty years ago, and I will tell you that it can never be mastered. All you can do is keep moving in the right direction. I'll explain this in more detail when the right time comes. Despite the truths I'd learned, I was not getting better, so I had to do something. At my lowest point in golf, I realized I had to change drastically."

"But if you had the best mentoring, what had to change?" I felt I was missing something.

"Good question. I had to change my whole perspective and my complete personality when it came to golf. My belief system had derailed me with all the failure it absorbed. If you play badly for long enough, you will find it a chore to get out of bed in the morning. You will fear the golf course, the tournaments, the other competitors, everything. It's a terrible state to be in."

"There are some prominent players on tour going through that right now. Do you think you could help them?" I asked.

"It's hard to say, because it's always up to the individual. If they were open-minded I could probably lead them back to their natural potential. It's my experience that people can usually get back on track from there. For me, I had realized I had to do something and decided to take action on what had been, up until then, the lowest days of my career. I also knew no one could help me and I had to figure it out for myself. It took a lot of time, but eventually I came full circle. When the realization dawned on me that I wasn't alone in these sorts of problems, I decided to develop a program to help others get back on track, too."

I began to wonder how someone could be so honest about his own failures. I guess Joe Burlington was so secure in his experience that it didn't matter that he had, at one time, failed miserably. He wasn't ashamed of failing. He had no pretense about how good he was or how much he knew. He definitely wasn't trying to impress me: When Burlington spoke, he spoke with humility. I was used to teacher-student relationships that cast the teacher in a starring role and the student as a supporting player, as if the teacher's glory might rub off on the student with the proper attention.

But Joe Burlington spoke to me on the level, with no superiority, no condescension. Even with me probing for information, Burlington didn't seem bothered—he volunteered information genuinely and naturally once he'd gotten his motor started. He didn't seem to mind being bombarded him with questions.

"Anything else contribute to the change?" I probed.

"Well, things got real ugly, and I don't mean just my performance. I mean my attitude—especially on the course. One day, while we were playing in Texas, my brother told me, 'You know, Joe, you're no fun to be with on the course. No one wants to play with you. You're so miserable and you hit some of the worst drives I've ever seen. I don't think you'll ever get it.' He was partly right. I would never get it if I kept going about it the way I had been. I was playing scared from the very first tee and it didn't get any better.

"But I was very angry with him for saying that—I felt he had disrespected me. I had worked so hard to improve myself and help him as well. Anyway, I should have thanked him because he supplied my spark for change. What he said was true—and sometimes the truth hurts."

"What happened next?"

"I decided to go out the very next day with the attitude that no matter what happened, I was going to enjoy myself. Sounds stupid, but it was the first glimmer of hope I'd had in a long time. My brother's words gave me the energy to prove him wrong. So I drastically changed my way of doing things, first in my head and then in my body. That was the beginning of my transition and of seeing a smidgeon of my potential again.

"My first step was to find something to enjoy while I was on the course so I could relax a little. I had gotten so anxious about golfing that I needed to find a way to calm down. If it wasn't in the way I played, it would be in the birdsong, a cool breeze, or the way the light filtered through the trees. I had to take the focus away from my problems and myself and find something delightful in the moment. It is this attitude—which has nothing to do with golf and everything to do with my *performance* in golf—that allowed me to begin turning myself around."

"Well, then what happened?"

"That turned out to be my first glimmer of hope about what the solution could be. I played shots that day that were up to my potential, just a few, mind you, but it gave me hope. Though I didn't understand why on earth it worked, I decided to go further with this positive attitude. I designed a self-help program that might work for me—and for others, too."

"What did you do, specifically?"

"I'd repeat positive statements in my mind to obliterate negative thoughts. I would picture success in every shot and swing. I'd tell myself that this was easy and that I'd done it well a thousand times before. This program put attitude first and didn't allow a player to judge results."

"How can you improve your game without judging results?"

"Simple," he said. "By being aware of what's happening."

"That seems like the same thing."

"Oh no, Geoff, it's very different. You see, awareness has nothing to do with right and wrong or good and bad. It's just what is."

"Sounds interesting," I said, still puzzled. "Could you tell me more?"

"Not just yet," he replied.

3

THE LESSON BEGINS

Burlington suddenly switched gears. "Enough about me. Tell me about yourself, Geoff." In a flash, he had turned the table and now I was the one who needed to be brutally honest. Caught off-guard, I said nothing. He rephrased the question. "Tell me a little more about what happened to your golf and your teaching."

OK, I've come this far.... Jumping in with both feet, I recited the preamble I'd practiced in my head. "I feel I've run into a roadblock. Although I'm considered a successful teacher, I still don't think I'm very good."

"So you came here because you figure there's another way?"

"Well, yes; that's part of it."

"Well, what is it that you really want?"

"I really want to improve the way I teach and how I swing and play so that I don't feel like a fraud. If I can't do what I'm talking about, I feel like a phony."

Burlington nodded, taking in what I was saying, then challenged me again. "Tell me again: What do you want?"

"I want to feel authentic. I want to *be* authentic. I want to be able to perform consistently as a golfer what I teach my students and to be a complete coach to them. I'm hoping that the problems I've run into lie with my program and not with me."

"I see."

"For example, at the summit, I saw that as teachers, we're all going in the wrong direction and none of us seem to have an alternative approach. There is very little difference in our methods—although we all claim to be different. To me, we're six of one, half a dozen of the other. It's all about body positions, the core, and nothing else matters. In one camp, you have the big muscles controlling the swing, and in another, the small muscles. The whole thing has turned into a great debate, almost muscle by muscle and bone by bone, on the mechanics of the swing.

"Let me tell you, not only are the players in golf competing with each other, but now teachers show up at tour events and are competing for students. It's turned golf upside down. And these summits—" my voice was rising "—have turned into popularity contests. My talk was a typical uninspired session: I talked the talk. Maybe we are all doing the best we can with what we have, but we don't seem to be getting better!" I slapped the arm of my chair. A moment later I was a little sheepish. "I hadn't realized how strongly I felt until this moment."

"OK, so we need to get you organized. Let's begin with a simple history of your experience. You, Geoff, not those other pros. How do *you* view the true nature of golf and golf teaching?"

Wow! I've been waiting for that question all my life! Encouraged, I began. "I grew up learning that golf and the golf swing were inseparably tied to feel and the use of one's imagination. It wasn't so technical. The whole learning experience was supposed to be natural, not to mention a lot of fun. The way things are now, so complex and competitive, it seems that something has been lost. The mechanics and all the debate seduced me, too, though. But I just don't like the way I teach golf anymore."

Burlington raised his eyebrows. "I agree that things are out of balance, but complaining about what's wrong won't get them back in balance. You need to do something positive about it."

"That's why I came," I said, not hiding my irritation.

"I understand that," he said quietly, "yet you keep referring to approaches that don't sit well with you. By the way, they don't sit well with me either. But you need to let it go so you can open up to what is possible for you."

I noticed a different expression coming over Joe's face, as though he was thinking back and remembering. There was another long pause before he spoke. "I agree with you, Geoff. I, too, was deeply concerned about the direction golf instruction was going in some years ago. I chose to slip into the background, to drop out in a sense. I didn't want any part of what was happening. I had new trails to blaze and I'd never minded being different. But that's another story. Right now, we need to help you get your instruction going in the right direction. We need to get you to be authentic and confident so you can become as complete a coach as you've told me you want to be."

"I'd like that," I responded. "Can I ask you a question I've asked many other teachers, but not gotten what I consider a complete answer?"

"Fire away!"

"What do you consider to be the most important fundamental in teaching? Some people say it's the ability to teach someone to turn, others say rhythm, and still others talk about the total path of the club. What's your opinion?"

"I think some of those answers have their place, but they're certainly not at the top of my list. In my experience, there is one quality that is a must." There was another pause as he leaned in closer and looked me straight in the eyes as if to make an important point. "*Listening...*"

"That's right!" I interrupted, before he could finish, in total agreement, I thought. "I never thought of that, but you're right, Joe. My students constantly interrupt me. They don't listen. If I could ever get them to listen, we might make a lot more progress in a lesson."

"Well, no," Burlington chuckled good-naturedly, "I wasn't talking about you teaching your students to listen. I'm talking about you learning to listen."

I tried to pry my foot out of my mouth, face red.

"You see, nothing is more important in a teacher than the quality of being a good listener and an astute observer. The only way to get on the wavelength of a student is to listen to his or her story. You need to learn about the student—not vice versa. You need to draw from each student what's within them. It's an inside-out approach, rather than a cramming-it-in-from-the-outside method. A teacher must be an exceptional observer and listener, taking in what they're saying and how they present themselves. These are the only tools available to us to truly get onto our students' wavelength."

"Seems simple," I said.

"Yes, Geoff, it is a simple principle, but you would be surprised how much golf instruction either violates this principle or is completely unaware of it. If you listen between the lines of what your students are saying, they will give you a clear picture of the source of their problems. The answers are there in what the student says and in their body language. The students' eyes, their hands, their facial expressions, and their words are invaluable clues to help your students solve their own puzzles."

"But isn't solving their problems my job?"

"No. You need to allow them to do the work. It's like the old saying goes, 'Give a man a fish, he may enjoy one nice meal. But teach him to fish and he can eat for a lifetime!' The goal is that a student learns to trust in his own experience to become a solid and independent self-coach."

"So, in a sense, the teacher facilitates learning, but doesn't instruct?"

"That's right," he replied. "The art of it is that the student begins to believe he has always had the ability—which of course he has."

"Joe, I can understand an accomplished player accepting this approach, but what about a beginner?"

"Well, of course. With an accomplished player, you are essentially removing stumbling blocks that don't allow them to see clearly—in a sense, getting the player back to the potential they seem to have misplaced. Beginners absolutely have to gain experience with club in hand from the beginning of their natural swing, but we'll get into that later."

"So the most important ingredient in golf teaching has nothing to do with golf itself?"

"That's right," Burlington confirmed. "The universal quality of all teaching, whether it's sports, music, dance, whatever, is listening! And the student's words and actions must fall on unbiased ears and eyes. Being outwardly focused really takes practice—I've worked on it every day of my career. And when you're focusing on your student's words and actions, your life and your experience must fade into the background. You must, in a sense, detach yourself from yourself."

It never occurred to me that as a golf teacher I needed, first and foremost, to work on listening skills. This sounded like something Claire would say, something she worked on as a social worker. I bounced the idea around in my mind. "Kind of like a psycho-physical therapist." I said.

"Yes, Geoff. I'm glad you included the physical too because being involved in athletics, we need to have an in-depth knowledge of how the body learns its skills."

"Like, balance and motion?"

"Yes, that's part of it," he agreed. "As a golf teacher, you need to be well grounded in the physics of the club and the body's responses, but you shouldn't be teaching that to your students. Only you need to know it. You see, often teachers try to prove to their students what they know and how good they are, but this doesn't serve the student. The instructor really needs to concentrate on observing the student's learning process so that accurate adjustments can be made."

"Is that what you mean by 'awareness'?"

"Exactly. Awareness is just noticing the details and the nuances—waking up rather than being asleep. That's why you need to get your students to train their minds to practice self-inquiry. The onus of development is on them; you merely open the door and let them do the discovering. You help students discover their own ability. That's your only job. Your experience and knowledge are instruments to facilitate discovery. When your students discover for themselves, they can never be fooled or misled because it's their own experience that gave them the answers. And that's the kind of learning that's never forgotten. To discover your own best swing allows you to play with trust and confidence.

"And instructors must use diverse approaches to relate to all the different backgrounds of their students, their individual ways of understanding, perceiving, and interpreting. You must be able to relate to each one's individual nature. You can't pigeonhole them or conform them to your nature—you must teach them to embrace their own."

"OK, but after listening and observing, and letting the students discover, what next?"

"I believe in using a bare-bones approach so as not to confuse the student. While you must cover everything, you have to pare it down. You must only speak of essentials."

"Which are?"

"The essence of the golf swing is to create an environment of swing motion for the release of energy into the impact. And what is an environment of swing motion, you ask?" He seemed to read my mind. "It's a tempo and rhythm, a flow with a consistent path pattern," he explained.

"Yes, that's it!" I had a flashback to the seminar. That was the answer that really excited me. It had become my Holy Grail.

"Great golfers have all kinds of ways of swinging, Geoff, long and short, flat or upright, but what is essential? What is universal? They all have a rhythm and a path, and they release the energy into the impact consistently. We can get into some detail later, but that is as simple and complete as I can make it."

I absorbed this new idea while he paused. He was about to speak when I blurted out, "I've found that I get into ruts in my teaching, Joe. It doesn't make me happy, but I get stuck in routines and, even though one isn't working, I rarely seem to break free of it and then..."

This time he interrupted me. "Have you ever noticed that you seem to be teaching students the same things the same way, lesson after lesson?"

"Well, yes—all the time. I never questioned why. They all need to learn the same skills, don't they?"

"But the same way?"

"And why do my students need to learn the same things over and over?" I asked. "They keep coming back with the same problems. I know I have told them correctly what to do to improve."

"Because you told them what to do. It's that simple. You haven't gone through the lesson as a discovery process. You just gave them their adjustments from your treasure chest of knowledge. You did the work for them and they were very grateful. You were great; that is, until they fail again. It becomes a vicious cycle and you become the object of praise—or slander—depending on the outcome of their performances. I've said it many times: Never take credit for a student's success or the failure."

I raised my hand to plead for a pause. I needed him to slow down. There was so much meat here. I couldn't digest it all at once. I was processing his words, but still hadn't put all the pieces together.

Burlington took my cue and didn't give me the chance to ask another question. "Geoff, you can observe a few lessons, up close and personal; I think you'll begin to realize what's possible when things come together through this discovery process. You will have the opportunity to see new students and a couple of players that I've worked with before who wanted to come back. Hopefully, you will get the whole enchilada and, at some point, maybe it would be helpful if you experienced this type of lesson for yourself, as a learner. As you said, you want to improve your own game too! Anyway, you can decide later if that would be helpful for you."

"I'd like that!" I volunteered prematurely. I sat for a few minutes, absorbing it all, before I continued. "I was also wondering if you could clear up a few more questions about the common golf swing talk and the corrections that golfers and teachers make—you know, your take on the typical responses to a golfer's mishit or misdirection."

"Sure," he smiled, "fire away."

"Thanks. There are a lot of things said about a golf swing that are confusing. In fact, I have a whole list of them. For instance, one that I hear all the time is about keeping your left arm straight."

Burlington smiled. "I assume you're talking about a right-handed player? Naturally, that's based on observation and really has no ground in our fundamental program, and I'll tell you why. The first fundamental of motion is to be fluid-like, right?"

I nodded in agreement.

"Often, when a golfer concentrates on keeping the left arm rigid, it leads to rigidity throughout the body. It tends to destroy the very pacing control the golfer's looking to achieve because, physically, he has become somewhat numb. That's detrimental to control—not good at all."

"But let's say the player's left arm does collapse," I said.

Burlington swiftly refuted. "Then our golfer is lacking a good arc of the club in the swing; the problem has nothing to do with strength or a consciousness of rigidity. The key to having a good swinging lever is being able to picture the club's travel route or swing arc—and visualize the desired path. There is an arc to the handle, too, so you need to notice how it travels back. The answer is to free up the entire body so it can move to support the arc, and if you do, you'll never have a problem with an arm collapsing."

He caught his breath before continuing. "The arm actually stays relatively straight—simply by knowing the fundamental arc, or where you would like to swing, and the angle at which you would like the club to swing. Fact is, Geoff, the left arm is attached to the left shoulder and for arc momentum purposes, the lead hand and arm begin the swing back. The trailing arm will naturally bend to accommodate the circle of the swing and the limitations of standing in place while swinging in that direction. In other words, based on the swing, one side of the body folds and the other stretches. Therefore, knowing the arc, and seeing how we're put together anatomically, it would be virtually impossible to swing the club in an arc and collapse the arm."

Joe stood to demonstrate. "Notice how my right arm bends in the swing. Because the swing is progressing in the direction of my right arm, it must bend to accommodate the swing direction and arc, just as my left arm may stretch as the swing progresses away from its starting place at address. The left side of my body is being pulled by the momentum and direction of the swinging hand, arm, and club.

"Watch as my swing progresses. Notice how my torso moves naturally to accommodate the arc and path. It can all happen naturally to satisfy the club's dynamic needs." He winked. Was he being good natured or sarcastic about explaining the extension of the left arm? I could see that Joe Burlington could go toe to toe and beyond with any so-called golf intellectual. But he acted like their various philosophies were useless chatter.

"There are all kinds of degrees of arm straightness, Geoff. It really becomes personal; it's not fundamental. I have never suggested any learner try it, yet I don't have chronic arm collapses in my students' swings either," he said matter-of-factly.

I was beginning to feel somewhat irked with his simplistic responses to what I believed were complex questions, and I wanted to move on. "I've often heard that a golfer should begin his swing by turning his shoulders..."

The arc of the handle.

GB

"Yes," he interrupted, "I've also heard that lately and, again, I think it's very dangerous."

"Why?" I challenged. "It seems to work with some students."

"Well now," he scoffed, " 'seems' is the key word here. Geoff, it's first a question of intimacy."

"Intimacy?"

"Yes, intimacy. When the player's swing is controlled, or more aptly put, dominated by attempting to feel in the shoulders, then they're working with a part of the body that is not designed for that task. Also, that part of the body is not directly associated with the club or hand and handle's action. Golfers who go this route will eventually lose touch with the action of the club. To elevate awareness, golfers must have an uninterrupted intimate relationship with the club; it's their dance partner while swinging. A golfer who's no longer feeling what's going on with the club is headed for trouble, don't you think?"

Joe waited to let his question penetrate. "The golf swing has to be linked to your proprioceptive awareness," he explained.

"What?" I had to raise my hand at that one; I didn't understand the term. "What is proprioceptive awareness?"

Joe looked at me as though I hadn't done my homework in human physiology or something. But he indulged me. "Proprioception comes from the Latin word *proprius*. It means 'one's own' and of course, perception is one of the human senses. Proprioception is our sense of the orientation of our limbs in space. Without proprioception, we'd need to consciously watch our feet to make sure we stay upright while walking. Proprioception records fine muscle movements and sends the signals back to the brain.[2] That's why the fine muscles are concentrated in the hands and feet. The brain regards shoulder muscle movements as coarse. In other words, the torso is not linked to the brain in the same manner as your hands. Those parts of the body have not evolved to make the fine movements required in golf or music or dance. That's a major reason I believe so much in the hand control of a golf swing; there are no proprioceptors in your torso. Your torso relies on your inner ear for balance and center of gravity; it has absolutely nothing to do with the speed, place, or motion of your extremities.

"But of course the club is attached to an extremity! The club is an extension of our proprioceptive hand, which is perfectly designed to carry out the tasks of a golf swing. It makes no sense to try to redesign the mind-body complex in an attempt to gain awareness or consistency through the comparatively dull senses of the bulk of the body."

I felt I'd been given a heavy dose of understanding. But still Joe continued. "You cannot circumvent the most valuable feel network in the body. The hands have the tactile sense, the sense of touch and proprioception. I can't even believe there is a debate about this. You really need to get your colleagues up to speed on the sensory system." He shook his head in disbelief.

Joe got up, took a club from my bag, and made a few more swings as he spoke. I felt mesmerized by his ease and gracefulness. "In my opinion, exceptional proprioception is one of the main reasons some people have an outstanding feel for a swing right from the get go. The good news is, it can be learned and developed. My experience is that focusing on the torso can fool a player for maybe a few swings, particularly a player who tends to swing the club in a very narrow vertical pattern. However, that shoulder fix—and that's exactly what it is—is very short lived. Soon the swing becomes very horizontal or flat to the ground, and, as I've said, the player loses touch with the action of the club. Consequently, the club face rotates out of balance with the swing path, and that usually leads to an almost completely closed club face.

"Did you notice how easily my shoulders rotated when my hands and arms swung on a fundamental arc around and up behind me? Why would you want to place your attention on something that will occur naturally? Trying to rotate your shoulders, or to consciously turn them, is not a fundamental! It is a function of the action of the proprioceptive hands and arm swing. If you approach the golf swing this way, you will never sacrifice control or energy. Working with consciousness placed on your torso is a good way to dull your sense of feel."

"Then how do you get a vertical narrow swing, as you said, to become a better arc and path?"

"Geoff, there are several exercises you could teach to demonstrate it and never leave the handle-head relationship. In developing awareness, how much the player turns their shoulders, again, is unique to their body breadth, size, and flexibility. The answer is to swing the club and notice the action of the handle and head. This way, you'll never sacrifice club awareness."

"OK, Joe, I get it. Can we move on?"

He smiled and said, "Be my guest."

"How about this classic statement: When a golfer mishits the ball, he's told, 'you lifted your head' or 'you moved your head.' In a lot of cases, the player knows he didn't, yet he still missed the ball."

"They're not still saying that, are they?" Joe mocked, incredulous. Then his smile turned serious. "To focus solely on the ball is very dangerous because it really doesn't encourage club head awareness. It tends to restrict the free flow of the swing as it progresses to the finish, too. That statement, Geoff, more than any other, is one of the most destructive pieces of advice a golfer could get while learning to swing the club!" he said forcefully.

"Why?"

"Because it leads golfers directly away from developing club awareness. When golfers first learn to swing, the ball often distracts them from feeling the swing. After all, the ball is not moving. In fact, as you must have heard, I teach most of my students to swing with their eyes closed to develop the proprioception with club in hand. It helps them become aware of what's moving—the hands, the club—and the club's relationship to the ground, the target, and the ball.

"So never tell players to concentrate on the ball or to keep their head down or still. Those are natural consequences of fundamental club action."

"You've never held a club up to a golfer's head to help keep them still?"

"Absolutely not." Joe was emphatic. "That usually causes a golfer to freeze, just like keeping the left arm straight. I've never needed to do that; if their club is OK then their head is OK, right? If the golfer swings on a sound swing arc, the center is a result of the orbit. The outer orbit creates the center."

I pushed the subject in another direction. "OK, Joe, I hear this one from just about everyone and it seems that no one is able to give me an answer that covers all the bases. Everyone seems to swing differently, especially the tour players. Yet they get similar results. Where does all that power come from?"

"That's a very good question. You need to realize that there are different ways to generate power or, more precisely, optimum club head speed at impact. You might add the glide path of the club head, which includes the square center contact on the face at a good strong angle, but let me just address this question of speed for now. As you've noticed, golfers do have differing techniques. To keep it simple, I'll tell you about the two differing approaches to generating club head speed. The first, which you hear about so often today, is power generated from a completely synchronized system of torque and resistance of the upper and lower torso. Of course just based on what we've discussed regarding feel, I question the prudence of teaching this technique. Really fine athletes, with outstanding body flexibility and superb body awareness, can generate tremendous speed this way. They will still never have high energy in the impact without the timing for release, which is centered in the action of the hands and wrists. Anyway, to me, it is a very unstable approach, particularly for the club-level player. And it lacks intimacy, as I mentioned. The risk is not worth the reward, because the chance of mistiming such a volatile system reduces a golfer's consistency greatly, not to mention the physical and mental strain it places on him."

He stopped long enough to make sure I was following him. "The other way to generate power or club head speed is through timing; that is, through momentum and centrifugal force. This type of energy reduces stress on the body and really poses no physical or mental risk to anybody. Basically, one just knows the direction and speed of the flow and allows the rest of the body to respond. The beauty of this approach is that it's like riding a bike. Once you feel the synchronization and energy of these forces, you will always know them and have no need to manipulate your swing. It is really the only way for the club-level player to learn to swing. And it never sacrifices the intimacy or feel for the club," he added with a wink.

I agreed that it would be difficult to teach a golfer to swing by torque in the upper torso and resisting with the lower torso while at the same time asking him to feel the speed and direction of the club. "It would be real overload, and yet I know it to be one of the most popular approaches out there."

"Yes," he nodded, "I know, but for me, the whole body's flexibility, suppleness, and elasticity are where I get my club head energy, and I teach it that way too. Geoff, it's as though your muscles and joints become warm like soft taffy on a hot summer day; as you swing, your muscles and joints need to stretch, rotate, bend, and flex. I rely totally on the synchronization of my whole body's movement during the swing in conjunction with the club's pattern. That's what I rely on for generating power. Most of my students are very consistent—even though they don't have to practice much once they get the principles." I nodded my agreement.

He continued. "You also always need to remember that they will be on their own when the lesson's over, which means you really need to keep it simple! And, as I said, you're not compromising power, you're just making it available more often—differently, more simply, and certainly with less strain on the mind and body." This time his pause seemed to indicate that he was finished making his point.

"One last question, if you don't mind, and this is a big one." Maybe I was getting ahead of myself, but Joe looked at me expectantly. This particular problem was one I'd considered monumental—with emphasis on the 'mental.' This aspect of the game has baffled golfers since the beginning. I tried to think of a way to articulate it elegantly, but gave up. It all boiled down to this: "How does one get confidence? I mean, how can you regularly feel confident? I know it's easy to spot confidence in a player, just as easy as it is to see the lack of it. But how does one get it?"

As he slowly nodded, his brows lifted. The muscles spanning his forehead formed deep, curved lines. Was my question out of line?

"Yes," he responded, but not to my unvoiced thoughts. "Really, it is an easy question. And it has an easy answer. However, it has been made out to be complex and mysterious. Many teachers simply believe that some people have it and some don't, but I don't agree. The good news is you can get it and it doesn't need to be a difficult process. Yes, you can nurture it within yourself. Over time, your confidence will be sustainable and when it wanes, you can build it up again."

His answer surprised me. He paused in his usual manner then began to explain the source and truth of confidence. "You must simply learn to deliver the club: Know the release."

"That's it?"

"Know it by feel, know it by awareness, and learn to trigger it. Yep, it all boils down to that. It just so happens I've learned how to teach each and every golfer this release so that they'll be able to get it time and again. If a golfer learns how to do this, confidence is a natural result of it. Of course, you need to believe in it too, but I've found that any player willing to practice both the physical and mental triggers will ultimately practice and play with solid and genuine self-confidence."

The simplicity of his answer surprised me again. He made it sound so easy. I said it to myself in my head: Know the release and believe in it.

He continued. "Confidence is the positive feeling that things will go well. For example, when a golfer sets up to hit a shot, the instant before he swings is when he knows whether he's confident or not. He gets a feeling about the swing and the anticipated impact and can fairly accurately determine the chances of pulling it off. That feeling is the golfer's confidence level. The way to feel positive is to have a keen awareness and be present to the feeling of the release of energy into the impact. And there you have it! We've circled right back to 'an environment of swing motion for release.' The psyche and the physical swing are unified under the umbrella of knowing how and believing in your ability to impact the ball."

"And what are you present to?" I asked.

"You are present to the feeling throughout your whole body, Geoff. Ultimately the sense of release must be centered in the hands, those parts of the body holding the club, right? You notice as soon as a player picks up a club whether or not he is confident; you really can't hide that. The hands connect the body to the club and the mind and it's that connection that's a conduit to your whole system. It's like electricity, like plugging a light into wall socket. When you grip a club, the light can turn on and now there's current flowing through the whole system. It's like a current traveling from your brain to your hands and from your hands to your brain. Your grip on the club is the most accurate communication system for golf swing development."

"I know you explained about the differing roles the muscles and joints play in a golf swing; just tell me again so I can get it once and for all," I asked. I needed to reinforce his system in my brain. He seemed a little frustrated at my questions, but I wanted to have all his ideas, all the proof, and all the different ways to express this beautiful philosophy about what is real control and power in a golf swing.

"It's like this. Relative to your hands, your torso muscles are dull. Physiologically, in terms of the network of nerves and the sixth sense that operates on a subconscious level—proprioception—the hands are the only part of your anatomy capable of giving you accurate fine-muscle feedback on the speed and direction of the club. They are also uniquely designed for the task of making any necessary adjustments."

"Often I hear golf teachers speak as though the hands are unreliable and dangerous," I challenged.

"Hogwash," he said matter-of-factly. "Of course, they need to be trained, but no other part of your body can replace their role in a golf swing."

"But then why do so many golf teachers and skilled players say the larger muscles control the swing?"

"Do you want the truth?"

"Of course!"

"Fear. Fear coming from a lack of understanding. They have no knowledge of how the mind and body communicate; I mean the circuitry and design. After all, most of the golf swing takes place out of sight, but it doesn't need to take place out of mind. The proprioceptors take care of that for us. A basic lack of understanding is why these folks cannot fathom controlling the fast action of the swing through the true source of the swing. They hope and pray that the hands will behave, if they don't mess with them. Really, that's a very defensive way to go about swinging a club, and anyone who does it is setting themselves up for a fall, because you can't play any sport well in defensive mode. You've got to be proactive and aware and present to what you want; don't expect good things to happen without sound training. Your hands cannot be eliminated or glossed over in your training program. They are a rich, dense, fertile sensory garden."

These seemed like solid opinions backed up by science. Obviously Joe felt strongly about these conflicts in learning that golfers had had to endure in the past few years. But it was exactly what I needed to hear.

He had more to say, though. "I'll tell you another reason folks miss out on the truth: The hands and wrists move so fast during the release that it's hard to see what's going on. You asked about power and you and others have equated golf swing power with size. Sports are heading dangerously in that direction, but there is no direct correlation. We need to re-evaluate how we observe the body during the golf swing. What are we looking at? It's easy to see the larger slower-moving parts of the swing—the shoulders—and assume they're in control and provide the power. But that's not the source of the swing at all. Your torso moves a relatively short distance during the swing, and it moves slowly, so there's no way it can conduct the other parts of the body through greater distances, changing angles, and huge speed."

"Then what is the role of the torso?" I asked.

"The torso simply supports the swing pattern—the speed and direction—of the hands, arms, and club. Like a swing set, the frame allows the seat and chains to swing and supports them because it's anchored to the ground, like the torso is through the legs. The beauty of this system is that if you know the action of the hands and the club, then your mind-body system can respond in kind."

"You know, Joe, I tried to work with the hands years ago, but I found that most golfers' swings became narrow, weak, vertical in swing pattern, and extremely unstable in the wrist action. So naturally, I tried something else, because I couldn't get a student to develop any sense of club control that way."

Shaking his head, Joe responded, "You simply didn't do it with enough understanding of how the hands needed to be placed on the grip and how they function throughout the swing. You know, the hands are capable of deft control, and of course, if not taught with proper care and understanding, their action could create disastrous results. What you really needed to do was try to understand how they're supposed to work, not leave them to fend for themselves in developing a swing. To assume, when you concentrate on hand action, that the swing would become too 'wristy' is to really not use the hands in a fundamental way.

"For example, the beginning of the swing of hand action is to feel the arc of the handle that combines the lead hand and arm in a unified swing action." He demonstrated again how the handle has an arc. "That's certainly not too wristy, is it? The lead arm moves naturally in conjunction with the lead hand to create a swing arc that's useful." His hand and left arm swung back and his torso moved in kind. It was silky smooth. I could not tell what controlled what.

"Notice how my whole body responded to this arc. This is how one puts together a swing through the proper use of the hands—without sacrificing club head awareness. This way you gain total control of it." He demonstrated again. "You notice I have a swing arc that has great potential. Would you agree?" I nodded. His backswing was classic and potent. "However, my swing has no potential without a sound release, has it? One still needs to know how to deliver the club."

"So is this arc and a smooth swing the environment for it? Wow," I said, "that sounds great, but how do I do it?"

"We'll get into the release triggers in due time," he said. "Anything else?"

"I do have more questions, but maybe we should take a break."

Just then, the dog, who had been snoring steadily throughout our discussion, let out a sound that could only be described as a sighing yawn. He had obviously heard this discussion before and seemed glad it was over! Otter stretched his long legs and blinked at Joe. Joe gave him a pat and looked at his watch, excused himself and said he had to put some more lapping compound on the reels he was sharpening and would be back shortly.

My mind was ricocheting all over the place as I processed what I had learned. My negative vibes about Joe Burlington and this place had dissolved. There was a lot he could teach me—maybe it would get me out of my rut and take my mind off the break-up with Claire. It all felt good. It felt proactive for my game. Besides, my alternative was a bitter winter in New England, indoors, golfless, watching movies without anyone to share my popcorn.

4
AWARENESS: FEEL OR ANALYSIS

Burlington returned ten minutes later with two bottles of grapefruit juice and a few triangles of buttered breakfast bread. We sat down in the shade of some large trees near the building, and I thanked him for arranging for me to observe some lessons. "I know you don't teach much anymore, so I really appreciate it."

"It's not that I don't still love teaching," he said, "but many do not want to take the time to process and integrate the changes I suggest. It takes some real stick-to-it-iveness—if that's a word—and faith! In most cases, they'd rather be spoon-fed information and fixed and adjusted than acquire changes through their own practice. Spoon-feeding students is very empty, very boring to me. Desires are being served, but not true needs. That approach doesn't breed confidence and self-trust. Students who want that look at a teacher as a wizard performing magic on their minds and bodies. To me, though, that's sacrilege—when instructors take credit for talent that students already have. Big egos are being fed at the expense of the student!"

Burlington took a breather to eat his snack. My guilty conscience wondered if Burlington had lumped mine in with those other oversized pro egos and if his silence was to emphasize his point. The pause hung in the air, and except for a soft breeze from the east, we were a still life painting. These conversational gaps were uncomfortable for me, but Joe seemed to need and enjoy them. I picked up another piece of bread to keep my mouth busy before he began again.

"Golf is meant to be fun. It's played all over the world in the most beautiful settings. Yet so many players seem so frustrated most of the time, especially the ones who spend a lot of time practicing. The perception is that if you didn't learn it as a child, then forget about learning it now. That's misleading, and it's very limiting. Naturally, learning when you're young is a great advantage, but golf can be learned by anyone willing to take a good look and apply some principles of awareness." I nodded my agreement, still chewing on the bread.

"The golf swing needs to be learned," Joe explained, "through development of a personal physical feel, and relationships between the club, the ground, the ball, and the target. It's like developing an extra sense that combines all physical and emotional feelings—balanced to optimal potential. If you take golf analysis, it's like therapy, isn't it, Geoff? Fixing the golfer's physiology to conform to a standard. But that aside, the analytical approach, even though it's so universally accepted and praised by adult golfers, is of very little value and likely sends learners down the wrong road. An instructor needs to enlighten the student to the fact that figuring out every posture and move involved for each situation is of little value, especially if it means changing their nature. Analysis is too slow and awkward. It's unnatural! A great performance never relies on such a slow and clumsy tool. If a golfer is relying on intellect, trouble is lurking for sure."

I caught his wink, but I was still chewing. He took a swig of juice and continued. "Once you have imprinted an engram, a pattern, you can become accurate yet work subconsciously. Then you can begin trusting your own senses and experience. How it feels to you is all that's of value when you play golf, or any game for that matter. That's once the club is OK, right? I call it 'learning feel.' It is where your focus should always be when you teach and practice."

"But how can a golfer learn to feel? How do you show someone to rely on instinct when each learner's makeup is different? I'm sorry, but I don't understand your theory, Joe."

"It's not a theory, Geoff, it's natural and the best way a human can learn. You can learn just by paying attention to the action of the club and then asking yourself what it is to you, at that moment. In most cases you need to begin very gently and slowly so that accurate coordination is developed—like Tai Chi swings! At this speed, muscle overflow or 'trying hard' with muscle tension won't likely occur and your students will begin to get a sense of ease and timing from the get-go. Some teachers prefer to begin with shorter clubs and swings, but I prefer the longer whippy clubs and full swings at extremely slow speeds. It's a matter of preference, really, and it depends on the student. I like to begin right from the start cutting and grooving those neuropathways with the whole swing pattern. And practically anyone can do it at Tai Chi speed. The key is to make it a total quality exercise so the coordination is learned immediately.

"Through your suggestions of swing patterns, they'll start to get an imprint of the swing. It will take a conscious effort at first, but with enough repetition the proprioceptors will learn the swing and create such familiarity that conscious practice will give way to unconscious trust of the new pattern. Just like riding a bike or skiing down a slope: At first you may fall, but in due time, with repetition, your body will learn the balance and almost never fall again. It's muscle memory."

Questions popped into my head but I didn't want to interrupt him.

"Anyway, because feel is flux, it can be confusing to a student. They'll ask why they can't do it every time. Remind them it's like each day of their life: Every day is different, so they need to be ready to adjust based on their starting point. That's why you must teach them the fundamental action of the club—that's constant. They will learn to trust in a swing without consciously trying hard. The more opportunities you give them to discover on their own, the greater the likelihood they will be able to sustain their improvement. Simple as that.

"Ultimately, when they possess this confidence, they need to learn to simply observe, to not be part of making a swing. Their consciousness becomes an audience to their unconscious swing. They must trust it and let it perform. That's high-altitude confidence."

I finished my juice and put the cap back on the bottle. "Where can I throw this—do you have a recycling bin?" Burlington took the bottle and tossed it in the direction of an uncovered dark-blue bin outside the shed, a good twenty feet away. He scored an effortless three-pointer. "Good shot!" I exclaimed. "How long did you practice that one?"

"Geoff, that's exactly what I've been talking about! I knew it before I threw it, based on past experience. I never would have made that shot had I analyzed how to position myself and choreographed every move. You need to trust and rely on feelings when you practice, same as when you're teaching. I know people say you can't teach someone to use their feelings without analyzing the mechanics of their swing, but that's just not true. Once you go through the learning process you can let go of 'trying to do it.'"

Burlington smiled. He knew he'd gotten my attention. I returned the grin, and told him, "You know, Joe, you're making perfect sense to me and I realize that youngsters will be able to follow your feel technique, but I doubt I could convince most adults. I just don't believe that adults will accept your discovery learning approach, employing those proprioceptors and swinging with their eyes closed. I don't know if I could teach that way. Adults seem to want to fix their problems with mechanical adjustments and analysis. They want more obvious solutions than trusting their senses. Besides, they love to relate to positions and parts of a golf swing. They want something more concrete for their bucks!"

"That's true, but it's really your job, as the instructor, to do whatever it takes to help change this attitude."

"That's easy to say, but how do you go about doing it?"

"How do you change someone who's used to achieving success if they just follow directions by reading the recipe, memorizing the map, or mimicking a pro in a video? Most leisure golfers don't have the time to learn to feel. They want to purchase the answer key. That's why they hire a pro, no?

"Sometimes it's difficult, but I've found all kinds of ways to teach students to feel. My best example is that I used to be that way myself. In fact, I doubt if anyone was a more frustrated golfer than I. You wanna talk about mechanical issues? I had in my brain more swing analyses and recommended positions to integrate and sequence during my swing than there are grains of sand in that sand trap over there. I had been traveling in the wrong direction for so long I really didn't know where I'd gone wrong. It was my own miserable failures that made me take a good look and notice what was happening. I got to the point of having such self-doubt that I wondered where I ever got the idea that I could play and teach this game for a living."

Burlington's words mirrored my own recent thoughts. Were his pauses deliberate punctuations, allowing me to fill in the blanks with my own realizations? I stayed quiet and he began again. "I had lost all the things that had made me successful as a junior golfer. By the time I figured it out, I was miles from my best athletic self. You see, Geoff, I kept trying to perfect my swing. No matter how good I was, I wanted better. My preoccupation with perfection had a reverse effect. All the scrutiny and self-criticism diminished my swing's effectiveness.

"I had nothing to lose. The first thing I did, as I said, was change my attitude. I decided that no matter what happened on the golf course, I wasn't going to let it bother me. I made a commitment that I would just go on. I stuck to it. That was the beginning. Then I had to get rid of all mechanical thoughts—no more manipulation. I had to become techniqueless. Think about that," he ordered, giving me enough silent time to absorb his words.

"I imagine that's how the very first golf swing was taken anyhow, Geoff. It was probably a mighty lash that knocked that first Scotsman right off his feet. Just think what joy he must have felt when he shared his discovery of the game with his friends! Those first swings, those feelings and attitudes, need to be experienced again today. When I realized that I had left that approach in the rear view mirror long ago, it was a step forward for me.

"The people who brought us this game were earthy and natural. They were shepherds, farmers, blacksmiths. They never studied it. They were definitely not intellectuals. There was no technique in those days, Geoff. People played instinctually. There was no mechanical analysis. The ones who developed the most feel and trusted their own instincts won the game. That principle holds true today."

I visualized those earliest golfers. Golf with play! Playing golf! I couldn't remember when golf had lost its sense of play for me.

"Those first golfers were beautiful in their simplicity. They were in touch, Geoff, and to me it is this connection—this sensory approach—that I needed to return to also." I nodded with true understanding "Geoff, just think about it. The first golfers had no teachers. Their swings ranged from the rhythmic to the mighty. They were shot-makers and they had fun! They relied totally on their senses and intuition. That's exactly what we all need to get back to. So I agree with you: Things have gotten out of hand. Rigorously defining 'proper form' and using so-called mechanics excessively," he continued, "constrains your students. The result will bear little resemblance to an athletic performance."[3]

At the risk of frustrating him, I asked again, "But how does a golfer learn totally by feel?"

"How does a teacher teach totally by feel?" he countered. "You have to be creative. After all, you know the absolute fundamentals, the physics of the club for the shot desired. Help your students develop the swing qualities necessary for them to sustain positive growth within those dynamics," he explained.

"But there's so much to know," I protested. "The fundamentals, I mean."

"I beg to differ. There are only a few things to know very well." I asked him to explain. He looked at me a little puzzled, as if this were elementary. He took a sip of juice and continued. "All you need to teach a student is the speed and direction that the club head needs to be traveling through impact, then the shapes and speeds of the swing that make that action more possible more frequently. Each student needs to satisfy the physics component to the best of their mental and physical ability, realizing their own potential. Once the physics are satisfied, just ask them how it feels. All your questions will drive at their awareness of what is happening with the club.

"You need to ask a lot of 'feel' questions to get them to tap into their senses: What does it feel like physically to swing over there? Ask them what different speeds feel like, etcetera. Get it?" He smiled encouragingly. "But again, Geoff, they will ask you how to do it. And, if you're tuned in, you can make a guess at what they're feeling, and while you're observing, you'll find out how close to reality they are. Remember, it's your job to just wake them up, not rebirth them. They must view you as a coach, not a wizard or guru. Otherwise they will become dependent on you, which, in teaching, can only mean failure."

"But there must be some mechanics."

"Anything you want to categorize as mechanics can be covered under Feeling the Physics 101," he laughed. "After God, everything is physics."

"I wonder, Joe, if you could show me how you practice teaching feeling, becoming aware of it."

"Glad to," Burlington responded. He got up and pulled out his one iron. That was a surprise. I'd never heard of beginning a practice session with a one iron. He made a few practice swings in slow motion right there, as though he was feeling every muscle in his body. He began to swing, again very slowly at first, like Tai Chi exercises. Then he closed his eyes and continued to swing. His action was super fluid. Its shape seemed perfect and I wondered when he would begin hitting shots. Suddenly he stopped, took a mighty swing, and brought with it a divot of turf almost a foot long just below the surface of the grass. Then he placed a ball into the middle of the divot, took the one iron, looked once at the target, and took a swing. He hit it thin directly toward his target. At first, I wasn't impressed, but then in another instant he was into his next swing. He struck that shot a little heavy, but again toward the target. In another instant, Burlington placed the ball in the middle of the divot and swung again. This time it was solid, but a little to the right. He was into the next swing, no hesitation—wham! There was another crisp shot, only this time it split the pin. Another swing again—hit solid, right at his target.

The next few minutes were a display of one-iron shots off hardpan like I had never witnessed before. Burlington finished most of the bucket without saying a word and there was a definite groove to his play. What he did next really took me by surprise. He bent down and picked up the divot that he had slashed from the earth and replaced it. You could hardly tell he'd practiced there.

Impressed and excited, I thought here was a guy whose actions matched his words. I hadn't seen that very often. I thought back to some of the tour players I'd worked with. They can hit it, for sure, but when they try to explain how you can do it, they're at a complete loss. They relate only to themselves; they haven't a clue about your perspective, and therein lies the problem. And then there are teachers who can describe in detail how to go about it and yet can't hit it. But Burlington could practice what he was preaching. How he hit those shots so quickly and accurately was a puzzle to me, especially since he didn't even seem to look at the target. Yet the balls went directly toward it almost every time.

Next, Burlington pulled out his driver. Skepticism crept back in; this I wanted to see. At Tai Chi speed, Joe teed up six balls in a line and, one after the other, he hit them with barely a second between shots. The first ball flew about a hundred yards a little off-line; then he hit a little to the left and not quite solid. Then a little right, more solid, and then just right. Then to the left again. He finished the first set, and just as before, you could see he'd reached his groove. In the next set, each ball landed almost on top of the one before. Only now the speed was increasing. The balls were flying long. Burlington still didn't say anything. He kept swinging and the balls kept flying. As the display of shot and swing control continued, it became a marvel to observe. Burlington hit about thirty drives. After the first six, the accuracy was so good, you could have put a blanket over the balls.

Then he took his wedge, picked a target, and shot balls toward the base of the flag. I was astonished. He began to change the trajectories of shots and alter the spin. Some hit the flag, while others bounced just beyond it. There was clearly a ton of creativity and control in his shots. He could only be doing this by feeling and trusting in his swing. What also struck me was that this is exactly how everyone should be playing! That truth had been obscured by my own dismal past.

Silent as he performed, Joe Burlington smiled from time to time, emerging from the game he was obviously playing in his head. I desperately wanted to get in on it. This was the real deal. He took one last swing. "That's it," he said. He put his wedge back into the bag and sat down.

"How did you do that?" I asked.

"Do what?" he teased.

"You know, make all those swings and hardly take a breath."

"Oh," he replied, "you mean how fast I practice?"

"Yes, and why in the world would you begin with a one iron? What are you thinking from shot to shot?"

"Hold on there, Geoff; one question at a time. The one iron lets me challenge myself right from the start. It's one of my favorite clubs, but you know it requires a high level of awareness. I've learned that it tells me the most about my swing, so I begin with it to find out my baseline for the day. It helps me notice my patterns and my timing for the impact."

"But what about all the other contributing factors, like setup, grip, and plane?"

He lowered his voice. "Those things are rote," he whispered like he was embarrassed to have to clue in a big boy like me. "We learned those things a long time ago. There's no need to concentrate on them now. Besides, there's too much to feel in the impact zone to be distracted by things that we learned as children. Right, Geoff?"

"I begin slowly," he continued, "so as to wake my feelings and senses up, but once I get what I'm looking for, I just begin repeating. If I get something I don't want, I just cancel it out in my mind. I don't verbalize anything as I practice because I never want to engage the left brain in a session. Again, it's a discipline that keeps my mind in the right place—asking the right questions so that my senses, intuition, and body awareness can discover the feel of a sound swing for that day, based on the physics. I'm playing a mental game, a mind game, if you will, the whole time. I figure if I can time a one iron, a driver, and a wedge, that covers the whole ball of wax. Don't you think?"

Holding in a chuckle, I shook my head with amusement.

"What's wrong?" he asked

"I just find it very amusing," I replied. "Practically everything you do is contrary to how I learned to practice golf."

"Thank you," he responded with a smile. "I will take that as a compliment. But let me tell you in more detail what's going through my mind as I practice, Geoff. The questions I ask myself are fundamental. The fact that I begin with a one iron is just a challenge and fun to me; I wouldn't recommend it to most golfers."

"Oh, you don't have to worry about that," I quipped. "No one would take me seriously about that anyway."

"Good," he said.

"One other thing came to mind as I was watching—the speed at which you practice the routine for developing feel. I've always wanted to develop a clutter-free way of swinging and playing, and..."

"You're pretty sure you were just watching it?" he asked.

"Well, yes, I think you could say that," I said humbly.

"You'll get your chance to see how to teach and swing that way. Some of the students will be filled with ideas that are, as you put it, cluttered. We will definitely address 'monkey-mind syndrome' when the time comes. I agree that being uncluttered is a real good place to be, both physically and with one's psyche. Of course, the psyche always comes first."

"But back to what was going through your mind when you first struck those balls not so solid and off line."

"Actually," he said. "I don't remember them. I forget them right away. I chalk them up to being unaware in that moment of swinging the club. Really, I just say 'cancel' to myself and go to the next one. I do notice what they are and adjust according to my awareness, but that's all I use them for. They help me get in balance. I don't waste a second on what went wrong. They don't mean anything in terms of how I might play."

"It would have disturbed me a lot if I'd started that way."

"Really?" Burlington's eyebrows raised and he feigned surprise. "Those warm-up shots give me an accurate assessment of where I am at that moment—feeling-wise; it's like tuning in to my inner frequency. Missed shots are stepping stones, not stumbling blocks. Just because those shots weren't what I wanted doesn't mean they're wasted.

"Let me ask you this, Geoff: When you get up in the morning, does everything happen perfectly from the moment you leave your bed?"

"I guess not," I answered.

"Do you fret about it or do you just go on?" Joe asked.

"I usually don't pay it any mind. It's just part of the day."

"Right. There's nothing you can do about it, so your only option is to go on. The ball is always in your court when it comes to choosing how you're going to react to anything. You can either dwell on what didn't work or you can choose otherwise and move on." He turned his palms up, weighing the choices. "You'll probably see exactly what I'm talking about in a student this week. Looking in from the outside will make it easy for you to see clearly which choice was the best one. The same thing needs to happen in your own golf, Geoff, whether it's on the course or on the practice tee. I've found it to be a healthy way to handle learning and playing golf, and for that matter, handling life itself."

He laid down another one of his long pauses. I was starting to get used to them. Then abruptly, he stood up. "Excuse me, but I need to take care of a few things; you can stay here and practice if you like. I'll be back in a while."

5

JUST FLY THE PLANE

I sat there, trying to absorb what Burlington had told me and shown me. I didn't need to hit shots; I needed to think about what he had said and done. He had hooked me with his maverick attitude and his unorthodox, yet simple, technique. He was definitely unconventional, but his eccentricity was not the issue; I'd been accused of that myself. And it was obvious that as an athlete, Joe Burlington could do with a golf club exactly what he was talking about.

My own practice sessions were the antithesis of Joe's. I'd spend an hour hitting the same bucket of balls Burlington had hit in a few minutes. I'd developed a sort of slow ritual of checkpoints. I would always begin with a wedge or other short club. I would begin going down my checklist—first my alignment, then my setup, then my takeaway, ending with my top-of-the-swing position. When I think about it, I hardly ever got to feeling and knowing what I wanted at impact. I had always assumed that you needed all the other things to come first. Yet Joe claimed he never left impact with his awareness presence. I could never get to the one iron or the driver. Compared with Burlington's, my approach seemed backwards. To top it off, I would have been exhausted—and that would have shaved off confidence rather than building it. Joe was fresh. The whole time he'd been practicing, he was improving his feel and his confidence. Wasn't that what it was all about?

I had been digging myself into a deep hole, analyzing each swing and what was wrong with it, and then trying to extricate myself from that hole. My practice never seemed to have an end, either. There was always something else for me to do; I never felt ready to put it into action on the course. If I had a good day of practice, the doubt would cast a shadow over the next day.

Would my swing be there tomorrow? How many years would I have to practice to ever feel ready?

This rush of honesty pivoted my mind to Claire. I was crazy about her and would do just about anything to make her happy. But my social life had always come second to golf. When Claire had shown up for her lessons after Jason dumped her, I was angry that he hadn't recognized what a prize he'd won in Claire. I only wanted to make her laugh again. And when she finally let me know that I could do more than make her laugh, I'd felt like I'd won the lottery. Yet I'd kept telling her I wasn't ready. "Life happens, whether you're ready or not, Geoff. All we have is the moment. Sometimes waiting for 'ready' is not an option," she'd told me before saying goodbye. I could have agreed with her, if she'd waited for a response.

Joe Burlington was right. I'd let too many meaningless things bother me— like the way things went when I first picked up a club, or how I'd feel if my swing deteriorated as a session progressed into the second hour. It stopped being fun when I didn't feel ready. My students complained about that, too. At times they would begin on a good note, but after a few minutes, things would take a turn for the worse. Sometimes no matter what they tried, and despite everything they knew, nothing worked. That's when it stopped being fun.

I hadn't thought about it before, but most golfers don't know how to practice to get better, me included. Oh, we know how to complicate the game and end up worse off for the effort. I remembered students—I'd done it myself—taking a hiatus from golf, and then doing pretty well for a while after resuming the game. But very quickly, the same patterns would emerge and things would go downhill. I kept thinking of how much time I'd wasted. I wished I'd met Joe Burlington years ago.

Before I had time to let my thoughts drift to other parts of my life that needed fixing, Joe returned with Otter, two containers of coffee, and a brown bag. It was closer to lunch than breakfast and Joe must have anticipated my stomach grumbling. As he sat, he proffered the bag with one hand and a napkin with the other. "Sorry it took me so long. I needed to check a few things in the shop."

And I had needed the break to process what I'd learned. Maybe it *could* get me out of my rut. I took a cookie from the bag.

Burlington sipped his coffee and relaxed in the chair next to me. Otter sat down at his feet, lowering himself slowly, leg by leg. He let out a deep groan. Joe broke off a piece of cookie and Otter made it disappear without blinking. Joe continued to share his cookie with the dog, balancing his coffee on his knee.

After a bit of small talk, I took the opportunity to regurgitate my ponderings. "You know, Joe, since I watched your practice session, I've been thinking about the differences between your routine and mine. When I was very young, I guess I learned your type of practice, but I wasn't aware of the process—or how my senses and 'feel' figured into it. Now that I think about it, as I got older and developed my analytical thinking, I abandoned my natural and intuitive self—and for the sake of trying to improve! You've made it clear that that's exactly how I lost my confidence. I became very unsure of myself and that snowballed. My skills plateaued when I began to get mechanical, and it all went south after that. Oddly, I had confidence in most parts of my life, except in what I wanted most—to be a really fine golfer!" As I said that I felt like I was sharing a great golf epiphany.

"I can relate to that," Joe said. "Your practice strategy was a stumbling block instead of being a stepping stone to your progress, Geoff. As your confidence eroded, so went your swing."

"Yes," I concurred sadly. "I understand now. When I reached the point where I had no place to go, the only strategy I had was to learn more and practice harder. I couldn't seem to get going in a positive direction." I really wanted to hear more about how Joe had gotten himself back on track and to hear in more detail about the changes he had made during the transition. I wanted a roadmap. I asked him, "What exactly did you find out about how to develop your confidence and how to get rid of your insecurity in golf?"

"Geoff, my mistakes were similar to yours—and to almost everyone who picks up a club to learn to swing better! You see, I also thought knowing more about the mechanics of how to play and how to swing would give me confidence. Boy, was I wrong! It's very difficult for people to understand, but knowledge is the opposite of trust and self-confidence. The more I thought about my golf swing and really knew how it worked, the worse I performed. Knowledge of how things worked, in fact, increased my self-doubt."

"How could that be?

"I guess as I learned the intricate mechanical details, I began to micro-manage everything about my swing. Now I knew how many things could go wrong. But knowing all the mechanical minutia would never provide me with the trust I needed. Remember, Geoff, I'm Irish. Murphy's Law, a given for anyone Irish, was at work!"

He laughed heartily and took a sip of his coffee, then tossed the last piece of cookie in Otter's direction. The dog snapped it down in one swallow that went straight to a yawn. Joe patted Otter's head and put down his cup. "Let me tell you a story about trust that illustrates what I mean. It comes from eastern philosophy."

Otter let out another yawn, but Joe continued anyway. "A master would frequently assert to his disciples that holiness was less a matter of what one actually did than what one allowed to happen. To demonstrate, he told the following story." Joe lowered his voice to a dramatic whisper.

"There once was a one-legged dragon, who said to a centipede, 'How do you manage all those legs? It is all I can do to manage just one.' 'To tell you the truth,' said the centipede, 'I don't manage them at all'."[4] Joe chugged down his coffee as I nodded a dim understanding.

"In the case of a golf swing, a lot is happening, and it's a matter of trust that we allow it to happen. So often, we think we need to be in charge of everything—as if that would really give us total control! But that control is an illusion, Geoff, and the odd thing is, we keep doing it and it keeps serving us poorly. We have to pause, examine, and change the way we do things.

"You see, trust and knowledge don't necessarily work together. It's not logical, but neither is any belief system. It's harbored in our unconscious, complex and often illogical. When one is learning, one is not necessarily getting more confident. That was hard for me to understand because I believed that the more I worked and the more I knew, the more successful I would be. You must develop your confidence, your trust in yourself, at the same time that you are becoming more aware. Many people fail to accept this principle."

He hesitated for a moment. "It's like spirituality. Have you ever asked anyone to really explain their faith? To a believer, that faith makes perfect sense. But to a non-believer.... Because if you have faith, you don't need an explanation, and if you don't, then no explanation will ever satisfy your intellect. If you don't have it—that instinct or feel or faith—you can't get it through knowledge or logic!"

During the pause that followed, my cell phone rang. I turned it off, embarrassed, and apologized. Joe dismissed it with a wave and a single nod and continued to speak. "So we cannot get trust through intellect. It's a matter of belief. You need to become a bit of a mystic, Geoff. Get to the point where no explanation is necessary. Have you ever noticed an athlete's response to either a great play or an unusually poor performance? Most often, they can't explain how it happened."

"So then what can one do to get better?"

"You build up your awareness, your in-the-moment ability to feel, and you believe in that. You don't need to know why or how, conceptually or intellectually. The trust component is vital when it comes to improving and needs to be developed while improving one's swing and playing the game. It's like when we learned to walk. We had to keep trying and, at some point, believe that we wouldn't fall down. After a while, it was automatic because we were designed to walk. We just don't realize how we learned to do it or how we developed our belief that we could. And now we don't question our ability to walk or run. The same thing can happen with your golf swing, but you need a program that covers all the physics and, at the same time, enables a golfer to become confident. Because as humans, we were designed to play golf, right?" He smiled.

I nodded, but really didn't know what I was agreeing with. "Physics. I have another question. When my students take lessons, they usually do fine with me. But when they get on the course, or if they practice alone, things don't work as well."

"Yes," he responded, "that used to happen to me all the time. If they're in balance with their swing, you could point directly at their trying too hard, which is, again, a trust problem. But if they're not trying too hard, and they *are* trusting, but it's just not working? What's happening usually relates to an imbalance of focus."

"Huh?"

"OK, I'm going to explain using an old physics theory from the 1930s." Otter sighed loudly. He had, no doubt, heard Joe tell this story before. Joe scratched Otter between the ears. "This story may be useful when your students are puzzled by their practice and play. You see, Geoff, focus is a two-edged sword! It may get you to change something for the better, but it may also disrupt something that was good before you zeroed in on it. Micro-focusing, compartmentalizing, often does not allow you to see the forest for the trees. Performance suffers because of this incomplete awareness, and then you get confused about the value of your changes. You may end up believing you went down the wrong road.

"Do you know the first thing pilots are trained to think when they have an in-flight emergency? Fly the plane. Don't get so into the emergency that you crash, having fixed the problem. In golf that translates into 'swing the club.' Don't get so into improving some aspect of your action that you don't swing the club well!

"Anyway, back to physics. Have you heard of Heisenberg? The guy who turned the physics world upside down with his uncertainty principle back in the thirties?"

"Uh, no, not really."

"Well, Werner Heisenberg came along when there was a great debate about light, classical physics, and the new quantum physics. The question was, 'is light a particle or a wave?' It caused great consternation among that branch of science. In one camp, you had the wavers and in the other, the quanta or particle fans. Heisenberg disputed both when he said that light can be both—it has a dual nature, and what it seems to be depends on how one looks at it. That principle kind of goes with everything we look at, doesn't it? Essentially, Heisenberg said that you cannot determine the momentum of light and the position of it at the same time, so when you look at light one way, it is a particle in a small space, but from another perspective, it can be a wave covering a very large area."

I wondered how this fit into our discussion of the golf swing. My puzzled look prompted Joe to say, "Bear with me, Geoff; there is a point to this story." I nodded politely and tried to look less confused. "The wave camp pooh-poohed Heisenberg's idea and, of course, so did the particle camp, but he was right."

I couldn't restrain myself. "How does this relate to golf?"

"Well," Joe said, "it relates to how we look at everything. Let's say you looked under a microscope at two words."

He took out a pen and wrote on the paper bag, very large, *momentum* and below it, in very small letters, *position.*

"If you focus the microscope on the word *position*, the smaller of the two, *momentum* goes out of focus, right? Heisenberg to the tee! The same thing happens to golfers, Geoff! In teaching, all you need to figure out is what's more valuable to your students. I'm sure you know where I stand on this. Momentum relates to a whole motion and of course position relates to static parts. To me, learning a golf swing through feeling motion and the sequence is the key.

"Anyway, back to Heisenberg. When we focus on one area, the others get fuzzy. If you only care about your flow in a golf swing, if you focus on it long enough, it's likely you'll become unaware of your path! If you concentrate on path, it's likely you'll become unaware of your timing. Now regarding practice, it's the concentrated way you look at things that can throw off the other fundamentals. That's why it's best to spend a few minutes on each discrete area in order for the whole works to stay in balance. When your students are not trying hard and they seem not to be making progress, it's usually a question of focus."

"What do you do then?"

"You give them a simple balanced program. Ten minutes of flow, ten minutes of path, and ten minutes of timing—and maybe ten minutes of nothing to do except swing to see how things blend."

"It seems that after the setup your program is all motion. I learned to swing in a totally different way."

"How so?"

"By getting my body and club into about eight distinct positions to create a fundamental swing action."

"That surely is popular, Geoff, but just like Heisenberg, you have to include the point of view of the observer, the student. Then ask the question. What POV gives them the most complete picture and the possibility of a sound swing action? Remember, your students are going to be on their own and need a way to go about it when they're alone on the course too."

"You seem to have a real aversion to teaching the golf swing in the separate parts that most instruction adheres to these days."

"You're exactly right, Geoff—this is a very important aspect of my paradigm shift. Have you ever noticed how much you can tell about a swing from a distance? I mean, it's easy to see the flow and path patterns from 200 yards away."

"Yes, I have noticed that I can tell who's on our practice tee from a distance."

"And that's a view of the whole, not the parts. Coming from this perspective allows you to help a student develop a swing from a totally different point of view. Teaching from a position development standpoint tends to shut down the mind-body sensory system because it lends itself to analysis. Feel comes to a grinding halt. On the other hand, the whole swing motion development, momentum, which the mind-body system relates to instantly, gives feel feedback continuously. Avoid the minutia and wake up the sensory system.

"Granted, for a teacher, it's a far more challenging way to go and requires a lot of experience and creativity, but in the final analysis (no pun intended) it is superior and longer lasting. Your students will be very well served.

"I'll give you an example. I had a student, Tony, who'd been playing for a few years and loved it. He played OK but felt he could do better, so he came to see me. I questioned him about his game and what programs he'd tried. And I asked him about his swing thoughts—what was on his mind while he practiced and played.

"He said he had many different swing thoughts for all occasions. He described it as putting out fires. For instance, he said when he wanted to hit it far, he used to load up on his right side—you know, increase his shoulder turn. But most of the time he'd get mishits—until a friend told him some magic way to hit it far and never to the right. He had all kinds of different adjustments friends and teachers had recommended.

"So I asked him to just show me his swing. This was almost an alien concept to him. He asked me what he should think about and how I wanted him to approach it. He had a lot of trouble with the idea of just being 'mindless' and hitting a few shots. He'd never made a swing before without a litany of things to think about.

"So I tried another approach. I asked him to show me his routine, and to swing, and tell me everything that went through his mind from beginning to end; from before he made the swing to when he executed the shot."

"So what did he think about?" I asked.

"It was quite something. First he lined up the club from behind the ball, then he walked to the side and begin working on his posture, bending his knees and sticking out his butt and kind of wiggling into position. You could tell his lower back had tensed up and he wasn't comfortable. Then he took hold of the club with what he described as 'good pressure.' He said if he wanted to hit it far, he made as big a shoulder turn as possible."

"Anything else?"

"Oh yes. He said then he had to really concentrate on coiling his body, keeping his head down on the ball for as long as he could and on trying to keep his left arm as straight as possible, and keeping his wrists stiff. And lastly, he prayed. Which is not a bad idea.

"And remember, Geoff: One manipulation begets another."

"What do you mean?"

"If Tony had to think of a step one movement, then he would have to deal with step two, three, four, and on and on. It never ends. He'd tied himself to a series of simultaneous manipulations. I watched him go through his whole routine, and he made solid contact. His swing looked like it took a lot of work, but you could tell he was pleased with the results. But after a few more swings, he was very erratic. His excellent start disintegrated into a hodgepodge. He would hit the ball solidly toward the target every fourth shot and chastise himself for every mishit.

"I asked him to swing with a longer club—a four iron. With that, his contact became seriously unpredictable. I remember he practically stuck the club into the ground, then hit it way left, way right, and also very thin. As he swung, his upper body coiled. The downswing seemed like springs in a motor wound as tightly as possible. The club flailed recklessly at the mercy of his unharnessed force. He was about one for ten using the longer club. He had no way of controlling the club's direction. His club face was really shut, too. That's a common result of a dominating torso torque in the backswing.

"So what did you do?"

"I told him he didn't have to think a thought at all."

"How did he take that?"

"He said it would be strange, and that his thinking it through was what allowed him to play well. 'I beg to differ,' I said, and told him it was exactly why his swing and shots were so erratic. I asked him how many of his swing thoughts dealt with the club."

"And?"

"None. So I told him that it was totally unnecessary for him to think about the things he was thinking about and that it was actually a detriment to his natural athletic ability. I mean, all he had to do was swing the club! That's the first order of business. Just like pilots need to first concentrate on flying the plane. Tony was so micro-focused on all these details that the big picture went out of focus.

"I explained to Tony how he could get back to a natural swing. For the swing to be repeatable, it needs to have a quality of fluid motion for consistency. In Tony's case, I suggested he begin to lighten his hold on the club and allow the club swinging to dominate his muscles and joints. He needed to see how supple he could feel throughout his body."

"At first he was concerned that if he held the club lightly, he wouldn't gain control over it or that it would fly out of his hands, but I told him that a golf swing needs to be graceful. Look at the best swings throughout golf's history.

"I got him to try a few practice swings and he began to loosen up and swing the club as though it were not so heavy. Then I had him tee up about six balls, six inches apart, and swing consecutively from the first ball to the last without stopping. Tony went right through the six balls and made solid contact with four of them. He teed up some more and went through four sets that way. He struck the balls solidly, for the most part."

"Because he stopped trying to focus on all those adjustments?"

"Yes. And he also discovered a nice bonus. He said that before, using his routine, he would have been tired and sore if he'd made that many swings, but he wasn't. I pointed out that this was because his body was very smart when it was swinging the club with such a rhythmic, fluid motion. There's just no need to be forceful. I then asked him what he had been thinking about while he swung through those four sets of balls."

"And?"

"He said, 'Nothing'. Just swing the club."

I heard a car and looked. A green pickup truck was coming down the dead-end road bordering the golf center. It pulled into the back entrance of the maintenance area. Joe followed my gaze. "Oh, that's my friend Bob. He's gonna be annoyed at me for not having prepared the loader for repair. We planned on replacing the seals on the lift arms. They've been leaking oil. I hate to end our session now, but it's a two-man job, and I need to help."

As he got up, Joe said, "You can practice here if you like; we can meet tomorrow, nine AM sharp." His mind had switched to his next task. I thanked him and we shook hands. I pulled out my money clip, but he waved me off. He had spent several hours with me and he didn't mention a fee. And he invited me to come back tomorrow. I thought surely I needed to pay him. But he was already on his way to his tractor. I guess we could do business later.

It was still early but I didn't feel like practicing. I got my stuff together and made my way to the car. I mapped out a plan for the afternoon. First, get some groceries for the week. At around four in the afternoon I would head to the golf course to try my technique-free swing. Nothing to do but swing.

I went to Publix and picked up cold cuts, rotisserie chicken, potato salad and rolls, filling my basket with my favorite foods, plus some wine and beer.

Back at the B&B, I sat down at the kitchen table overlooking the ocean, made a sandwich and had a cold beer to wash it down. After a short nap, I headed to Pompano, ready to try out a little Burlington philosophy on the course. I could play there anonymously.

After checking in, I went directly to the first tee. No one was around. This time of year the sun goes down around five-something. There was only an hour of daylight left, so I had clear sailing for at least nine holes; that's all I had time for anyway. I decided to improvise on Burlington's idea of all feel, no technique. I would go full Technicolor and pretend I was in Scotland with the original golfers; the craftsmen, herders, and fisherman. Here it goes: the beginning of my new golf game.

I pulled out my driver, walked to the championship markers, and teed up a brand-new Titleist. As I looked down at the ball, a swing thought leaped into my mind, but just as Joe advised, I shouted 'cancel' to myself. The thought dissolved. Amazing. That little shout from within shut down my misbehaving mind and allowed me to focus on this mental game of feel and imagining. Part of me felt uncomfortable not thinking about a position in my swing, but another part felt relief. I was determined to stick with it no matter how uncomfortable I got. What did I have to lose?

As I looked down the fairway, I pictured Scotland. It wasn't hard, because Pompano resembled a links course. It was rough, there were just a few trees, and sand dunes lined the fairways. Of course being near the Atlantic, the wind was gusting at a good 20 knots, too. After one more look at my target I proceeded to nail it down the middle of the fairway. Wow! It worked, technique-free! I had a half wedge again, rehearsed the feeling of the swing. This time, I put the ball just under the hole—almost exactly where I pictured it. This could be fun, instead of a struggle. I played the next several holes well, hitting each fairway and green and canceling swing thoughts as they entered my mind. That's how it's supposed to be done.

I couldn't believe it: I was getting good at this already. This must be the 'let-go' mode Joe had been talking about. I was two under through seven—not bad. Darkness was approaching. The eighth hole was a long par four dogleg right; the wind was blowing left to right. It was the most difficult of winds for me to make a swing. I couldn't help but try to keep the ball from flying too far to the right so I told myself, don't go right and just like that, I hit a wicked block out of bounds to the right! I couldn't believe I lacked the confidence to hit it somewhere down the fairway. But when I thought about it, that's exactly what should happen when you try too hard.

I needed to keep trusting, but I felt I just couldn't be techniqueless in this situation. My history in this wind had taken over and I had performed my 'trying hard' swing perfectly. I shook my head; that's exactly what Joe was talking about. Insecurity was written all over this swing.

I teed up another ball and said to myself, just swing. I did, and struck it solid and square. The wind barely touched it. It ended up far down the right side of the fairway. OK, good lesson. It was getting dark now. I drove to my ball on the right side of the fairway, leaned over to my left and snatched it off the turf without slowing down. I wanted to return the golf cart so the cart guys could go home. I could remember when I used to work the carts what it was like waiting for the last one to be returned.

I felt like I had found my first strategy to get out of my funk as a player. It was all mental, too. Maybe I was finally on the right track. But it was still too early to say. At least I'd seen that being techniqueless could work. And I knew

Burlington's ideas of proprioception were right, too. Without any technique I could feel the action of the club through my hands, from driving to putting. It was total feel. I couldn't believe the difference in how I felt about things after only one day.

Optimism was becoming my mantra. I drove home elated. I nuked my chicken in the microwave and pulled the potato salad and a beer from the fridge. I was feeling pretty good, except for one thing. I was alone. I had come home to no one. It was now exceedingly clear to me that I needed a companion, a partner, an intimate partner. I thought about calling Claire, but it was still too early in this odyssey for that.

6
A NEW DAY

I arrived at the golf center, eager for more. Joe's whole approach really appealed to me now. I went directly down to the barn. Joe was ready for me, sipping hot coffee with Otter at his feet. As he sipped he occasionally tossed a morsel of his muffin to the dog. Otter concentrated on Joe until the last bite was gone.

Joe had set up another stool. I sat, gratefully accepting the coffee he handed me. I felt much more comfortable with him today. My impression was that Burlington was never uncomfortable with anyone.

"Let me ask you a question," he asked quickly.

"Sure!" I said, eager to begin.

"Since we're discussing fundamental learning, what atmosphere do you think we need to cultivate to really get the most out of our time with our students?"

"Atmosphere?"

"Yes. What do you think is most important to everyone in this world?" He hesitated a moment, then continued. "What I mean, Geoff, is what do you think is the best condition to be in, to grow, the most desired feeling in the world?" He looked around the shop as he waited for my answer. His question took me by surprise; I hadn't a clue where he was coming from.

Then Burlington said, "Everyone is seeking more freedom, aren't they?" I nodded. I guess that seems right, but I was fuzzy on it. He recognized my uncertainty but continued. "The more you understand the truth of this principle, the more you will understand what I'm doing as I share my experiences with you. If you make freedom part of every aspect of your interactions with others and never attempt to control them, you will always be assured of doing something good." He paused dramatically and took a long slug of coffee while searching my eyes. I was silent, not wanting to interrupt, waiting for his point to crystallize without silly interruptions from me. "In other words, if you don't limit the freedom of others, and if everyone else respects that too, the world is a better place. So it goes in life or in golf. When you are free, you are fearless. Defensiveness is eliminated because there's no need for it. And when you're fearless, you own both trust and confidence. In teaching, once you elevate trust, the student loosens up. You free the spirit, the swing loosens and they become, as you say, clutter-free. Ask yourself how straitjacketed you felt when you were struggling with your various swing techniques."

His voice dropped and he put his finger to his lips as if getting ready to tell me a sacred secret. "I hope you'll see it happen this week in the lessons you observe. Maybe you'll even experience it in yourself. You see, Geoff, when you understand this and experience it, you can relate it to practically everyone and everything in life."

"I'm looking forward to it," I responded sincerely. But I realized I was a little disappointed that he still hadn't spoken much about the fundamentals of the golf swing, except in very general terms. Even though I had experienced some success being techniqueless, I realized I was still somewhat attached to the angles, torque, and position adjustments of the body during the swing. Yesterday afternoon, on the first tee, I had fallen back on those elements. It was hard to let go of them, even though I realized that a comfort zone can be detrimental. Conditioning is a weird thing: Even when it doesn't serve us, we cling to it because it's familiar.

I had lived my life this way for too long. Claire had tried to enlighten me to this principle, but somehow I couldn't let go of old patterns. I knew it was time to change and that required commitment.

Joe awakened me from my thoughts. "I know you'd like to get into the physics more..." The way Burlington seemed to respond to questions before they left my lips was beginning to freak me out. "...the fundamentals of the swing and how they need to be taught, but it's important to reinforce our underlying purpose. You need to set up the conditions that give you a peek into a golfer's authentic swing." His hands framed the word *authentic*. "Otherwise you end up observing their trying-hard, heavy-effort swing. Really, there's no use attempting to work on adjusting that, right?"

That question didn't really require an answer, but Joe waited. I nodded.

"So a condition of ease and lightness needs to be woven into a lesson from beginning to end, with no pressure to perform. At this stage, we want only to discover. So, before we get to the swing, we must have a clear understanding of that."

"OK, I understand, Joe. It makes sense. Let's talk about the students," I prompted. "Where are they coming from?"

"Hold your horses. First, I have a story I think you'll find interesting. Learning is a process, Geoff. Everyone processes at a different speed. As a teacher, you must give the process time and not interfere with it. Do you have any experience in drawing?" *What?* He continued without waiting for my response. "I once read a book by an art teacher, Betty Edwards.[5] She studied the learning process intensively and from a neuroscience perspective. The brain is governed by its property of plasticity. Ongoing discoveries have proven that, though we know the brain does have specific areas of expertise, designated for particular tasks. The brain is all connected, but for our purposes we will separate the parts to determine the tools best suited for the task at hand. I can elaborate later. Betty Edwards claimed that she could help anybody learn to draw better in only a few minutes. You know how some people say they can't draw? Well, Betty was determined to obliterate that belief. She believed everyone had the ability—if you could write your name, you could draw."

I was still trying to catch up and asked, "How did she do it?"

"It's mostly a matter of perspective. She figured there was something going on in the brain that caused people to either be able to draw well naturally—or not. Light enters your eyes and the brain interprets and processes information. For our purposes, let's combine the brain and eyes and call it seeing! When we see, we automatically perceive. Our life experience typifies our responses and gives them a frame of reference—what we are familiar with is always a factor. The brain has an amazing capacity to fill in the blanks based on experience."

Burlington paused before continuing his lecture. "The brain can learn to see, and it can continue to learn to see better and more clearly throughout your life. In golf, it can then interpret things more accurately, know where to go, anticipate obstacles, or see openings, and will always be able to make good decisions based on seeing better. Betty Edwards caught an inkling of this nature of seeing. She identified left-brain judgments as interference: We don't have a vision handicap, we have an interpretive one! It's in the brain! She designed exercises that turned on the right part of the brain so it could not be interfered with.

"How did she do it?"

"There's a well-known example you've probably seen—the vase-profile exercise. She got students to turn a drawing of the outline of a vase upside down. When they did that, the brain didn't label it a vase anymore. Edwards obscured the brain's interpretation of the picture so that the picture was just a couple of curvy lines. That's when the magic takes place. Without a label, without being familiar with the form, and without preconceptions of what it is and how to draw it, the students began to examine the relationship between the lines. When they drew it, they drew two faces in profile. They learned to see things for what they are exactly in terms of the picture—one line's relationship to another. When the vase is no longer a vase, the brain's— the left brain's—interference is eliminated—it just sees the lines.

"What this proves to me is that when we have problems, our interpretations, the perceptions on which we base our understanding, are flawed. It's using this basic strategy of labeling and mind jumping that throws us off."

"I get it." I said. "They couldn't see the faces when it was right side up, because they saw a drawing of a complete object instead of the relationships between the lines."

"Right. It's all in the interpretation. They bypassed the line relationships and skipped right to the fact that it was a vase or a tree or a person. It happens so fast—the eye-brain interpreting process—that we're not conscious of it, and then we can't understand why we can't accurately do something seemingly so easy."

I was on the verge of an a-ha moment, but he continued his lecture. "Sound familiar from golf, Geoff? You see, players also interpret instead of just looking. For example, they make a swing, the ball curves and they call it a slice, a negative label. They rarely see it nonjudgmentally as a relationship between the club's path, face, angle, and target. If they did, they would adjust and the slice would be gone. But then golf is a little different than drawing;

golfers also have to deal with another conundrum. They have an unconscious belief about the dynamics that create the flight of the ball that's skewed. You can tell by the change from their practice swing to their actual swing.

"Of course, golf teachers explain where the path of the club must be, but as soon as students attempt to strike a ball they return to the old familiar swing. So just knowing the better path is not the solution. Even though they know the path and face angle necessary for positive change, you have to let the belief system believe in positive change. It can occur in seconds with a dose of the right medicine, so to speak, but I will tell you more about that later. All I am saying, Geoff, is that in golf or in life, we miss a lot based on fear of the result or faulty mental judgments. We have to learn to see differently, to see the true nature of things. And that takes training. The beauty of it is, we have a way to go about it."

He clasped his hands behind his head and squinted at the sky. He could see I was taking in every word, but then he stopped abruptly. "Let's continue this later, maybe over dinner at some point. We had better get into the actual swing dynamics. Give me a few minutes to do some work in the shop, then we can get into it."

He left, and I sat there once again trying to understand this whole aspect of golf I hadn't ever entertained. But it made so much sense now that I'd had it explained to me—though in my mind, I still questioned the statement that someone's slice could be dissolved in a few minutes. I felt as if we were really getting somewhere now. I was beginning to like Joe Burlington, with his out-of-the-ordinary manner and way of relating to others. But I knew I was unable to communicate golf with words the way Joe could.

7
THE PHYSICS—
AND THE FEELING

Joe returned from the maintenance shed with ice cold bottles of water and a Publix bag. He took a few lemons out, rinsed them with a squirt from one of the bottles, cut them neatly in quarters, and then put them into tall cups he'd pulled from the bag. He then spooned some instant tea into the cups and filled them with bottled water. The resulting drink was icy and refreshing and hit the spot—especially since it was unusually warm for a winter morning, even by Florida standards. Once the tea was made, he began again, and we got right into the swing, but not like I anticipated.

"Where were we?"

"You referred to golf swing dynamics."

"Oh, yes." He picked up right where we had left off without skipping a beat. "As a golf teacher, you'll see the relationships of the club—that is, the relationship of the face, path, speed, and the player's way of handling it. As a golf physics expert, you need to know the probability patterns. You need to know the path/speed boundaries, so to speak."

"How do you mean?"

"Well, there are boundaries between the club, the ground, the target line, and the wielder, as I like to call the golfer. There are probability patterns of path and another probability pattern for success based on speed. And there are points of no return."

I looked at him quizzically, not comprehending. "What do you mean by probability patterns?"

Joe took a deep breath and more than a moment to figure how he could impart this concept to me. "When it comes to the physical aspects of the golf swing, what I mean is as soon as a student places their hands on the club and aims, an experienced teacher knows instantly the probability pattern of the swing path and face relationships quite accurately."

"You mean as soon as your students place their hands on the club and aim, you know what the swing will be like before they swing?"

"Yes, pretty close to what it will be like. I observe the student's way of handling the club and how they move it as they approach the ball. I can pretty well tell how the club will behave in terms of face, path, and angle of the swing just by the student's grip and aim."

I shook my head in disbelief, but asked him to continue.

"We can therefore know the probability of a golfer achieving the results—the ball flight—they prepared for, based on these relationships. So we're ahead of the game before they've even struck the first ball. I'm not always right, but I like to play a game in my head and see how close I come, and my observations rarely fail me. Anyway, that's why it's important to get a student going in the right direction fast.

"When you know the probability patterns of the speeds and directions of the handle and club face relationships, it's easy to suggest an adjustment for each pattern. Aim this way, hold the club in this manner, posture yourself this way, swing on this path or feel the face angle like this. It really is easy; the challenge is to get the students to picture, know, feel, and believe!"

"You know, Joe, I find most of my students are stuck on aiming their feet and bodies square to the target line. How do you posture your students?"

"It depends, but an important principle is that the foot alignment or body position has to be connected to the path pattern desired, not just square to the target. You could think of it this way: The club face is for target, but the body is for path. That's why I so often close the stance and body so my students can easily swing in a curve rather than a straight line."

"How does that work?" I asked, still puzzled.

"You see, Geoff, the student has come to you because he or she doesn't know or is not aware of these relationships as they're swinging. The students are simply not present. When students are unaware, you help them become aware so that when they become conscious of the imbalance, they can adjust. All the while, you're attempting to get them to feel the relationships—not as though it is right or wrong, just what it is. Everything points to the action of the club. With a golf club, there is right and left, up and down, fast and slow, wide and narrow, and all things descriptive of its physics. It's your job to create a strategy to get students to balance the club's relationships to those boundaries for their shots. Once the students are there, their swings will be a function of them seeing with this different perspective.

"With this approach to the golf swing, we can identify the true relationships between the physics of the club and the shots we're trying to create. You see, students are discovering and becoming self-coaches and, all the while, they're gaining confidence in themselves and their performances. I love it when they begin saying that it's not so hard. They've really learned, rather than just being fixed."

"That sounds great! When do we begin?" I asked, my excitement filled with new understanding.

"We can begin tomorrow, as I have a lot of things to do with the irrigation pump motor. I have a friend coming over to help me and I need to assist him."

"Anything I can do to help?" I couldn't believe I'd asked that.

"No," he said, "we can handle it, but thanks anyway. You can practice your golf right here, if you like. But while you're practicing, Geoff, begin to notice. Notice how you feel. Begin by asking a good discovery question, like are you in balance throughout your swing? Can you sense the pace changes during your swing? Does it feel effortless and powerful? Those are all good awareness questions to begin with. See if you can come up with your own questions. Let's meet tomorrow morning, bright and early."

Again, I was disappointed that our session had ended so abruptly, just as I felt we were getting into the golf swing now. But I knew he had a lot to do— the machines, the grass, the grounds, the whole business. Now I really understood how little time he had. I still wondered how he could do so many different things and still be such an excellent teacher.

I took Burlington's suggestion and began to practice what we'd spoken about. As I was swinging, I began to realize that I had never really practiced naturally—as Burlington termed it, discovering feel. I'd always had an agenda in my swing. My practice never dealt with feeling where I was, but rather where I wanted to get to mechanically. I wanted to give Joe's approach a shot.

I began with one of his eyes-closed exercises to feel my whole swing, the shape and the rhythm of it. I closed my eyes, swung and really felt the pace. For the first time, I felt my rhythm. I was not distracted by the results since I couldn't see them to judge. I just felt, and to my amazement, I didn't feel a need to fix anything. I just grooved on feeling it. I was present with my golf swing and I was enjoying the process.

As I continued, with no fixing and no intent to change, my pacing improved. It was hard to believe, but it felt wonderful. Maybe Joe Burlington was right. Change was a matter of course when we're aware and impossible when we're not aware, no matter how hard we try. In fact, maybe it's the trying that gets in the way of awareness and change. This was the first time I'd thought this way. Was I truly discovering? I felt like I was. My mind was alert in a new way. I was discovering my swing, not interfering with it as I usually did.

My shots gained consistency. What a high! It felt like I'd only been practicing about twenty minutes. I looked at my watch, surprised to see that two hours had passed. I wasn't even tired, although my grumbling stomach reminded me that I was starving.

It had been the most satisfying time I'd ever spent practicing my swing. I absorbed the feelings like a sponge. I knew I had to get home and get something to eat, but before I left, I stood for a moment and took it all in, felt every sensation, just being. It was so different from being on the go, programmed and performing! I couldn't wait to tell Burlington about it.

I went back to the B&B with positivity swirling inside me. I felt the need to share it. I parked in the driveway and sat in the car looking out at the ocean. I dialed Claire's cell. It went straight to voice mail, so I left a message. "Hi, how are you? I really want to chat with you. It's just that something new is happening to me. I can't fully describe it yet, but I wanted to share it with you. Anyway, you don't have to call me back, I understand. Be well... I love you." That last sentence came out of my mouth just as the recorder beeped. I hadn't meant to say it, hadn't thought it, it just fell out. I didn't know whether to hope the machine had cut me off or not.

8

IF THE CLUB IS OK, THE SWING IS OK!

I awakened before dawn with excitement brewing inside me. The prospect of finally moving forward in my golf didn't allow for a deep sleep. I didn't feel like making my own breakfast, so it was a perfect day to visit Lou at his diner. I set out down the street and hoped he would be there this time since I hadn't caught up to him yet on this trip. I was looking forward to his freshly ground coffee as I made the short walk.

When I arrived, Lou was standing with his back to the counter, cooking bacon on the flat top. Hearing the jingle as the door opened, without turning around he said, "I'll be with you in a minute." The smells livened my appetite, bringing back Sunday morning memories of my youth, when my dad used to brew fresh coffee and fry up bacon long before the rest of the house got moving. The aroma became our Sunday morning wake-up call.

I had picked up a paper outside, and planted myself on a stool at the counter. Lou turned and registered surprise. "Geoff! When did you get in?"

"A couple days ago, Lou." Lou grasped my hand in a firm grip developed from years on his shrimp boat.

"So how's it going?" Lou put down his bacon fork, turned around to grab a pot of coffee, and poured me a cup. "Claire still sleeping?"

"Ah, no Lou… she, ah, didn't make the trip."

He paused for a moment, standing still, looking straight at me, still holding the coffee pot. "Remember, Geoff, you're talkin' to me. What's up?"

I had to tell him. After all, he knew us as a couple. "We broke up."

Lou just stood there for a few seconds and then said, "I'm so sorry to hear that. She is such a special lady. What happened?"

"Let's just say the timing was off."

"Really? I always thought that of the women you brought down to Florida over the years, she was the class of the field."

I nodded. "She was."

"And you let her get away? You know a girl like that doesn't come along too often in a lifetime."

"I just wasn't ready, Lou. I had too many problems; you know, with my golf and all."

Lou shook his head. "Your golf? What does that have to do with it?"

"I felt that I didn't want to commit to anyone before I got my own house in order."

"Geoff, you know me long enough to know I'm a straight shooter, right?"

"Yeah, of course."

"Let me give you a little advice, or better yet, tell you a little story." I nodded, since I knew I was going to hear it anyway. "It happened to me a long time ago." Lou's voice lowered; he got a serious look on his face. "I once had a special gal, and I let her get away." He shook his head regretfully. "And she loved me, if you can believe that. I've had my ups and downs, Geoff, but one regret I still harbor was letting her slip away. Sure, I've had a decent life, and I really can't complain, but I believe it would have been a wondrous journey if I'd taken just a little different road.

"At the time, I was livin' on my boat. I was shrimpin' off the coast of Charleston. During the season of course, I'm working seven days a week, on the water maybe fourteen, fifteen hours a day, sometimes with not much to show for it. I was new in the business then. I could only afford one mate; I needed three. After a catch, in the evenings, we would make the deliveries to the local markets and restaurants.

"Getting a foothold in the business was tough. I had to lower my prices to get any business at all. After paying for fuel, my mate, and the mortgage on the boat, I was practically working for nothing. Anyway, you get the picture."

"Yeah, Lou, I get it."

"Anyway, one day while making a restaurant delivery, I met this girl." Lou's face took on a peaceful look and a smile came over it. "She was good looking and intelligent. She had the most carefree attitude. Being younger than me didn't seem to bother her. Soon we began to date a little. Our first date was a picnic at the old park near the water. She was creative that way. We never went out to dinner at a restaurant; we couldn't afford it. We were a good match, though; both of us worked hard. She spent her days in school at the College of Charleston and most evenings waitressing at her stepmom's restaurant; me on the water. The little free time we had, we spent together. I got to know everything about her and found out that life at home was not rosy. Her mom had died suddenly when she was very young, and her dad took care of her by himself until he remarried several years before I met her. Anyway, her stepmom was tough. Jenny couldn't do anything right. No matter how hard she tried, her stepmother made things very difficult for her.

"But we enjoyed each other's company. She even began to work with me on her days off; it was a calm respite from being home, I guess. Geoff, no work on board was beneath her. She would do anything that needed doin' on that boat. As time passed, I guess you could say we were fallin' in love. Our friendship had become a love affair. Anyway, things got real bad at home, and she realized she needed to get out. Naturally, she wanted to come stay with me."

"What did you do?"

"I did just like you did. Fear got the best of me, and I just couldn't let her come. I got cold feet. I wanted to keep seeing her, but I wasn't ready for a live-in. Being on the water all my life, I figured I couldn't afford to be tied down with a wife. I was afraid of commitment."

"So what happened?"

"Like I said, she had to escape the situation at home, so she ended up quitting school and moving away to live with a cousin. I felt terrible about it. By the time I realized what a horrible mistake I'd made, it was too late. I've been living solo ever since. I never had a companion like that again. For me, it's too late, but you still have time. If you're really in love with her, and she loves you, find a way to make it happen."

"But," I stammered, "how can I be sure, how can you know?"

"Geoff, I just gave you the best advice I can give. What are you lookin' for, a guarantee?" He rolled his eyes like I was being ridiculous. I could tell he was a little annoyed with me. Then he perked up again. "Actually, Yeats said it better."

"Yeats?"

"As in, William Butler. In his poem 'Brown Penny.'[6] Google it, you might learn somethin'," he said with minor disdain.

I wanted out of this conversation, so I agreed to look it up. He sighed with a look of regret. "I wish someone had told it to me when I had my chance. But that's life." He left to help some other customers. Lou's story was sobering. He knew Claire and me well enough to give me that advice. I knew I had to fix that part of my life; I just didn't know how.

In a few minutes Lou returned with my breakfast, and I tried to enjoy it, but his words reverberated inside my brain. As he set down my plate, he asked, "What are you doin' down here anyway, practicing for the winter tournament series?"

"Actually, I came down to work with a golf pro."

"Who?"

Lou wasn't a golfer. "You probably never heard of him. Joe Burlington."

Lou stopped short and turned to me with a wry smile on his face. "Never heard of him? I used to fly fish with the guy in tournaments. What an angler! He can find fish where nobody else can. My friends used to have me invite him because he had some kind of extra sense when it came to fishing."

"It's not just in fishing."

"He can cast a line pert near 75 yards. We knew he was a golf pro, and had a driving range near Pompano, but he never really said anything about it."

"Typical," I muttered.

"So he's teaching you golf. Interesting! How's it going so far?"

"At first, I was skeptical, but he's opened my eyes to a whole new way of swinging a club and playing the game. It's simple and beautiful. I think that by week's end, I'll be far enough along to begin working on those other parts of my life."

"That would be good; I want to see you two back together." Lou was an exceptional guy. He had said as much as I needed to hear. He'd made me believe that somehow, I was going to find a way to win Claire back. I finished my breakfast, said goodbye to Lou, and walked briskly back to my place, emotions churning, then headed for the golf center.

I arrived earlier than I had yesterday. The dew was still on the grass and I saw tire tracks spaced about twenty feet apart in a grid across the whole property. I guessed that Burlington was on the tractor early that morning fertilizing. He seemed to take great pride in the condition of his turf, though it didn't look very plush to me.

Unlike yesterday, it was a bit chilly for Florida, but I figured the fog would burn off when the sun got a little higher in the sky. I looked down toward the maintenance barn and could barely make out the form of someone swinging a golf club. The first swing looked great, very fluid, like a professional golfer. But the next swing looked like a first-day player without much talent. Then it was super fluid, and then erratic again. I couldn't see well from so far away so I figured Burlington must be teaching a beginner and demonstrating rhythm. As I got closer, I saw Joe standing nearby, so realized it wasn't him swinging. His student made another swing. It was a thing of beauty, as though every movement was blended and all his muscles were moving in cooperation with each other. It was flawless. By the time I approached, the student was packing up and saying goodbye to Joe.

I was feeling pretty good about what I had learned from the day before. I blurted out, "That looked great, but what was up with that terrible swing before? It must be a real challenge to teach someone like that." Burlington ignored me, so I repeated the question.

He looked me in the eye and said, "I heard you the first time, Geoff, and, at first, I wasn't going to address your assumption. You remind me of some other students who watch novices taking lessons, with eyes totally focused on results. They will rarely recognize talent or what it looks like when a student is making the first step in awareness."

Uh-oh; looked like I was going to have to extract foot from mouth again.

Joe was as close to annoyed as I'd seen him, yet he remained calm. "But it is a good lesson for you. That was actually my student's attempt to be totally out of balance and then totally in balance."

"Could you please explain?" I asked, humbled once again.

"Sure." He got serious. "Do you realize what you just did?"

"No," I replied innocently.

"You broke a cardinal rule of teaching." I braced myself for a reprimand, but thinking a little humor would soften the blow, I said, "I thought listening was the cardinal rule."

"OK, this is cardinal rule number two," he said with a grin. "When you observe a lesson, you must not assume what its purpose is."

"What do you mean?"

"You assumed my student's erratic swing was a failed attempt at his best swing rhythm—to the point that you thought it was a terrible failure, indicating lack of talent." He waited for me to consider this and I nodded for him to go on, contrite. "But you see, Geoff, you didn't know his purpose. You presumed you knew what was going on and judged it based on your own criteria of a good swing versus a bad swing. Remember me saying that there is no right or wrong in awareness learning?"

"Of course, but I really didn't understand it entirely," I admitted self-consciously.

"Well, just then, I asked my student to produce an erratic swing. That was the purpose. It's just an exercise in awareness. If he identifies what feels erratic and what super fluid feels like, then he has the parameters or boundaries down. He can discover perfect balance and fluid motion from an exercise like that."

"OK, I think I'm getting it. You've defined the two ends of the spectrum between super fluid and erratic."

"That's right. It's like getting a note in tune if you're playing a piece of music. When the fiddles had trouble with a note, our conductor used to have us play flat or sharp intentionally so we could distinguish what was in tune. When we were conscious of the tones and could hear the flatness or sharpness of them, we could find the note we wanted. We rarely made the same mistakes twice."

"Your conductor?" I asked, wondering how many hats Burlington wore.

"Yes. For years I played fiddle in a local orchestra."

"Wow," I exclaimed. "That's really different from golf."

"Oh, but it's not. Playing music, more than anything else in my experience, takes exactly the same qualities that one needs in golf. Mostly, Geoff, you must be present to the task at hand. A measure of music takes a period of time and, especially when you play in a group, everyone must move along together. You can't stop to fix something or take a break to analyze what went 'wrong.' A golf swing also takes a certain period of time. I like to set up a tempo for students to get the idea that no matter what, their swings take this much time."

"I'm not really sure I get it."

"I like a three-beat tempo: Da, Daaa, Daa. Each beat takes a slightly different amount of time to reflect the distance and speed the swing travels from the beginning, to the change of directions, and finally to the end, but the total time is always the same."

"You mean a putt takes the same time as drive?"

"That's right. They have different ranges of motion and speed, but the amount of time in each direction is the same. Tempo is time. Of course you want to have a smooth pace in between the Da's, but the amount of time in the swing, for all the great golfers, from putting to driving, is the same."

"How does this tempo exercise work?"

He obliged me. "The first beat, you just get ready. On the second beat, you swing back, and on the third you swing through. Da, Daaa, Daa."

Da   Daaa   Daa

GB

"Knowing you're going to take this finite amount of time for each swing direction reduces the urgency in the swing," he explained. "It's a great tool for discovering your rhythm and pace. When you have a student making his or her first swings, you need to wake them up to the tempo, because the swing is nothing more than a synchronized sequence of motions in a finite time and space. An awareness of tempo needs to be imprinted right from the start.

Consistency depends on being aware of the feeling of time and the pacing of the whole system, Geoff. Very often, if you focus on a part of the system, it's likely to disrupt the whole. I don't want to get too technical," he emphasized, "but knowing the whole pattern of speed and direction of the club can create the desired behavior of the parts of the body."

He added one caveat: "If you let it. The focus and picture must be panoramic, not microscopic. Let's get back to purpose in learning. You were surprised that a fundamental sequence of learning could be taught and defined in a few short sentences."

"State of mind is something I recognized as important before, but not that critical," I admitted. "Being present, as you call it, was not in my vocabulary. Until I practiced yesterday afternoon, I had never experienced it. I had a real epiphany yesterday during my practice session," I told him proudly. "I've actually begun liking my swing. I mean, the image I now have is much more positive."

"I was hoping that would happen. What surprised you the most?"

"I didn't try to be or do anything except feel my rhythm and I was able to do it! My swing changed for the better, just as you said it would, once I allowed myself to become aware of it."

"I'm glad you experienced that feeling. There's no really good way for me to explain it that would come close to you experiencing it on your own. It's like you could read a book about swimming and study what others have said it feels like in the water, you could know everything about it through words and thoughts, but not until you hit the water could you ever really know what buoyancy means." I could relate to that. Words are really clumsy tools when it comes to feeling.

"But I'm an experienced player," I said, hedging a bit. "I still find it hard to believe a novice could learn that way. I just can't see someone learning all those fundamentals. There are so many to learn, aren't there?"

"Well no, once someone gets to holding the club in a good zone and sets up to be athletic and ready to swing, there are only three, as far as I am concerned. You just build a 'swing house' out of this simple triangle of awareness. Begin wherever the player happens to be—which is at his or her athletic baseline. Once hands and alignment are in good order to begin the motion, there are only three fundamentals..."

"But..." I tried to interrupt, but he wasn't letting me in.

"The foundation of the motion is flow or rhythm. The frame is path. And the roof is timing the impact. That's the swing house."

"So flow, path, and timing cover the whole swing. And you're supposed to learn it totally by feel?"

"Yes. Think about it. None of us could ever get too good at our rhythm in a swing, or have too good a path pattern, or time the impact too well, could we? That makes these fundamentals universal in my book. My students cycle through those fundamentals. They first develop a fluid quality of motion—motion that seems effortless and very well-blended so you can't tell what causes what. There's an imperceptible change of force. Once that becomes a constant, we need to determine the direction this fluid energy is going in—the path pattern from beginning to end. Lastly, once the energy is traveling in a consistent pattern, a golfer needs to time the club face's direction and angle of delivery for the ball flight. That's the physics of it all. It's simply the action of the club. It's the club's dynamics."

"That sounds simple enough," I said, "but what do you mean exactly by timing?"

"I'll explain that later, Geoff, if you don't mind."

"OK." But I felt a little stung by his putting off answering. "But if the swing is so simple, then what's all the hoopla about body positions and planes and all that jazz? And all the mechanics I see the tour players fixing all the time during tournaments? What's that about?"

"Let's not go through that again."

"I promise this is the last time."

Awareness Triangle

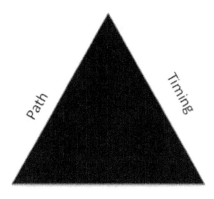

Flow

"OK, I know, one could really get messed up that way. Even superior players end up believing they can't play well anymore because they have bought into that approach. They're up against a mental wall. Following this block, there is a typical scenario. They hit the panic button and begin to follow a convoluted litany of fixes prescribed by the latest greatest wizard, so they no longer tap into their natural athleticism. Getting that technical erodes their confidence. They're using an approach so foreign to their natural talent that they probably *can't* play well anymore. Having thoughts like that streaming through their minds challenges their natural abilities."

I could see that my question had stirred something in Burlington. "Geoff, golf instruction has gotten so far away from making things easier that there needs to be a paradigm shift." There was that phrase again; this time I would get clarity.

"What do you mean?"

"I mean we need to completely shift out of a paradigm that breaks a golf swing down into minute individual pieces and then fails miserably when it attempts to put the puzzle back together. We must discard this Humpty Dumpty sort of thing, shift away from this Cartesian approach. The athletic mind doesn't process that way. The evidence is clear that it doesn't work for the vast majority of golfers. In fact, it's exactly why golfers end up frustrated and quit the game. They never give themselves a chance at seeing their potential."

"Cartesian?"

"Yes, the so-called scientific approach. Descartes was one of the fathers of breaking things up to discover their fundamental building blocks. But it just doesn't work in golf!"

"What approach must we use, then?"

"Basically, we need to teach the complete opposite. In other words, that the *whole* swing creates the behavior of the parts."

"How exactly do you do that?"

"It's like when you take a trip in your car. Mentally, you know where you want to end up, you know the route, and then you unconsciously drive the car to get there. You make the turns, you stop and go, based on where you want to end up. It can be similar in golf: Begin teaching the whole swing and watch as the golfer's body parts learn based on the whole swing pattern.

"Of course, you must set up the boundaries. My Pathfinder helps with that. Other than that, have your students pay attention to the flow of the swing without any care about anything else. Develop the complete path by showing the two endpoints and where the club must pass through the Pathfinder in the impact zone, and then learn the impact trigger. You don't have to reassemble the machine from scratch—your students arrive with an already well-oiled machine. You need to show them what they need in golf, where they want to go.

"The old paradigm reminds me of a situation involving one of the greatest golfers of all time. I once heard of Jack Nicklaus describing in an interview what it had been like working with Jack Grout. Toward the end of Nicklaus's playing career, he was having a devil of a time with his swing. One summer, just after the British Open, he had experienced one of his worst performances as a professional. He seemed dejected and probably wondered how he had arrived at such low a point." Joe paused to sip from his water bottle.

"Apparently," he continued, "golf teachers were flooding Nicklaus with input about how to fix his game and get out of his funk. Jack Grout had passed on at least ten years before. These self-proclaimed gurus were trying to get Nicklaus to change his swing to what they thought would be more effective. Apparently it was a complicated change, foreign, and difficult to perform in competition, especially at this stage of his career.

"Reflecting on his time with Grout, Nicklaus realized Grout had spent very little time talking about the golf swing, just the fundamentals, and of course there aren't many of those. Nicklaus seemed to be longing for one last conversation with his friend that would liberate him from his problem.

"As Nicklaus told it, Jack Grout had been plain spoken. He would have spoken first about the day, maybe the weather, family—a normal everyday conversation with a friend. But then he might interject a suggestion or ask a question for Nicklaus to contemplate, like, 'How's your aim today, Jack?' Or, 'How does your rhythm feel?' Grout said so few things to Nicklaus that every comment was essential, and they were easy to remember. He never wasted any words.

"You know, Grout helped Hogan too! Those original teachers were very well-rounded, and most of them could really play, too. Heck, Tommy Armour played the fiddle."

"Like you."

"Something like that. Anyway, as the interview went on, Nicklaus spoke about really missing his old friend and his approach to golf and life, so fundamental and simple, yet complete. It was very enlightening to me and, at the same time, a little sad to see Nicklaus so dejected. I believe he felt a little duped by this episode in his career. I had watched Nicklaus play as a younger golfer when his talent and ability bore no interference. His complete talent was something to marvel at; his work ethic, composure, concentration. Jack Nicklaus really had very few weaknesses, if any, and back then he seemed invincible. And contrary to what some teachers have said, he did have marvelous swing action. His swing exemplified what we have been talking about all along—freedom!

"For Nicklaus to be listening to these self-proclaimed gurus puzzled me. It isn't rocket science, Geoff. Yes, there seems to be an inordinate number of fine champions who, as they say, seem to have lost their touch in the past twenty-odd years. You know golfers used to be taught to get on the tour, but now with the technical complexities and all, there have been several champions taught off the tour! Many get confused. But they really haven't lost anything—they've just misplaced it. You could say it's lost within them."

I felt like one of those pathetic lost golfers and nodded in total understanding.

"It can be recaptured, Geoff. The problem, your problem, is you keep looking outside yourself to find solutions. Redeveloping awareness is always an inside job! The route to one's potential can never be found outside oneself. People believe their problems are complex and require complex solutions. Really and truly, most problems are actually simple. As teachers, we cannot afford to miss the boat when it comes to simplicity and awareness." He stopped speaking and looked me in the eyes and let his words sink in. "Simplicity is the ultimate sophistication. You know, sometimes I think it's better to be a little unorthodox."

"You mean like Trevino or Palmer?"

"That's right. They have decided on a way to play, and they don't mess with it, and nobody messes with them. Sure, they don't swing classically, but they are effective and never confused. That was probably their greatest asset. They didn't try to perfect their swings according to some model, they perfected their shot-making and knew how to produce it for themselves."

"What have you done to make it simple?"

"One strategy I use is to reverse the way we learn. The principle being, if the club is OK, then you are OK."

"Could you illustrate?"

"Sure. Usually it blows my students' minds. Let me ask you, Geoff: Where do you begin teaching a golf swing once the setup is in good order?"

"With the backswing, of course," I told him, as though it were obvious.

"Well, that's the opposite of where I begin. Did you know that starting from the finish can create the perfect backswing through momentum? Or with a more experienced player, that knowing the downswing approach of the club into the impact zone could create the backswing?"

"How can that be? The backswing happens before the downswing."

"Yes, that much I do know," he grinned mischievously. "But the backswing can be like taking that trip in your car. In fact, the beginning of a trip or a swing can begin at the end both physically and mentally. All the while, in the back of your mind, you're picturing where you're going. And because you know the club needs to strike the ball, it's on the route too."

"That seems right," I conceded, "but to work from the finish or the downswing first still seems backwards to me."

" 'Seems' is the key word," he told me. "It's the fastest and most effective way I know for the student to develop a feel for the shape and effortlessness of the swing. There's no need to exert force or use tension and strength to create the swing. And at the same time you awaken their feel for momentum and centrifugal force. You see, you're so bogged down in the new technical approach. There are umpteen steps and the belief that says, if you have step one, the setup, and you move on to step two, the take-away, and then three, a good top-of-swing position, it's likely the downswing will happen. Right, Geoff?"

"Well, yes; that is how I teach it."

"It's hogwash! I will tell you this: I have seen a lot of good backswings with inconsistent and erratic impacts. Besides, clogging your mind with too many things to do will surely send you down the road of confusion. On the other hand, when I see a consistent impact, I don't much care about the backswing."

"So you never teach the backswing?"

"I didn't say that. It's the way you teach it that will dictate whether or not your students will change for the better and sustain it. Instead of a multitude of steps and body positions, I help a golfer to change by suggesting better patterns of the club. If there is anything in the way of this, it is usually tension and the fear of being out of control, but they usually discover that control is letting go, both mentally and physically. They come to me thinking there are a lot of rules to swinging a club well. When they feel safe with me taking all the responsibility for the results, the freedom in their swings is quite remarkable."

Joe shook his head with a look of bewilderment, seemingly wondering how golfers could accept the complex 'rules' dominating golf teaching today, especially regarding the backswing. "Now let's talk about your backswing. You can get it by knowing where you're going—that picture and feeling can give you a direct route that includes your backswing. And it takes into consideration the uniqueness of every golfer." He picked up a club and swung it forward, first toward a target, then continued into a backswing through the air from there; the orbital pattern looked perfect. As he swung forward the club brushed the grass where a ball would be and then it continued around and up to where he began. This seemed like a lot of motion to control; would a beginner be able to do it?

The front end.

GB

"This is a way to get your students to pay attention to the swing rather than being distracted by trying to impact the ball. Have them notice the club action only, where it's going, with your two endpoints as references. You could call them A and B. That's the beginning of getting the mind in the best place. The pattern will begin to take shape and smooth out as their bodies begin to learn. Of course all students will vary to some degree."

"Right—I mean, you wouldn't argue the fact that all the tour players' swings are different, would you? Of course they all take a different route to the impact, don't they?"

"Of course. They all look different and yet they achieve similar results. You see, Geoff, all their bodies are different in size, strength, flexibility, and suppleness, not to mention their unique psychological and emotional makeup. Most of the swings you see on tour are dramatically different. To me, that means there's no right or wrong in a backswing.

"On the downswing, there's effective and ineffective, and if a player's on tour, they must be effective. In your teaching, you must allow for the diversity of each student's physical, psychological, and emotional levels. So then really, the only close similarity from player to player is the club's physics near impact. That is, the speed, angle, path, loft, and so on. In short, if the club is OK, then the swing is OK. That means that the club has satisfied its physics at impact to produce the shot. I will tell you more about that later," he promised as we sat down for a moment. He pulled two bottles of lemonade from a small cooler and we refreshed ourselves with a few sips.

Soon we saw a man walking across the grass toward us. Joe turned to me with a smile and said, "Geoff, let me show you a good example of the simplicity of my approach."

Joe got up and tossed a golf ball toward the approaching man. The fellow reacted—he leaped like a cat, and he was no spring chicken. He caught the ball and seemed as proud of his athleticism as the littlest of little leaguers. "Come on, Joe," the guy said, a little out of breath. "Don't keep doing that to me every time I come to say hello."

Joe looked like Peck's Bad Boy, with a sheepish grin. "Just proving a point, George, and hello back." George continued on his way, shaking his head.

"I think I get it," I said.

"Go stand over there." Now my athleticism would be tested, I guessed. Joe picked up another ball and tossed it just out of reach. I leaped, stretching, and caught it, relieved I could show him I was athletic, too. "You might be surprised at all the things that go on to enable you to make a catch like that, Geoff. Actions you weren't conscious of happened automatically. If you analyzed how you caught that ball—if we broke down everything that happened in a split second to catch the ball, you'd realize it was pretty amazing. Just having a goal and trusting in your experience initiates the action without you even considering it. Think about it: All you really had to know is where your hand needed to be, and you had a shot at it.

"You can learn and teach golf in a similar fashion, taking all this unconscious athleticism and letting it work for you and your students." I felt my understanding growing. "In the golf swing, the club mirrors the hand action throughout. The club is nothing more than an extension of a golfer's hands. The back of the lead hand mirrors the action of the club face. There's a direct correlation there unlike any other part of the body." I watched closely as Burlington swung his hand and arm back, around and up, and then down again, his wrist flexed as I had not seen before as he went through the motion. "When the hands travel, they're the outer orbiting component of the body's swing. And they travel the farthest and the fastest. If they're functioning OK, then the club is OK. And if the club is OK, then the swing is OK.

"In other words, any action of the club is a reflection of the action of your hands, of what's holding the club—of what truly controls the club. It's an intimate relationship that must be nurtured!"

There was that point about intimacy again.

Concentric arcs.

GB

I must have looked like I was making progress because my hands gripped an imaginary club, as if to confirm what Joe was saying. I noticed him observing me as he paused to chug down the last of his lemonade. "I mean, all the core issues you hear about—shoulder turn, hip turn, etcetera, etcetera—it's really not necessary to be conscious of them; they can literally be placed on autopilot." Burlington had made his point.

As I thought back to catching the ball, I realized my whole body had reacted to place my hand in the space of the ball's anticipated position as it flew toward me, without me being conscious of my preparation. Everything happened without me consciously directing anything. I tried to understand and dissect everything that went on mentally and physically with that simple action. I saw the ball and just wanted to catch it, so my feet, legs, and lower body all pivoted to go in the direction of its flight. Then, through my shoes, I felt my toes grab the ground, my knees and ankles flexed downward, and I pushed off to jump. My left arm stretched out and up and my fingers opened to touch the ball. My right arm extended the other way so I could keep my balance—all without any conscious effort, except the mental goal: Catch the ball. "And the whole golf swing can be learned this way?"

"Of course, Geoff! Your mind and body learned this a long time ago. What I'm trying to get at is that our golf swings are already very much predetermined by our past athletic development. From an athletic standpoint, why should anyone begin from scratch when, for the most part, he or she already has what it takes to swing a club? We don't have to be conscious of every move. Why not make it simple?" There was that word again. Simple. "Just know where the club needs to get to with whatever speed and then allow the whole body to support that action. Again, the club is just an extension of our orbiting hands, or at least it swings in an arc in direct ratio to their movement. If they're OK, then the swing is OK."

My body knew exactly how to catch the ball and just did what it had to do to achieve that goal. If I were to try to break down the physical action that had just occurred and apply that approach to learning the golf swing, I would be completely confused. The golf swing is a lot more complex than catching a ball. But maybe that was all the more reason to simplify and not complicate.

I realized in a flash that complicating was exactly what I had been doing in my playing and teaching. No wonder I had trouble; who wouldn't? "So I don't need to know all about the rest of my body when I am swinging a club?" I questioned, emerging from my introspection.

"That's right," Burlington replied. "You can learn it, and then teach a person to swing clutter-free just by getting them to know, feel, and picture what the club must do, especially at impact. The rest of the body's action supports in leading or following or anticipating where the club needs to go."

"So the rest of the body is involved, of course," I confirmed. "I mean, it's all connected. But you don't need to get bogged down in all the inner workings that have been worked out for you since you were a toddler learning to run, catch, and throw. Just because you're swinging a golf club doesn't mean you need to reconnect your body. It's actually a waste of time and a distraction to really becoming aware. The golf swing can really be learned like that? It has so many moving parts." I sounded stupid, repeating the same question, but I couldn't stop myself.

"It's little more complex, but that pretty much covers it. There are ratios involved, but the mind-body system balances them beautifully, providing nothing interferes. Suffice it to say, if you know what you want the club head to do, and you use your hands as the sensory feedback center, everything else will support it. It really becomes easy. Just allow the rest of your body to move to support the energy and direction of the orbiting club. You just need to know the outer arcs or circles. Your hands represent the second-last outer orbit and the club head represents the farthest orbit from the swing center. The feet and legs, the support system, are moving to support the direction and momentum of the outer orbits, just like when you caught the ball. The torso is in the inner orbit, the center."

"OK, I can see that."

"When you caught the ball, your feet, hands, arms, legs, and torso—they all knew what to do, based on your entire lifetime of athletic experience. You didn't need to direct each muscle group consciously..."

"Yes, but—really, golf, this way...?" I tried to grasp what he was showing me.

"Of course," he smiled, "you do need to know the club's physics; otherwise, you'll surely get lost and confused, and so will your students. You see, Geoff, you don't need to know what's happening with all the circles, just the outer ones. The inner ones will respond in perfect balance."

"You just put the others on automatic pilot?"

"That's right.

"What about the swing center?"

"Autopilot!"

"Pivot?"

"Autopilot."

"Shift?"

"Auto. I'm telling you, man, if the club is OK, it's all OK! Leave it alone. Everything will naturally respond in leading or supporting the energy or force of the other circles, so that all the action of the core of the swing is a function of the outer orbiting club head and hands. The key is to get number one and two arcs, the outer arcs, going at a good rate of speed and path pattern. Arcs three and four, the center of rotation, are a function of one and two."

"That eliminates so much extraneous thinking."

"Thank the Lord," he said. "And that's the luxury of this approach. You have a complete method that's easy to learn and perform and, I might add, connected to touch. It's really that simple. It's exactly the same way you've learned every other action since you were a child! I could never understand why the so-called modern big-muscle, mechanical golf technique claims that we, as golfers, should not use this built-in awareness. It's an awareness we've been using daily since we came out of the womb!"

"That makes lots of sense, Joe."

Burlington continued his passionate lecture. "This is why children do so well when they learn golf. They don't have to be cerebral! They trust in a task by seeing it or feeling it! And children communicate totally by feel—they have no inhibitions and so they can go with their gut. Keep in mind, Geoff, learning to trust comes from early childhood; it's not something out of the intellect!"

I pondered it all. "It's hard to believe it's that simple."

"Oh, but it is, Geoff. You have got to stop trying to complicate things." Where had I heard those exact words before?

"But what about the fact that the lower body, the feet, legs, and hips, lead the way in the downswing?" I pleaded for clarity. Or maybe I didn't want to give up my investment in being right. After all, I had invested years believing the party line.

"Of course they do, but do your students have to be conscious of them? Depending on the athlete, you have to make choices on how much you tell them. It's very easy to ruin something good. In most cases you allow the feet and legs to move in response to knowing what you want the club to do on the forward swing."

"How do you do that?"

"Let's say you want to hit a knockdown shot that really bores the ball low into the wind. With that goal in mind, your body responds to the changes necessary in the club to get to that goal. I guarantee your feet and legs will shift and drive downward and more forward and squeeze the ball into the turf naturally. You see, your mind controls everything and if you tell it that you want the ball to fly low, your body will respond in kind.

"Someone once asked Sam Snead how he faded the ball. His answer: 'I see fade.' Asked about a draw, he said, 'I see draw.' Snead let himself perform totally non-technically! He was the epitome of non-interference. That's how I'm proposing we teach! Say the least and get the most by asking the best awareness questions."

"But you have to admit there was only one Sam Snead." I countered.

"Yes, and we should pay homage to his extraordinary awareness! Snead never interfered with his natural ability and he trusted his swing probably more than anyone. All we need to do with our students is show them how to learn this way. How far they get is uniquely personal. But I do guarantee that if they stick with it, they will learn to swing and play better than their wildest dreams!"

"Do you teach all your students this way?"

"As I said, students are diverse in their backgrounds and, as such, you need to find out where each one is coming from and get a feel for their unique histories. But the physics approach and awareness development is a constant. I just go deeper into the awareness as they progress. It's always about the club's physics and the feel and the action emanating from that. You need to facilitate this process for each student personally."

Joe wiped his brow with a handkerchief—the day had warmed considerably. Florida weather was still preferable to what I'd left behind up north, though. I adjusted my visor.

"You can't organize all the parts and hope the club is on autopilot and will be OK. You must be aware of the club and put the body on autopilot. You know," Joe concluded, "all sports are played well this way. Simply."

9
THE GRIP

"You've mentioned the hands; what about the grip? How do you teach that?" I asked.

"Good question! There is no greater physical influence over the action of the club and the outcome of a shot. Getting a person's grip placement and pressure points optimum for them is key."

"I've heard so much about the importance of grip and yet there seem to be so many ways to hold the club. How do you go about teaching it?"

"There again, it depends on the situation. Are we talking about a beginning golfer or an experienced one?"

"What's the difference when it comes to the fundamentals?"

"There's a big difference. If a golfer is effective with the position of their hands on the club, and they're conditioned to hold the club in a manner that imbalances the face or path during the swing but still consistently impacts the ball solidly in the direction they want it to go, then why change the grip position? Just to accommodate some teacher's impression of what's orthodox? You could destroy a golfer's confidence and effectiveness in one fell swoop! The only time to adjust would be if the hands are poorly placed on the club and not being effective."

"But that's what I'm getting at, Joe. What do you change the placement to, and how do you change it?"

"Another good question. I really take into account a person's hand dimensions—their palm and finger ratios, long or short. I notice whether their fingers are meaty or lean, thick or thin. Then I do tests, experiment a little. I notice path and face relationships as they swing. I adjust their hands to fit and balance out those relationships, and of course the grip size plays a role in all of this too."

"I don't mean to sound obtuse," I said, feeling very much that way, "but do you think you could show me what you're talking about?"

"Sure. The hands, wrists, and arms have limits to their degree of rotation, and of course, flexing potential is limited once one's hands are fixed on the club. There are tendencies that you really need to know. You see, if the face of the club lies square to the target—I mean looking directly at it while addressing the ball—and the person has never held a club before, I place their hands on the grip with good leverage for lead hand control and a neutral look." He picked up a club and walked a few feet away from me.

"Like this," he said as he demonstrated. "Here is the leverage; notice where the club lies in the hand and its angle in relation to the fingers. From this position you can control the club without excessive pressure. This position of the club in the hand is for control and the lighter pressure is for speed. So often golfers think that heavy pressure is for control; it's not!

Proper angle in hand.

GB

Improper angle in hand.

GB

"Now look at this grip," he commanded as he moved his hands. "Here, there's no leverage over the club. Notice the angle of the shaft in relation to the fingers and palm. Usually a player with this hand position cannot generate enough club speed because the hinging is compromised and they need excessive pressure to retain control of the club in hand."

Neutral grip.   Square face

GB

Burlington changed position. "Having a neutral hand position almost always simplifies the path-face relationship throughout the swing. Neutral, in this case, means there's a close directional relationship between the back of the lead/left hand and the face of the club. They are at a similar angle to the target and can be used as a reference for face direction.

"Now look here: This is what is often called a weak grip. The hands can rotate excessively from this position. Generally, the face of the club will over-rotate open as the swing progresses away from the ball and then under-rotate swinging through to add loft and curve the ball to the right. Also, the arc of the swing is often narrowed and the swing tends to become too vertical from this grip; it reduces the potential for high energy."

Weak grip.   Open face.

GB

Strong Grip   Shut Face

GB

He changed again. "Here's what used to be called a strong grip. I just call it another imbalanced grip. Look what happens to the club in this position." He showed me what I knew to be a strong grip. "The hand is pre-rotated on the club relative to the face and usually it will not rotate as the swing progresses. The hands, being fixed at this angle to the face, have almost reached the limit of their rotation—the joints and muscles can't turn any more than they already have, so the club face doesn't rotate with the path and it produces what we call a closed club face. This grip also often produces a path that lays off the club shaft, a dreadful pattern to say the least. Usually on the return, barring a recovery or compensation, the club face will arrive closed and often produce a wicked hook or left curve for a right-handed player.

"Your hands really do influence the club directly and the rest of your swing absorbs the balance, or the imbalance, in which they function. These are all tendencies an instructor needs to be aware of. It will make your lessons a lot easier."

"What about interlocking, or the Vardon overlap, or the all-finger grip?" I sputtered.

"Those are personal preferences and we have to allow a person to choose what feels right," he explained. "The key is the leverage over the club with the top hand, a balanced position relative to the face, and pressure that provides the speed and the feel of what's happening at the club head."

The shifting paradigm was getting clearer to me now. But it was so much the opposite of how I'd been teaching. Just then, Otter let out one of his famous yawn-sighs, revealing his formidable molars. The dog stretched. By now I knew this meant the end of the session. I still had many questions, but time had run out for today. I thanked Burlington and decided to return to the B&B to reflect on all that had transpired.

10
DEFINING MOMENTS

Golf was a simple game and learning the golf swing should be simple. I'd learned that it could be learned without complex thinking and analyzing. Less really was more. I left the golf center with those thoughts streaming through my brain.

I didn't feel like cooking so I ordered takeout from a nearby chicken joint. I devoured my meal with a hunger I hadn't been aware of until the aroma of the food hit me in the car.

There was nothing of interest on television and I wasn't sleepy, so I pulled a book off the shelf in my room. It was the kind of book I would never have taken time to read otherwise. But I enjoyed the story of a father and son and a wily brown trout. It was heartwarming and it almost put me to sleep before thoughts of Claire intruded. There was still no message from her and I wondered if she had even heard my fumbling 'whatever—I love you' message. And if she had, did she hear my inadvertent confession? I didn't know if I was ready for her to hear it.

I did love Claire—that was never the issue. I just kept thinking I had too much going on in my life, my career, and the time wasn't right. When I had told her I wasn't ready to make us more official and tried to make light of it, she hadn't laughed. In fact, she'd become dead serious. She told me she wasn't going to waste any more of her time; life is too short. I hadn't thought us a waste of time. We'd had fun together, we cooked, we hiked, we complemented each other's personalities.

Claire was a few years older than I was, and in no uncertain terms, she had told me to grow up right before she walked out. "Oh yeah," I had brusquely retorted, "and be old before my time and serious and no fun, like you?" I hadn't expected the hurt on her face to assault me as badly as the door slamming behind her assaulted my ears.

Lou was right. I needed to mend things soon or forget it. I rewound my mental videotape to sweeter moments and drifted off.

After a deep and satisfying sleep, I awoke to my alarm, right away thinking about my golf lessons. I had come to some pleasing conclusions. I realized now that it didn't matter if Joe ever saw me swing again. I was learning principles that would always be available to me. I just needed to apply them. I also realized more than ever that I didn't want to lose Claire. The same mantra that helped me find Burlington was rolling through my mind about Claire: she is the one, there is no other one. I would figure it out, and hope I wasn't too late.

With Burlington, I was getting much more than I'd hoped for. That thought caused me to wonder briefly what kind of price he put on his time. After all, we still hadn't discussed his fee.

I dashed over to the golf center, arriving early and hoping to try out the 'if the club is OK, the swing is OK' approach. Joe was already there and Otter was wide awake. Miraculous! The dog was barking incessantly at the ducks on the shore of the pond, showing more signs of life than I'd thought him capable of. As I approached, I noticed Burlington had set up for us to begin. He was wearing a fresh outfit but almost identical to yesterday's khakis, yellow sport shirt, and moccasins, minus socks. No surprise in the wardrobe department; that aspect of him was already predictable.

"Good morning, Geoff. I set up early so we could finish early. I have a little running around to do this afternoon," he explained.

We took our seats, including Otter. "I really think your whole approach is beginning to sink in." Otter briefly diverted his gaze from Joe, who was munching a muffin, to sniff out my sincerity. Joe tossed a morsel to the dog and the muffin won back his focus. "But how do you begin a lesson with your by-discovery approach versus the traditional way?"

Joe took a moment to think. "I begin by getting to know my students. I delve into their background, I really want to know their own version of their history. I try to learn about their experiences so I can begin to understand how they interpret and perceive things.

"For instance, are they self-critical? Do they assume things based on hearsay? Are they really aware? Do they judge harshly? That kind of thing." He squinted into the sun and pulled his sunglasses from a pocket. "That's what I use for the basis of my strategy to get to a higher awareness. Without their cooperation, the lesson is doomed. Their success, as I said, has nothing to do with me."

"Have you always taught this way?"

"No, of course not! I'm always learning. I'm evolving as we speak," he said with a grin. "I've had my share of guinea pigs and I'm sure I've screwed up a few people in my time, Geoff, but I was always looking to improve my approach. Over time, it's gotten better."

I wanted that attitude. Burlington seemed to possess equally large quantities of confidence and humility, without a trace of arrogance. I asked him, "Do you remember your first experience of teaching through discovery and awareness?"

"Ah, my first experience," he sighed. "You mean, when I knew something different was happening?" Burlington's expression changed. He looked joyful and a contented almost trance-like smile came over his face. He snapped back to reality. "Forgive me, Geoff. I just had the clearest picture of a lesson I gave a long time ago. It was very different from a normal day at work. I guess you could say that for me it was a defining moment in my golf instruction."

I was on the edge of my seat.

"I was living here in South Florida when I received a call from a lady in Rhode Island. She and her husband were good golfers. They had a son about to enter college on a golf scholarship. He was a having a very bad time with his golf. Their son's teacher was a nationally recognized pro who, sadly, had recently died in a plane crash and the young man was left in the hands of the pro's assistants. Anyway, the kid had developed some serious imbalances in his swing that were obvious to anyone watching him. Instructors were able to identify the problems, but no one seemed to be able to resolve them. In fact, the harder he tried, the worse they got.

"Everyone had an opinion. They first contacted my friend Bob, who was a colleague of the kid's late instructor. Bob referred him to me. It was Thanksgiving weekend, and though I had planned a trip out of town with my family, I was in no position to turn down a series of golf lessons over a four-day weekend—I was having some financial difficulties at the time, even though I was already working four jobs." It surprised me to hear that Joe Burlington had ever seen lean years. I nodded in understanding and waited for him to go on.

"Anyway, this young man's mother seemed desperate. I changed my plans and decided to stay in South Florida and work with him. Mr. C, the boy's father was a well-known practitioner of the golf swing and was well-schooled in techniques and all the modern terminology. The young man's mother also warned me that Arthur, her son, would test me. He didn't just accept canned ideas and statements, so I had better be able to back up anything I said. Interesting situation, eh?" He winked.

"When the day came for our first lesson, I drove to their very upscale golf and country club in my old green Chevy Nova. The young man's parents had arranged for me to teach there instead of at my public driving range around the corner. I pulled up to the security gate. The guard looked me over good. I guess I looked like I'd made a wrong turn. After he checked a couple of lists, he let me through. I was a little out of my element. I was accustomed to the public courses and driving ranges. Back then, golfers like me were called trunk slammers. We never went into a locker room to change shoes. We always went from the car directly to the first tee." Burlington chuckled at this memory and it made him seem younger, like he had become the young pro of his story.

"Anyway, this fine-looking woman pulled up next to my Chevy in a Rolls Royce golf cart and introduced herself. She waited while I changed my shoes in the parking lot. I think she was surprised I was so young. She told me Arthur was already practicing on the driving range and she would take me directly to him. As I looked around and took a deep breath of the fresh, crisp morning air, I realized how fortunate I was to be working in this game of golf under these amazing conditions. It was a beautiful morning and this was a stunningly natural setting. The country club had perfectly manicured Bermuda turf, colorful flower beds, and lush shrubbery. Next thing I knew, we were off to the end of the driving range where Arthur had been warming up.

"It was a very private place, with tall Australian pines lining the fairways. We pulled up to meet young Arthur's father and a few friends of the family. I was introduced, and they scrutinized me pretty closely." Joe smiled at the memory. "As I was about to begin the lesson, a great blue heron sailed gracefully across the range just a few yards in front of us. I remarked on how graceful it was. Then behind us, I noticed an osprey in a tree munching on a sunfish. There was a mockingbird singing about ten different songs. I just couldn't stand there and not notice these creatures and the intense beauty of the blue sky and this setting. It was a glorious moment! Are you getting the picture?" He waited for me to nod. "This Mr. C. was a real go-getter, though, and was already getting impatient.

"His son, my student, was a handsome young man, slender with a thick crop of dark wavy hair. As we began chatting, I remembered his mother's warning, but Arthur didn't seem to be testing me yet. At least he wasn't trying to impress me, which I appreciated, considering I was out of my league socially. He and his father knew all about golf swing mechanics. Arthur had gotten great professional instruction early on. But I wasn't concerned about being challenged about golf. After all, I had studied for many years myself.

"Growing up, I had devoured the old Scottish classics in golf and anything else golf-related I could get my hands on. But as I matured, I began to find my own way. I had come to believe that while these books were interesting, they were filled with empty facts. I realized that without the feel and trust to perform, a golfer couldn't place much value in volumes of minutia about picking out positions at some arbitrary point in the swing—that sort of stuff.

"Anyway, I got into a conversation with young Arthur and he seemed to be enjoying it, too. Yet there was definitely some tension building behind us between the parents. Years later, his father told me how he had doubted me from the beginning of the lesson but how he was won over by the end. So, Arthur's father was impatient with me. There I was, for at least ten minutes, just taking in nature all around me. Then I started in on music. Arthur had told me he played the violin. We talked about that for a few minutes while Mr. C. paced behind us. He must have thought the golf lesson would never begin. He sighed and cleared his throat again and again, which I took to be early warning signals of his mounting impatience. After all, he was paying me by the hour!" Burlington chuckled.

"Of course, the lesson as he knew it would never begin! But I knew we were well into helping Arthur before he even picked up a club. I wanted to establish a rapport. I wanted to get to know him—in a sense, to enter his mind and his experiences in order for us to find some commonality. I continued to probe, asking questions to try to really understand how he had gotten to this point. I refused to even glance at his parents because by now his father was fuming. He told me later he was wondering where his wife had found this guy, and did we have to pay him? Did we have to listen to him talk for the next four days?"

I had some understanding of Mr. C.'s impatience. My first encounters with Burlington had me anxious for him to get to the point. His stories circled around and around. Although I enjoyed the way he colored in a story, I was accustomed to a more linear approach. But there was nothing linear about Burlington. In any case, it was turning me into a good listener, as I found myself wanting him to keep talking.

"Mr. C. knew Arthur had serious swing problems even with the so-called superlative instruction he had procured for the boy. The experts had exhausted their possibilities with little success and I was a last resort; that was apparent. Except for Dad's obvious displeasure, I was under the impression that things were off to a great start. So after our conversation, I asked Arthur to take a few swings. I heard his father let out a big sigh of relief."

"What was his swing like?" I asked, prompting Burlington to get to the meat of it.

"Arthur pulled out an iron and asked me which swing I would like to see. I thought, oh boy, this kid is really loaded down with things to do. So I told him, 'just make a swing toward that tree and don't think about it.' I told him our technique was to be techniqueless." Joe laughed. "'You mean, just swing?' Arthur asked me, incredulous. 'That's right,' I told him. He swung and I was amazed at all the different angles his club swung through. And he missed the target by a football field. He was really messed up. All the lessons he had taken and all the analysis had obviously buried his natural talent, and that's a nasty trap to free yourself from. I knew Arthur needed something different from just verifying that the club was laid off and shut—that was obvious. The question was why. Arthur felt helpless, he later told me. The answer to the dilemma lay in the experts' approach to solving the problem."

"So what did you do?"

"I decided to start from scratch. As he continued swinging, I hummed a little of a Mendelssohn violin concerto. Arthur stopped mid-swing to say he loved that piece. I heard another sigh from behind, so I figured we'd better stick with his golf swing. We could talk about music later. Back to the problem of teaching him to swing. None of Arthur's family, friends, or teachers, no one, had ever experienced learning from a discovery and awareness process. They only identified problems and assumed that if they knew what a problem was, they could solve it. Easy to change, right? Over time, they realized it was not that simple.

"So Arthur's present swing was probably a conglomeration of all his teachers' approaches to solving his swing imbalance. It got so he could only produce his 'trying-hard' swing. The natural swing had been buried long ago. But it wasn't dead! It was still in there breathing! If we could get back to Arthur's natural swing, he would improve immeasurably. I asked him to hit a few shots and I observed that he swung the club in a manner that required a lot of recovery to strike the ball consistently solid." Joe paused to demonstrate, as deftly as a mime, Arthur's failed delivery.

Left: Club face is shut and laid off—not desirable. Right: Club head is crossing the line open, *a la* Bobby Locke.

EW

"The club was shut and laid off, but every pro knew that, especially his father."

"As soon as someone tried to help fix the problem, it got worse. That was what was puzzling them all. I decided to find out just how much feel this kid had. So I asked Arthur to hold the club as lightly as possible to give him an opportunity to feel it as a sensitive instrument and to hit me a cut shot. As you know, that's very difficult with a laid off club shaft and shut face. At first, he just blocked the ball to the right. I pointed out to him that it was not a cut, even though it curved to the right. I told him that the cut must start to the left. Anyway, Arthur tried a few more times and the path of his downswing began to take on a different shape and direction. His path began to swing to the left of the target before impact, which was just what I wanted," Burlington explained cryptically.

"I was getting hopeful, but I still just went about the next step without even remarking about the swing path change that had already begun to take shape. The golf shot was still not exactly what he wanted, so those watching never noticed the improvement in Arthur's swing. You see, sometimes when you make a positive change, the results don't show up until later. There's a lag between the change in habit and the change in the results. The mind-body system is now processing something foreign and needs to be allowed to let that occur naturally, to let the athletic timing re-evolve.

"Most golfers are only result-oriented, not process-oriented, Geoff, and they miss out on what really takes place. It's a shame, too." Again, Burlington's eyes locked with mine, as if he knew how close he came to reading me. "A few more swings and Arthur's natural athleticism began to emerge from its long hibernation. It must have been a very long time since he had allowed his natural swing to surface.

"Anyway, Arthur's shots began to come too: one at first, then two, and then three in a row. Now things were quiet in the background. I asked him to see if he could hit it higher. Naturally, the face began to open more and more on his backswing—another improvement without thinking about how to execute it. Arthur just reacted to my request to fly the ball higher, and his mind-body system, not cluttered with things to do, responded. After a few more swings, the club face began to match the path. It was getting less and less shut, as Arthur practiced the cut shot." Burlington mimicked Arthur's improvement with his imaginary club and continued speaking.

"Now I needed his path to get more in line with striking the ball straight. I reversed the shot. I asked him to hit a high hook. He gave me a puzzled look, as did everyone else. I guess they thought I was going to confuse him, and his swing, but I was just working on the redevelopment of his feel and balance with the club. Arthur's feel for his golf swing was really beginning to activate and he seemed right at home with the approach. I think he was starting to have fun, something he probably hadn't experienced in golf for a long time. The shaft began to cross the line and the face was still open." Joe pretended he was Arthur again and demonstrated.

"What did you do then?"

"I thought, great, we have a nice orbit to this path and the face was getting in balance. After a few more tries, Arthur hit a high draw. His swing had been completely revamped in about fifteen minutes and yet I hadn't told him anything in particular about his swing. I had only asked him to feel, to notice, differently shaped shots. Then his athleticism made the adjustment! I could hear some remarks in the group of observers—they were getting excited! I still get goosebumps telling you this now, Geoff, and that was twenty-five years ago!

"The group had by now gathered in closer. They actually started applauding after each swing as the ball soared high from right to left into the target, an ever-so-slight draw. I don't think anyone noticed the swing changes, but everyone sure noticed the ball flight. People thought it was a minor miracle because they knew what Arthur's shots had looked like a few minutes earlier. But they hadn't heard me speak to him about his swing at all. They missed the process. It was a quick one, I'll grant you that, but it was still a process occurring in Arthur's swing. No one could figure out how it happened. He was getting where he needed to go, totally by his feel for the shots."

Burlington's story mesmerized me. The pieces of my golf puzzle were gradually clicking into place. I prompted him to keep going.

"Understand, Geoff, he already possessed the ability, but had buried it by over-thinking and analyzing everything he was doing. Arthur's God-given talent and all his athleticism were replaced by some experts' concepts of how to swing." Burlington paused to let that statement sink in and to take a sip of water.

Balanced path and face.

EW

"Arthur's father was looking interested, but still had his arms folded in front of him. I could feel him leaning over my shoulder; I turned and whispered, 'Club face isn't shut or laid off anymore, is it Mr. C?' A huge grin came over his face as he realized I had known what the matter was all along."

"Did he apologize for doubting you?"

"He didn't need to; his smile said it all. Later he told me that this lesson was so far removed from anything he'd seen or experienced before that he was put off at first. By the end he realized it was much more advanced than his own approach, light-years ahead of his way of adjusting the golf swing. He appreciated that it was sophisticated in its simplicity. He told me, 'You hadn't missed Arthur's grave swing imbalances, as I'd originally thought. I had you pegged as an imposter for the first ten minutes of the lesson. I wondered how Bob could have recommended you. I just didn't understand. But you knew a different route to get Arthur on track and it seemed effortless and easy. And it worked! You obscured your strategy by never mentioning the problems.'

"Mr. C. admitted that by paying such close attention to the golf shots and by feeling so annoyed at my seeming casualness toward the problems, he'd missed the swing transformation completely. More than that, he said he'd realized that it was obvious that Arthur had the ability to change all along; how else could he have gotten it so fast? 'We just didn't know how to go about it,' Mr. C acknowledged.

"You see, none of those folks had any experience in awareness learning. Arthur already had the ability to swing exactly the way he wanted to, but his system rejected it, and those try-hard, fix-it approaches as well." Burlington threw me his famous unreadable smile. "It ended up that Mr. C. paid me double what I had requested for my time; they have sent me many students over the years and we still have a close relationship even though we rarely see each other."

"So what happened to Arthur?" I inquired.

"He went back to school and qualified easily. It was quite a moment for me, Geoff; I just kind of looked skyward and said thank you. The wind-up is that that day changed my teaching forever. And Arthur has never forgotten how to retrieve his feel again. I understand from his father that he still plays very well today, even without much practice."

11

BEGINNING PLAYERS: AIMING

The story about Arthur lingered with me. I could see that Joe's approach was the best way to get an experienced player back on track quickly. I wondered about teaching a beginner or even an average player, though.

But Joe explained, "You can use the same technique even though a novice hasn't developed any depth of feel yet. It might take a little more time because of their lack of experience, but you must begin exactly at the beginning, wherever the player is."

"How do you mean?" I asked.

"You mustn't gloss over the precision of handling the club, the grip. It can be painstakingly tedious, but you have to do it. It will save mountains of time and frustration for you and the student in the long run. Take the time to organize the pressure points and position of the hands right from the start. Often the rest of the swing will fall into place as a result."

"So how do you actually begin a lesson with a beginner?"

"I do exactly what I just told you," he said with a little irritation. "You'd be surprised how many golf professionals teaching the swing don't really understand this fundamental. Once the golfer's hands are well placed and their pressure and tension levels are optimized, you might just ask them to feel for a simple swing quality, like the pace of a short pitch, or the path pattern on a full driver swing at Tai Chi speed. I usually get right on the club with my hands covering theirs; then I can literally feel the tension and pressure points they exert on the club.

"And ask awareness questions about their hands and wrists. Or maybe have them make a full swing, allowing the club to dominate their joints so they bend and respond to the weight at the end of the stick. Any of these options accomplishes the same thing—it's just that your starting point is different. You need to help them find their feel. Discovery and awareness is still the route. As a coach you just need to determine where to begin."

"How?"

"You do awareness and discovery testing," Joe replied. "Find out how in touch your students are with their bodies. Notice how they respond to the club in hand. You need to find out how they interpret and process things, what their perception is, so you can help them to use their mind and body together as a team. That is their reality. See how they respond physically when you ask a question, then you can tell. Start with something elementary and let their awareness determine where to begin. The speed of learning is very personal and cannot be rushed."

This was a recurring theme in all Joe had said: Find out how students interpret. "What exactly do you mean by using the mind and body as a team?"

"You give a student a clear task, so he has that task in mind and needs to inquire of his body. The mind asks and the body responds. You watch how close he comes to achieving that goal. There is a dialogue going on between the mind and body that can elevate awareness, or of course go the other way. When you watch students, you can tell whether they have accurate perception—of rhythm, for instance. Now when you ask them to perform a task, you're communicating with them exactly how they need to do it on their own. A student can just copy the discovery questions you're asking. That is the beginning of coaching between you and the student. Your job is to get students to learn how to communicate with themselves."

"So what do you actually say in a conversation like that?"

"Ask the student to aim at a particular target. He sees the target, aims the club, and focuses his eyes. Standing behind him, maybe you know he's ten yards right of the actual target. His perception is off. Therefore, you need to go through a process of aiming exercises that bring him into reality and get him accurately aimed at the target. You know, Geoff, I find that almost all my students think they're on line and they are actually not aiming accurately at all. Unlike other sports, when a golfer swings, they're not looking at or even facing in the direction of the target. Their view as they swing is not directly from behind and toward the target, and their body is aligned to the side of the target line too. Your students simply need to develop an accurate sense of target from an angle."

"Yes, I know," I replied, "but could you explain why?"

"You're viewing the target from an angle. When we view the target from one side of the target line a parallax is created. That means the actual position of the target seems altered based on our point of view. The physical eye often misperceives because of this. Anyone can aim the face from behind the ball on the target line with binocular vision. But as they set up from the side to try and aim the club face, invariably they misaim. Even accomplished players do this."

I knew that most of my right-handed students misaligned the club face to the right of the target.

The golfer's eyes naturally see the target to the right of the authentic target.

GB

Joe continued. "Over time, I developed a method to train the physical eye to see accurately from the side. Some players can naturally compensate for the angle, but most have great difficulty. This way of aiming helps a student learn to aim accurately so the parallax doesn't interfere."

He drew a diagram. "You go way out to a very wide angle from the target line and begin training. Then when you go right near the target line, like in a normal setup, it's easier to see accurately. I get my students to pick a spot on the target line from this wide angle and usually they're surprised how far off they are, but it doesn't take long to get accurate." He pointed with his pen at the drawing. "Next I have them come back to the ball without looking at the target."

Taking a look from the wide angle.

EW

"Without looking at the target?"

"Yes. As they approach the ball and set up, I subtract the physical eye from the equation completely. They're forced to use their built-in homing device as they look only downward toward the ball and make a guess for aiming based on the original sight from the wide angle off to the side. It's amazing how they begin to use their real sense of direction rather than physically looking and being inaccurate. They are now truly using their mind's eye. Some students get so good at it that they don't want to look at the target anymore and they're aiming right at it.

"But let's say they come back to the ball and are way off. Then you go through a middle-of-the-road exercise without letting them look at the target. It works like a charm! I've never seen it fail. But you need to go through each fundamental to determine each student's needs. "

"A couple more questions about your teaching style, Joe, if you don't mind."

"Go ahead," he said. "Ask away."

"You talk about a light grip pressure and less tension throughout the body. Is that what you do?"

"Absolutely. Naturally all golfers hold the club with differing degrees of pressure and pressure points, but the grip is the absolute starting point of any physical instruction. As I've been saying all along, the golf club is an instrument and the golfer's hands are the feedback center for the action of the instrument. The only way to feel it accurately is to have them well placed, and for the pressure to be light enough, to give this feedback."

"I was hoping you could help me to teach the swing well without the litany of do's and don'ts that I've used in the past. How do you, in a positive sort of way—yes, through awareness," I stammered, "get someone to change their swing path?"

"Remember what I said about artists and drawing, Geoff?"

"Yeah."

"Well, as a teacher, you need to know the arcs and angles, and the source of the energy being exerted during the swing. You need to know the patterns thoroughly. You achieve this by asking the right question for the change you would like to occur. You could also suggest pictures or get your students to use their imaginations."

"Could you give me an example? I want to get this right."

"Sure. Let's say the swing looks stiff or rigid. It violates the fundamental of fluid motion, which is often the result of 'trying hard.' You may ask them to picture a graceful dance. Ask them what it feels like to be super fluid. You need to get them to let go inside. They need to discover real control, so they can be released from trying hard on the outside. We have a number of exercises to do this. You know, so often in golf, we teachers ask too much at one time. That causes a golfer to try too hard. Eyes closed is great for letting go of trying."

I changed the subject. "What about concentration?"

"That's a good question. I marvel at the ability of great players to stay focused, but I think it's a very misunderstood concept."

"How so?"

"Well, when we think of concentration, we often think of it as a grind. We focus singularly. I don't think that serves us well. You see, for concentration we need a panoramic view—being aware and at the same time, letting it happen."

"That sounds confusing," I blurted, bewildered.

"Let me give you a simple formula. We could describe concentration both physically and psychologically. The beginning of concentration is having a clear purpose. One needs to set up a goal. It could be a numerical score, a swing quality such as rhythm, or a ball flight, anything like that. The best way to get to that goal is feel—sensing it. Your body's response based on your experience rather than any figuring or analyzing. Then you must trust in your feel.

"Purpose, feel, and trust. To me, those are the three fundamentals of concentration. You can take that formula and achieve anything you want in golf! If you're missing any of the three, the performance is sure to suffer."

"Huh?"

He drew another diagram.

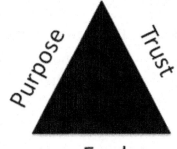

Concentration

Purpose • Trust • Feel

"*Purpose* is what you want. *Feel* is the vehicle to reach your goal, and *trust* means trusting in your feel. There are many strategies to develop each of these fundamentals of concentration. Remember what I told you about the physics of the swing? That, plus concentration, equals your best performance." He wrote the formula:

Flow, Path, and Timing + Purpose, Feel, and Trust = Performance

"I've never heard of a formula for performance. It's so different; I don't know," I protested.

It was beginning to sprinkle a little, a rare winter shower for these parts. We gathered our things and made our way back to the shop. There were two chairs and a small round wooden table already set up in his shop. Did he know it was going to rain?

12
TRUE FUNDAMENTALS

"But what are the fundamentals?" I asked when we got settled.

"The fundamentals comprise the club, ball, target, and ground relationships, along with you yourself. You see, to fly the ball a certain way, the club must arrive from a particular direction—angle to the ground, loft, face direction, and of course, the energy..." He began to use his hands to demonstrate. I must have looked puzzled because he said, "I see, Geoff, you're getting confused."

"Yes, how could you tell?" I still wasn't sure whether Joe Burlington was mocking me or whether he could read my mind. I went with the latter.

"Well, that's too much to think about. I never teach my students these things this way. What they need to know is the process of developing feel; *you* need to know the physics, the dynamic patterns of the club. Learn to avoid explaining it. You'll just put them off."

"How do you suggest I do this?"

"By asking the right questions. Let's say a student's club needs to be swinging in a more descending angle off a tight lie, making contact well before the bottom of the delivery arc. You could ask them what it feels like for the club to brush the ground more in front of the ball. Then you may notice the student's body moving to support a club head that bottoms out beyond the ball. You might notice a shift in their feet and legs; again, that's a function of the purpose of getting the club to do something different."

"Oh, I get it!" A new sense of understanding was dawning on me. "Your student wasn't shifting before, so the club had no angle to descend through impact and instead of talking about the shift, you reversed it by asking the question about the bottom of the club head's arc. Or asking in what part of the arc they'd like the club to contact the ball—descending or ascending portion?"

"You're getting it, Geoff. The shift isn't the problem, really. It's the club, the club, the club. I can show you how it works easily with my Pathfinder; it isn't only a Pathfinder, it's an angle finder too!"

He was referring to the foam tubes that could be bent to any shape needed to match a club's action in the impact zone. "In many cases the shift doesn't have to be discussed, and it happens. This approach allows the whole body to naturally blend the change rather than becoming disjointed."

I realized I would have discussed the shift, talked about the feet, the knees, the ankles, and hips, essentially each muscle and joint in the lower body, plus the left and right of it too. And most of the time my students would get totally discombobulated and the club would end up way out of whack. Burlington had pared it down so beautifully. Improve the club's action and the body will respond in kind. "I think I get it, Joe." I nodded with new understanding.

"We never want to interfere with the natural swing."

"But is there ever a time when you do discuss shifting?"

"Of course—when the student is locked up, or possesses exceptional body control; but again, by freeing them up and demonstrating the angle of the club's action, they usually begin to shift naturally."

"What else could you do to get them to know the angle of delivery?"

He answered without hesitation, but with finality. "I put them on a down slope and let momentum do the talking." He smiled mischievously.

It seemed our time was up. He gave no notice that the lesson was over for the day, but I got the hint. He lifted himself slowly out of his chair and began to clean up his shop. He picked up tools and put them away in the large red rolling tool box and placed extra seals and bolts into a wooden box labeled 'pump parts.' Finally, he picked up a wide straw broom that had definitely seen its best days, the ends frayed and worn. He swept the concrete floor slowly, with deliberate strokes, collecting the dirt tracked in from the yard. The broom seemed to be moving with the rhythm and pattern of a swinging golf club. I moved the chairs around so he could get under the table and emptied the garbage pail outside by the fence. When he finished sweeping, he suggested we take it up again tomorrow and wished me a good evening. I'd have offered to take him to dinner if he'd only keep talking. I made my way to the parking lot.

As I drove toward the ocean, I thought about all the things Burlington spoke about. I always knew that there must be a better way to teach golf, but before now I hadn't seen what it could be. Joe had thought long and hard about how to impart his understanding to any other golfer. I used to recognize improvement in my own play mostly when I didn't care about the results, or when I had taken a break, wondering why I was having trouble. But I just figured that was the way things were and accepted it. Now I believed I had really found a teacher who could help me, not only with my way of teaching, but with my game too. Joe Burlington was different—and special. He was refreshing, wise, and sincere.

The drizzle continued outside, so going to Pompano for a few holes was out of the question. I stopped at Starbucks, ordered a grande latte, and started reading the paper I had saved from this morning. I opened it to the sports page and knew instantly how I would spend my evening. The Bruins were playing the Panthers at 8:00. I could go home, shower and save my appetite for the arena. I decided to phone Tim to see if he would like to go to the game. I wanted to thank him for hooking me up with Joe.

I got home, stripped out of my damp clothes, took a hot shower and dressed. I drove a little south and picked Tim up at 6:30 in plenty of time to get to the game, get decent seats, and find something to eat. To me it was always a treat to watch hockey. I've always thought the best athletes in the world were hockey players. I had worked with many of them in golf. Once I had their hands well placed and got them to open the face as they swung back, it was Katie bar the door. They all seemed extremely talented at delivering the club. But hockey players have great hands. It's weird how sometimes we need someone to point out the obvious.

Tim was good company, a good conversationalist and listener. He wanted to know all about my lessons with Joe. I told him we hadn't done much swing work yet; we had to get the groundwork done first—meaning, Joe's principal philosophy of the golf swing, which of course spilled over into life itself, or maybe it was the other way around. I was glad to have some company, someone to talk to, even if we weren't paying close attention to the hockey game. I discovered that Tim was a machinist by trade and had his own business.

"Has Joe shown you his release technique yet? You know, the curl?" Tim asked.

"No, not yet."

His brows lifted. "Well when he does, you will understand why your hockey player friends play such great golf. Watch how they hit slap shots. It's almost identical to Joe's revolutionary release in a golf swing! I'm sure when the time is right, he'll show you. And man, you think you hit it long and straight now. You won't believe how reliable the curl release is. I added about forty yards to my tee shots, and my swing tempo is like Freddie Couples'. Now that's timing, eh? I'm sure it's in the plan. Be patient with Joe; he works on Chiros time."

"Meaning?"

"God's time; he never knows how long things take because everything he does flows. He's so absorbed and immersed in his activities. You know how everything he does he claims takes five minutes?" I chuckled at the observation. "Two hours later he's satisfied and can't believe what time it is. He believes time is meaningless. Just a human invention for ordering events. Pretty far out, eh? The only thing predictable about him is his unpredictability."

"I'll second that."

I began to watch more closely how the players hit the puck, especially the long shots. It happened so fast their action was hard to discern. We had a good time and good food, and the Bruins won, although it was a hard-fought defensive contest. I took Tim home. We made plans to meet at Pompano some afternoon later in the week to play a few holes. With a twinkle in his eye, Tim told me he wanted to see if what I was learning with Joe was paying off. I was glad I'd invited him.

I reached home a few minutes later and it hit me how tired I was! I knew that even with the excitement of my next session dancing in my mind, I would sleep soundly tonight.

13
DITCH DIGGING

I got up late. The rain drumming steadily on the roof all night made for a deeper and longer sleep. It looked destined to be a stormy day too and it was quite chilly when I arrived at the golf center. With the rain continuing, I wondered where we would be today.

I walked down to the barn and found Burlington brewing some Irish breakfast tea. I gratefully accepted a cup of the hot brew. The kettle, pale green ceramic, was definitely from Ireland. He had set it up on a Bunsen burner that, judging by what was scattered around it, also served as a melt for adding lead to clubs that swung too light. Joe had peeled and sliced a banana, and had even stuck toothpicks in the slices. He also had some Italian anisette cookies with the bananas on a paper plate. There were two places set at the little table. I found this very thoughtful, especially since I hadn't had breakfast this morning. Joe's offering was a nice substitute for the instant oatmeal I would have had to settle for had I gotten up earlier.

Otter lay flat as a pancake on the cold concrete floor. With his eyes wide open and body alert, he reminded me of an alligator lying in wait—in this case, for a morsel to fall so he could vacuum it up. We sat down. I took a sip of my tea, almost burning my tongue. The squawk box let out a ring and the shop attendant came on. "Joe, did you know we have a leak out in the field?" the voice crackled.

Burlington walked over to speak into the box. "Yes," he said, "I saw it this morning."

"I can't water the green like you wanted—no pressure," the attendant snapped back.

"Yes, I know, but the slow soaking of this drizzle should be OK. Don't worry about it. We're going to get to it soon," Joe responded.

We didn't say much as we ate our bananas and cookies and washed them down with tea. "I don't like to rush like this, but we do need to get that leak fixed, despite the rain."

"No problem, Joe. What do you need me to do?"

"Just help me get these shovels and things into the Kubota. This will only take a few minutes." I smiled to myself as I thought of Tim's explanation of Joe's adherence to Chiros time. But I was happy to help and set my empty mug down.

"Except for these last two days, we're in the middle of a drought. The water table is still very low. During the dry season we need to keep the irrigation in good working order." We walked around the corner of the barn, where there were two pairs of boots, two shovels, and a small portable pump, I assumed to dry out the hole we'd dig to repair the pipe. We hopped onto the carryall and drove across the middle of the fairway. Only a few people were practicing, but I was still a little concerned that a shot from the main tee might drill us. It didn't seem to bother Burlington.

As we approached, I could see that the pressure of the water had blown a deep, wide hole in the turf. We got out of the vehicle and slipped on our boots. Burlington handed me a shovel, and then he hooked up the pump to the battery. The pump would empty the hole, and then we could dig out the sand that covered the pipe and repair the joint.

The chill in the air felt good, especially when the breeze picked up. The rain had slowed to a gentle drizzle. Even though it was cool and wet, we broke a good sweat digging out the area to expose about three feet of pipe on all sides of the broken T-joint. I figured a little conversation couldn't hurt. "How did you learn all these things, Joe, like taking care of the turf and the machines?"

"Well, Geoff, I've had a lot of help from many friends along the way."

So there we were, essentially digging a ditch, me on one side of the hole and Burlington on the other. Otter wandered over to inspect the hole, but would have nothing to do with the digging. I guess he figured we had it under control. Joe seemed to be enjoying the exercise. I wanted to get back to talking golf. I really didn't fancy working up a sweat in this hole—especially with my nice golf clothes on.

Burlington's attitude was the same as ever. He chatted about how cool it was and what really nice weather we had for digging. Thank God it wasn't summertime or we'd really be sweating like pigs. But it was muddy, wet work. After a few minutes, my enthusiasm for helping had all but disappeared. This really wasn't what I'd signed on for.

Burlington seemed oblivious to my discomfort. He told me he appreciated the fact that he still had the physical ability and health to do this kind of work and wanted to take advantage of it. I marveled at his perspective. This guy was enjoying the act of digging and sweating it up in a ditch fixing a pipe simply because he could. He seemed so at peace. "You know, Geoff, you can learn a lot about patience doing things like this." His expression changed. I could tell he was recalling something from the past. I expected him to say something, but he didn't. Maybe later.

I could see his plan was to mend the T-joint from all three sides with slip joints. He examined it and made a mental measurement of the sides. He wasn't much for writing things down. Burlington motioned for me to give him the PVC saw and began to cut the pipe. It was like a knife going through soft butter. There seemed to be no resistance from the pipe. He performed the work faster than seemed possible. He measured the pipe just by looking at it and cut it to the right length. I was impressed; I had never seen anyone do that.

I realized that everything I had observed him do he had done with ease. He didn't seem to waste any energy. He didn't rush things; everything was casual, as though he had all the time in the world. At the same time, he somehow did things swiftly. He was consistent—he cut the pipe just as he swung a club and struck a ball, fluid and square.

I asked him if I could make the last cut. He consented but he didn't tell me what to do. As I got into the pipe, the saw began to catch. The pipe was pinching the saw and I could no longer get through it. I increased the pressure and changed my grip. I held the saw with both hands now, and with all my might, tried to cut the pipe. The saw came to a screeching halt and stalled between the two edges of the cut. After a few seconds of standing still watching me, Burlington said, "Would you like some help?" Embarrassed, I gave him the saw and watched him carefully. The saw went right through, as though the pipe were already split.

There must be a trick to it. "How did you do that?"

"Lots of practice," he said modestly. "Oh, it's just like a sound golf swing, you know. You get experience with the angle of attack as it cuts right through. This saw is an instrument and, to be effective, you must use it as it was intended. The teeth are effective only if there is some speed balanced with the friction and angle against the pipe. Did you notice that when you had trouble, you instinctively applied more pressure rather than allowing the teeth to do the work or adjusting the angle of the saw to continue cutting? Did you ever observe that in your students? When they have trouble getting distance, they give up everything that gives the ball flight distance—unknowingly, of course, because the club is no longer used as it was designed!"

"What exactly do you mean?" I asked, puzzled.

"Well, we know that angle, loft, speed, and center squareness are the elements of distance. Most people apply more pressure, which negates speed and usually reduces awareness. So when the angle, loft, and squareness are compromised, the result is an ineffective impact." He grinned at me as if it were elementary-school stuff. "You did the same thing with the saw, Geoff. Success comes with experiencing fundamental awareness of the instrument you're using.

"You know, Geoff, everything is connected. If you realize the true meaning of that, you will have found the secret of being in the here and now. Then you can really teach golf as it was meant to be taught." It was hard to believe that there was a direct connection between how I had tried to cut a pipe and how my students tried to swing golf clubs, but there Joe was, drawing lines between the dots. And he was right. When we have difficulty, we generally apply more pressure and then tension becomes the significant force rather than the motion being fluid and natural. I saw it all the time and yet I did exactly that when I had trouble with the pipe. Sometimes I couldn't understand how my students could swing with all that force and no sense of direction or balance, but now I understood. The golf club is just like that saw was to me—a foreign object—and I needed, as their teacher, to guide them through awareness to let the club work as it was designed to.

What Joe Burlington had, I wanted, and I realized all these sidetracks were not really sidetracks at all. I could learn from every experience—indeed, be present at every moment—but it was up to me, no one else. If I chose, I could be there. Or I could go through life waiting to be where I thought I should be and miss out on the lessons and enjoyment of the moment. I imagined what it must be like to be Joe Burlington and find something of value in every moment, or at least to be there wholly. If I could find that, it would be the end of my chronic complaining and my criticism of people who didn't see things my way—the final chapter of my belief that I was the director of my own personal universe. The act of being present was the trick that allowed him to do things so effortlessly, almost casually, so that he didn't even break a sweat.

We repacked the soil around the repaired pipe. The dog got up and pawed the ground, then went back and lay down. I asked if we shouldn't check it under a little pressure before we covered up, but he winked at me. "No need; it's fixed. If Otter approves, it's good enough for me."

It was already lunchtime and I had worked up an appetite. Time had run away, so we must have been having fun! But more than that, I was understanding Joe Burlington better and at the same time coming to understand myself better and seeing that the real source of my malaise had been me. My attitude was my problem. Burlington had shown me by example; that was the beauty of it. I didn't feel judged by him, nor did I feel criticized or unnoticed. I just felt more aware of myself, simply by observing him. I realized that if I took a good honest look, the answers were inside me.

Burlington was right: The clues to helping others come from within. The key to helping myself was coming from a reflection I was beginning to see more clearly the more we were together. I was beginning to figure out his trick: There was no trick! I badly wanted his attitude. It allowed him to be totally aware and free. I figured that if someone practiced that attitude for a while, well, imagine how free they might become, and really good at what they did, no matter what it was. They might even become good at love.

Back at the barn, Joe went to the washer-dryer and signaled me to cup my hands together to catch the drops of liquid laundry detergent he poured. With his free hand, he wiped the spill drips from the side of the container and used that to wash his own hands. I was staring, my hands sticky with detergent, so he remarked that he loved the smell of it and how well it cleaned his hands. We washed up and rinsed at the basin outside the pump house. He took off his boots and reached up and took down some fresh blue jeans and a T-shirt that were hanging from the electrical conduit. He put them on and said, "I'm hungry. Let's get some lunch. You earned it this morning." I finished washing the dirt from my nails and fingers with his brush and I dried quickly. I hadn't brought a change of clothes, so all I could do was brush the dirt off mine.

We left the compound and jumped into his pickup truck and took a short drive down the road to a little diner at the local farmer's market.

I thought about how I was beginning to get the picture about attitude. Maybe now we could get more into the action of the swing. I understood the ratios of the circles and what they represented, but how did Joe get his students to swing based on that? I wanted to know how he taught the physics of the swing. I needed to color in some of the outlines. But during the ten minutes it took to get to the diner, my stomach was the only one talking.

The aroma of home cooking hit us in the parking lot and made my mouth water. The hostess showed us to a corner booth and the waitress came over and recited the specials. They all sounded good. After some enthusiastic eating and two drink refills, I questioned Joe.

"You talk about the physics of the club, Joe. When it comes to the motion, how does one get started?"

"OK," he said, "I will tell you the beginning of the physics of the golf swing and self-awareness, but it will have to wait until tomorrow. Better yet, I'll let you experience it for yourself. Meet me at the golf center at five AM and bring a bag lunch. Wear a hat, sunglasses, shorts, and a T-shirt. We'll begin the physics of the motion at seven AM sharp."

"I thought you said five."

"I said to be here at five. It's about a two-hour drive to Flamingo, where you're going to learn the true rhythm of all things." I didn't ask any more questions. Joe signaled to the waitress for coffee for both of us. I passed on dessert, but he opted for coconut cream pie. We finished our lunch and headed back to the golf center. Though it was clearing, the rainy weather dictated a short day so we shook hands and parted. I felt a little cheated with the time, but again, I trusted there was a good reason for it. Maybe he wanted me to absorb the lessons on my own. I began to anticipate tomorrow morning and what was in store for me.

I drove back to the B&B and changed into a T-shirt and cutoffs. The dreary weather had passed and it was becoming a beautiful day; I was thinking maybe a swim and then there'd be just enough time to play a few holes at Pompano.

I went through the dunes to the shoreline. The ocean was calm and inviting. I swam briefly, but wanted to sit and think about all I had experienced in the past couple of days. I stretched out under a row of palms. The diner coffee had no effect on me; I soon fell asleep.

I woke up well before dusk and made my way back to the house to get ready to play a few holes. I was well-rested and slightly red from the sun that had emerged from its half-day respite. As I freshened up, I tried to picture where Joe and I were going with this learning and how he would begin teaching me more swing physics and awareness. I couldn't guess what he had in mind, but I was willing to go along with it. I was still a little disappointed that today had ended so abruptly. But I would try the attitude shift at Pompano; playing alone should make it easy.

I figured the course would be empty at this time of day. I signed in, got my golf cart and went directly to the first tee. As I looked down the fairway, I thought of what Joe had said: The ball is in your court; how do you want to proceed? You choose the attitude. I felt powerful for the first time in a long time, mentally strong, as though nothing was going to deter me from being positive. I set the goal of appreciating every moment on the course.

I teed up the ball with the intention of not being technical. As I peered down at the ball, a thought about my backswing entered my mind. I thought, 'Cancel!' Just set up and hit it! I hesitated again and another swing thought entered my mind. I caught it, and inwardly yelled 'cancel' again. Now I felt clear. I made two waggles, looked down the fairway again and swung. This time I did it before another technique could enter my mind. I hit the first drive solid but a little right, just off the fairway. OK, this is good. Techniquelessness is working. I drove down to the ball. I hit the green with my second and two-putted for par.

The wind was strong coming from the airport just west of the course. It was playing havoc with the light airplanes coming in for landing. The second hole was a medium-length par three, 165 yards uphill and guarded by three huge bunkers, front, left, and center. The pin was tucked to the left side of the pie-shaped green, all the way back. I dropped my ball onto the deck between the markers and took my six iron out to play the shot. I rehearsed a low punch shot to escape the wind pushing hard from my backside. This used to be my toughest shot. With no hesitation I punched the shot low into the wind. It turned slightly left against the wind and landed hole high. Two rounds in a row, having fun. This was cool.

But this time I knew somehow I could keep it going. This attitude made golfing easy. I really had a good swing; many people had told me as much. But why had I had such problems? Joe figured it out without even seeing me play. It was my attitude, my mental state, and my practice strategy. If things didn't go well, it always bothered me. Now, if I gave it my best shot and it didn't work out, I would just go on. What a simple solution!

I played the next few holes carefree. I missed a few shots, but I just let them go in my mind and moved on. As I approached the ninth, a long par four back into a crosswind coming from the right, I aimed down the right side of the fairway and lashed the drive a good 300 yards. The ball sailed and curved slightly to the left into the middle of the fairway. Problem was, one of those Scottish bunkers lay smack in the middle and my ball had landed right in it. I chuckled to myself. I just didn't care about the result. I struck the ball just like I had felt and pictured it in my practice swing.

Familiar thoughts pushed into my mind. This was great, but I was playing alone. What about with others or in a tournament; could I be carefree then? Was I ever going to rid myself of that kind of doubt?

Just then, a voice came from behind the tee. "Nice swing laddie, but a little local knowledge would have been useful, eh? You could have avoided the bunker!" It was Tim. He had walked a few holes and had to cut over to the ninth to get in before dark.

"Hey Tim, I didn't see you. Where did you come from?"

"Oh, I finished work earlier than I thought and since the rain stopped, I decided to come out and walk a few holes. The air is so fresh in the afternoon after a rain shower. And I get so much more out of walking than riding. I like to feel the earth through my feet when I play golf."

"I know what you mean. I took a cart because it was so late and it's the only way I could get in a few holes." He asked if he could join me for the last hole. "Of course, my pleasure; fire away." Tim walked up to the middle markers, set his ball up and took out his driver. He waggled twice and looked down the fairway. He had that Sam Snead kick start. He made a silky swing and hit a beautiful low shot down the middle. He smiled at me, picked his tee out of the ground and retrieved his Sunday bag. I went to my cart and caught up with him. I pulled up alongside him and drove his pace so we could talk as we went to our tee shots.

"How's it going with Joe Burlington?"

I had to think about it for a second. "To be honest, Tim, as you know, at first I was very skeptical. The place, his maintenance duties and all; he does things so differently from what I'm used to. He has expressed his swing philosophy to me with great clarity. It's refreshing, and there's no way I could have gotten what he's given me anywhere else. The lessons so far have been mostly about attitude and the general motion, besides the grip. Actually, now when I think about it, he has given me a lot of insight about the golf swing. It just didn't seem like a lot. I could practically repeat it all in about three minutes. I keep thinking there must be more to it than he's letting on. Don't get me wrong, it's far more than I expected and every day I get more surprises."

"Oh, he'll surprise you all right. What do you find to be the most interesting so far?"

"I don't know, really. He's just so unusual that it's hard to pinpoint one characteristic, but if I were to choose one I guess it would be his perseverance—you know, his attitude. No matter what, he keeps right on going, whether it's a golf lesson, an irrigation problem, a motor needing repair, or anything else that comes up. Nothing seems too big for him and yet he's so gentle when he's interacting with any creature. His compassion for everything is contagious. He's so appreciative of every moment, too. I guess you could say more than anyone I've ever known he appreciates the fact that he can breathe, see, speak, hear, communicate, and be outdoors doing it all day. I don't know.... Then you add in his golf swing, his music, his interest in science, and his love of life itself; it's beyond measure."

"You are getting a good dose of him, aren't you?"

"I guess you could say that."

We reached Tim's ball, and he pulled out a fairway wood and without hesitation lashed it onto the front of the green. He smiled and said, "Now that's what I wanted." I was ahead of him a good twenty yards. I got out a four iron, walked into the bunker, and proceeded to hook it into another bunker on the left side of the green, but I cracked a smile. It didn't matter to me; I had hit it solid. Tim looked at me and said "Why, that's a little different from the other day. Now get it up and down and we'll have a beer to celebrate your emancipation." I wondered how he knew that. I took my old rusty wedge, got down in the bunker and lofted it near the hole. Tim hit a beautiful putt that finished within inches of the cup. He walked up to the balls, picked them up, and said, "good good."

Tim set his clubs out on the rack outside, and the cart attendant cleaned mine up and placed them next to his. I tipped her and she smiled and ran back to wait for the remaining golfers to return. We went inside and found a booth. The place was set up like a British pub. They had all kinds of brew on tap. We ordered two Yuenglings and some fried calamari. "So you're getting a good dose of Joe Burlington. It shows."

"What do you mean?"

"For starters, when you hooked that ball into the greenside bunker, you didn't slam your iron into the turf."

"I know. I don't know how I got into such a habit. But I do know that Burlington wouldn't put up with it, and I just don't feel like acting like that anymore. I just can't be that serious and reactive after watching Joe practice. I'm committed to adopting his attitude."

I sensed that Tim was really relating to what I'd described when he asked, "I was wondering if you'd be able to spend some time with Jake. He was really taken by the way you played the back nine the other day."

"Sure. Tell him to come out any day around four PM; that's when I can usually get here. Would you like to come along?"

"Absolutely."

"OK, we have a date." We finished off the calamari and downed the rest of our beers. "See you tomorrow." Tim had to get home. He wanted to split the bill, but I told him to forget it. It felt good that Jake wanted to work with me. I believed I could impart some of the things I'd learned. He was by far the best golfer in the threesome. I left the pub, picked my clubs off the rack, and headed home.

When I got home I took another shower and hit the rack. I was exhausted. Meeting Joe at five AM meant a very early start for me. I still had a lot to digest about teaching and how to control a golf swing by just being aware of the club, but it definitely beat the lonely winter up north.

14
FISHING

I opened my eyes in darkness, showered, got dressed, then drove over to the golf center to meet Joe. On the way, I picked up my favorite breakfast—Dunkin' Donuts and coffee—bringing along enough varieties for Joe and his dog. It was still dark when I arrived at five AM sharp. With curiosity and anticipation, I wondered what was in store for today. I knew it must be something special for us to be getting up so early and planning to spend an entire day working. Burlington was already there and was just finishing hooking up his flats boat trailer to his truck. I parked my car and he motioned me over. I jumped into the cab with my bag of donuts. I served up the coffee and we began our trip.

The truck was roomy and comfortable, but the diesel engine clanked noisily, dugga-dugga-dugga, in perfect rhythm. Burlington filled me in on where we were headed. We were going down to Flamingo Point in Everglades National Wildlife Reserve, at the very southern tip of the Florida mainland. We were going to fish for tarpon, redfish, snook, or anything else we could get into with a fly. Joe had heard there were some good schools running and thought we could kill two birds with one stone. I knew from Lou that Burlington was an avid fisherman, but I hadn't figured I'd be going down near the Keys to fish and simultaneously learn about golf physics. I knew there was no use asking Joe why.

"I really like getting going early in the morning, before anyone is up. You can get in some good thinking, Geoff." I nodded in agreement, but this really wasn't my favorite hour to start the day. But the road was empty; we didn't see another car for miles. It seemed like we had a calm day ahead.

We drove down the highway, sipping our coffee without saying very much, which was OK with me. I was barely conscious at this time of day anyway. I had offered Otter his choice of donut, cream or old-fashioned. The dog sniffed both and chose the old-fashioned. I wrapped the cream one in a napkin and put it aside for later.

The coffee eventually started working its magic on me, but Burlington still hadn't said very much, so I decided to break the silence. "You really move to the beat of your own drum, don't you?"

"I guess you could say that," he said. "Don't you think we all should?"

"I guess so, but you are really different. How does golf physics fit into this trip?"

"You'll see soon enough."

"And you said I would be learning about awareness and rhythm."

"Yes, I did, and you will."

"I just don't see the connection. Why go through all this trouble to drive two hours in the middle of the night?"

"I'm sorry about the hour, Geoff, but we have to time the water. The fish will be coming in with the tide and it's no use starting at low tide going out, so we have to go early. You can go right back to sleep—just like Otter back there," he laughed. The dog had gulped down his donut and was now unconscious. I closed my eyes too, and remarkably did not open them until we arrived in Flamingo.

It was a rather rude awakening when it came: a sharp slap on my thigh and "Wake up, Sleeping Beauty! We're here!" I checked my watch. We had been driving about an hour and a half.

Flamingo really was the last stop on mainland U.S. All one could see south was the water, and it was beautiful. The sun was just climbing above the horizon. My eyes were beginning to adjust to the light reflecting off the water. I stretched and yawned along with Otter, who had popped up like a piece of toast when we parked.

We were going to go to the outer rim, where we could see the sand on the flats beneath the water. The sand was white as freshly fallen snow, just like you see in the high mountain country in winter—pure white! The water was about three feet deep and you could see forever.

To the right of the boat ramp was an old motel in disrepair. It had definitely seen better days decades ago. I guessed it served as a place to rest your head overnight, nothing more, nothing less. The setting was rustic and Burlington fit right in.

It's no wonder he was something of an anomaly in the golf industry. Everything that was important in American professional golf was meaningless to Burlington. He seemed more like what I imagined the old Scottish pros in the Hebrides must have been like. The attire, the props, and the overly polite greetings to members and media—all the cosmetic elements of the golf business—were just not his style. He seemed to reject the choreographed political correctness so prevalent among his peers. His golf center and this rustic place were typical of him—no bells and whistles, just the essentials. It occurred to me that maybe this principle and his way of doing things were exactly why Burlington was successful as a teacher.

We backed the trailer up to the ramp. There were already two boats getting ready to launch. Two of the men came over to greet Joe as if they were old acquaintances. "Bring a new friend?" one asked. "Good fisherman?"

"Yeah, he can do it all. Push pole, spot, cast, you name it." Joe said with a smile. I had no idea what they were talking about, so I just nodded hello and played along.

After backing the boat into the water, Joe tied up beside the floating ramp and pulled the truck back up into the parking area amidst long rows of enormous royal palms. There were so many of them that they actually provided shade. We got out and Burlington tied Otter up to the trailer hitch with about twenty feet of leash and set out a huge bowl of water. Otter went right under the truck with that big goofy dog smile on his face. "Aren't we taking him in the boat with us?"

"Oh no, he hates the water. Ever since a gator at the golf center nipped him, I can't get him to go in a puddle, let alone a boat in the ocean. He'll be happy right here in the shade until we return."

"Then why did you bring him with us?"

"Oh, he loves the ride down and now he's very grateful that he doesn't have to go in the boat." Otter watched as we headed toward the vessel. I just shook my head.

There were still a few things we had to do to get ready. Joe had to rig up the fly rods and put on the tippet and flies so he would be ready if we spotted one right off. It took about fifteen minutes, as he meticulously put everything in the boat and checked all our equipment. I just did whatever he told me to do. I saw that Burlington had a disciplined way of doing things—it wasn't haphazard. Lots of preparation. I noticed he had several rods and reels. He had thought of everything.

After putting on our vests, we slowly motored out of the dock area into the canal and around the bend; he found a channel that hugged the shore. There were old cypress trees overhanging the shoreline. Once we got out a ways, he killed the motor and got up on the platform mounted above the motor and began push poling—moving the boat with a long pole so as to move silently as we neared the fish.

He stopped the boat for a moment. Everything was quiet, no wind, the water glassy. The wildlife around us overwhelmed my senses, and it seemed as though it had all just awakened when we arrived. I figured I wasn't going to do any casting. Burlington put down the pole and reached for a rod. He made a few casts in the direction of the trees under the mangrove branches that hung out over the water. He made it look so easy. I thought, if I could cast like that, I could probably catch a fish; how exciting that would be!

Nothing was happening here, so Joe poled out between two small islands about 200 yards farther out onto the flats. He had tied a glades minnow onto the tip of his line. It was about two inches long, chartreuse and white, with a red eye on each side of its head. This fly was supposed to fool a fish?

"Just keep your eyes peeled for fish. We're looking for permit, bonefish, redfish, trout, or tarpon. We won't be picky." I acted as though I knew what they looked like and kept my eyes glued to the water, scanning across the bow. Joe was up on the platform looking out across the water and had a much better view.

Once I gave up my preconceived notion of what we should be doing, I had to admit this place was beautiful. The water was light green and the bottom starkly white. A soft breeze blew. I had to put on my sunglasses because the reflection of the sun off the water was blinding. I felt myself relaxing and forgot all about the golf swing and physics.

I was beginning to melt into the environment around us when Burlington spotted the dorsal fin of a tarpon meandering near some rock outcropping about fifty feet off the front of the boat. His voice became a whisper as though the fish could hear us. He cautioned me to be still. "Do you see him?" he asked. "Over there." He pointed toward a dark spot in the water. "You see the dorsal fin just breaking the surface." I was surprised to feel my heart beating faster in excitement.

Burlington lifted his rod gently. In an instant the line was running through the guides out in the direction of the tarpon feeding on the bottom. The line shot out about ten feet above the water and with each back cast, the line moved faster. The motion seemed almost poetic: Joe would shoot the line and roll it gracefully out in front of us. Then with his rod lifting in rhythm, he pulled it back and looped the line behind as though suspended in midair. A pause, and then he shot it over his head and out again.

The fly line flew out above the water and then, in rhythm, with his left hand Burlington pulled the rod up and back to about twelve o'clock, vertical, never further. There was definitely a particular pacing to keep it going. The pause was noticeable when the line straightened behind him and then cast forward again. As he did this, with the line running through the fingers of his right hand he would synchronize the pull of the line to increase its speed. He did this on both the backward and forward cast. On about the third false cast—when the line hovered over the water without being dropped into it— he shot it out beyond the fish.

It looked choreographed—like a ballet. I thought how sweet it would be to be able to cast like that. Burlington didn't look as though he was working hard, either. Then I noticed the rhythm of it. This is why he had brought me here—to notice the rhythm! And not just the rhythm of his cast! He was showing me the rhythm of nature and how we fit into it.

Finally, he let the fly drop ever so gently onto the water. He didn't move it for a few seconds to let it sink, and then began to strip the line in slowly on a retrieve. His concentration was keen, his eyes were laser focused, still and calm, oblivious that I was even there. The tarpon hit the fly. Burlington pulled hard on the line with a swift lift of his rod, a tail swirled, and the fish was gone. The rod flexed back straight and the line instantly went limp. He relaxed and just looked at me with his wry smile. "Lost him," he shrugged. "Nice start, eh? Looks like a very promising day, Geoff." We ventured farther along, searching the surface of the water for signs of life below.

He knew all the spots, and told me conspiratorially. "There are always a few good fish in this little channel between the islands."

"Over there." I pointed, spotting the tip of a dorsal fin, another tarpon. Or was it a small shark? I pointed again, as it was hard for me to tell. Joe cautioned me to be quiet and still. He maneuvered us around with the pole so we were casting directly into the sun. With the sun in front of us, he could obscure the shadow of the line, the rod, and his motion from the fish.

Burlington focused intently; I just waited. He got his rod in hand and began casting again. His action was smooth as silk and the line just lengthened toward the fish, which seemed to be casually searching the area for food. Joe let the fly drop softly to one side of the fish and then began retrieving it in a short staccato rhythm this time, sort of darting it toward us like a live minnow. We could see the fish turn. It began to show interest and engage.

"It's coming toward the fly."

He shushed me. The water was perfectly clear and we could see everything, but, apparently, the fish didn't see us.

Bang! The fish hit it! Joe lifted the rod with a powerful stroke to set the hook. The tarpon broke the surface and there was a huge splash as it rose and fishtailed back down. It made a ferocious effort to dislodge the fly from its lip, but it was hooked solidly. Still it wasn't coming toward us voluntarily. It was swimming rapidly in the opposite direction and Joe's reel was buzzing, first the line and then to the backing. He yelled, "Grab the pole and push hard toward it! He could snap the line!"

I lunged frantically to the back of the boat, picked up the pole, and jumped onto the platform. I stabbed the pole into the sand and pushed as hard and fast as I could. With each push I picked up momentum, but we were still losing ground and the fish had lots of room to run. It headed toward the brush that grew along the shore of the island. "If it gets in there, it'll snap me off and that'll be the end of our relationship, plain and simple." I looked up, puzzled. "I meant with the fish," he said.

Then the tarpon broke the surface again, as though it was trying to get a good look at who had done this nasty deed. It had slowed a little and seemed to be spending its energy. Then it took off again, this time toward us. It was moving fast and Joe was retrieving.

"Wow, it must be four feet long! A monster!"

"Just keep pushing," Joe yelled. As I pushed, Joe retrieved a few feet at a time. After a few more minutes, the fish was beginning to tire and we were gaining on it. It was only a few more yards to the shoreline.

"We got him now," I said.

"Don't be so sure. He's likely just taking a break." I was already tired from pushing, but Joe held tight. He got the line to about thirty feet. As the tarpon slowly circled the boat, Joe turned around with it, coaxing it toward us. The fish gave one last tail swirl, then Joe reeled it in completely; we had it to the boat. Joe leaned over the side and lifted the tarpon up gently, part way out of the water, and removed the fly.

We both just marveled at this beautiful creature. Its body shimmered silvery in the sunlight. I knew this would be an experience I didn't forget. Finally, Burlington let the big fish down and coaxed it back to life, pulling it back and forth to get water moving through its gills, and then released his hold. The tarpon swam slowly back to its feeding ground, giving us the side eye, probably wondering what that had all been about—just as I was. But the whole episode was exhilarating. No longer feeling tired by it, I could feel my veins and muscles popping as my adrenaline crested.

"OK, Geoff, it's your turn."

"Oh no, I can't do this," I stammered.

"Of course you can. Just feel it! Feel what allows you to cast with accuracy and distance. I'll help you. With a little practice, you'll get it. It's just a matter of time." This didn't appear negotiable so I picked up the rod reluctantly and began casting, if you can call it that, awkward and tight. "What are you feeling, Geoff? What does the rod handle feel like in your hand? Hold the rod as lightly as possible, like a golf club. That'll allow you to really feel what's going on at the other end."

I was too nervous and tense and couldn't feel the action. "I'm not feeling anything."

Joe disagreed. "Oh, but you are, Geoff, you just may not like it. Are you feeling tight and forceful?"

"Now that you mention it, yes, I am."

"What would it be like to feel smooth?" Joe questioned me with serious intent, probably just like a golf lesson.

"I don't know, Joe. You know I have no experience fishing."

"It doesn't take fishing experience; just be aware."

"Well, it does feel like I'm forcing it."

"What would it be like to hold the rod softly in your hands and just cast the line a few yards?"

"But that won't do," I griped, "the fish are way out there."

"Yes, but a thousand-mile trip begins with the first step. Now think back to your golf instruction. Does this situation seem familiar to you?"

Yikes; I sounded just like my students—the bottom-liners who just aren't interested in the process. How do I get started? How did he get started? How did he begin his lessons...the hands, the motion, rhythm, flow; that's it. I paused my thinking for a moment and replayed the movie of his lessons, including this trip.

I thought about his rhythm. I pictured each exercise and all the things he had done. He never seemed to be in a hurry with his golf swing or his casting, or push poling the skiff, cutting a pipe, or digging a hole. He slid into tasks with ease and an economy of motion, as if he were part of the machinery. Burlington even drank a cup of coffee in a slow, measured manner, savoring each sip with more pleasure than the brew deserved. His rhythm was almost exactly like that of the great blue heron I'd seen sail down onto the water earlier, or the osprey now soaring above us. They all fit perfectly into what they were doing in the here and now. I seemed to be the only one feeling out of place and missing something. All I really wanted to know was how to get into the right places at the right time—the here and now—and find my own rhythm.

"Are you gonna make another cast?" I shook my head sharply to clear my head as Joe broke me from my trance.

"Joe, how do you get into the here and now? How does one get into the rhythm of nature and life? I still don't know how to dedicate myself to each moment."

"It's kind of an unconscious thing, Geoff. You simply don't try, you just be. As my wife puts it, be a human being rather than a human doing! Just be yourself, and then you can appreciate every moment."

"Can you really enjoy every moment?" I questioned with a hint of skepticism.

"Well, that depends. I might appreciate every moment, but not necessarily enjoy them all, because some of the lessons can be a bit trying—yet still necessary. Growth is sometimes painful, even grueling. And it often seems illogical when we're in the middle of it. Most of us have to make mistakes to learn. That's part of life, don't you think?" He paused to take a deep breath. "Usually after some time passes, we look back and clearly see there was a good reason for the growing pains; if nothing else, we gain appreciation for what it takes to reach our potential.

"When young tour players find themselves in contention for a major championship win, it is rare not to stumble on the first try. But if they learn and persevere, their performance will eventually match their talent. Or how about your beginning students who lack experience? They try to do things that are really outside the realm of achievability and they get deeper and deeper into trouble. It's important to know your current state of awareness and choose goals that fall within that state. You've got to get to know yourself, Geoff."

Just then, we watched an eagle swoop down into the everglades and clasp his talons around a nice fish. "Boy, that was easy."

"Good observation," he concurred. "How does that relate to us?" (I'd noticed he always included himself when he spoke of things I needed to learn and do to be more aware, as if he were going through the learning process alongside me.) "Anyway," he continued, "when you teach and play golf, it's important to be yourself all the time. Look at Otter. He's a dog and he spends his whole day being a dog. He eats, sleeps, and walks dog. Every moment he is a dog. That eagle, and the fish we fooled today? The fish, the bird, the dog, nature, never run into the problems we humans do. The fish just swims, the bird just flies, but we humans so often try to be something we aren't. We waste so much time acting with a mask on. We spend our lives not heading toward a better place. This is how we lose our way, by playing the wrong game of pretend. It really gets in the way of being at our best and putting our focus on what needs work."

"But what does all that have to do with learning rhythm?" I asked, feeling a bit lost.

"Until you be yourself and know yourself, can you ever find your own pace? There's rhythm in everything. All these creatures have it because they never spend time pretending to be other than they are. Learn your unique tempo. You be the judge of what's best for you. Make progress at whatever speed is right for you, in your swing rhythm, or just learning to get your students to discover their best rhythms and not forcing yours on them.

"And right now, you can copy how I cast or you can develop your own way based on how the rod feels in your hands and how the wind feels at your back. The point is, as you practice lifting the line from the water, you will begin to notice the pace that's most effective for you, just like a golf club. With a fly rod and reel, you find out quickly what's an effective rhythm and what's not when trying to get the line to shoot. As you begin to feel it, picture the line straightening out behind you and you accelerating the rod just right. In fly casting, you're using the weight and aerodynamics of the line and the flex properties of the rod to shoot the line. If you try too hard to force the line out without rhythm or timing, you will end up with the line slapping the water in a tangled mess right in front of you. It's easy to know if you're doing it rhythmically or not, Geoff. Granted, we could have cast the line at the golf center, but isn't it more fun to catch a tarpon or a bonefish?" He didn't wait for me to answer. "Here, we can get into how far we need to cast and how to present the fly softly onto the water so as not to give the fish reason to doubt the authenticity of the food you're serving."

With that, he pointed to a shadow swimming not far from us. "You see, we need to blend into its environment, to let the line land on the water gently, or it will be gone as quickly as you can say 'whatever.' And for that to happen, the fly needs to be presented in a way that requires a smooth rhythm. We need to use the rod and line as if they were a fine instrument, like a Stradivarius. A Strad in the hands of an untrained artist doesn't sound like a Strad at all. It's the player, not the instrument, who makes the first difference. You know, Geoff, I once heard that Schweitzer used to play Bach on an old rickety upright piano while he was doing missionary work in Africa."

Burlington was about to head off somewhere, but I didn't mind. It was fun to hear these tidbits of history and unusual anecdotes, which all seemed to point in the same direction: Get the most out of what you have and be authentic.

He continued on the Schweitzer tangent. "When Schweitzer was caring for the sick, several of his friends would periodically make short visits to bring medical supplies in from Europe. They said that almost every evening, even after a long day, Schweitzer would play the piano in the main room of his residence. The piano was so out of tune that almost every note he struck was off. But it didn't seem to matter. Why?" He didn't wait for my answer. "It was the love, intelligence, and talent Schweitzer brought to everything he did that was evident in his piano playing, not the quality of the instrument. Infectious disease was rampant where he was working, there were no antibiotics, and yet Schweitzer was the instrument that helped cure many of his patients when everyone else gave up on them. And the cure was love! This love pervaded all his activities, and Schweitzer got more out of that rickety old instrument than anyone could imagine." He mimicked tickling a keyboard as we floated amidst a panorama that had never heard one.

"The self-love that allows a person to truly care for others shows he has a spirit that can't be broken. They live each moment with such a deep faith that they solve seemingly unsolvable problems. They always find a way. That's the attitude we need to adopt every day, Geoff. Never give up. Never! Just keep plodding with an optimism that opens you up to whatever is possible, always moving forward." Joe Burlington's enthusiasm was contagious. I felt a new, serene sort of optimism just listening to him.

"As you move forward you must be open to possibilities. That is exactly what allows you to discover every day, just as we have out here on the water today. Every moment is an opportunity to see and experience, so we need to stay alert to what's happening. I brought you here so you could witness the rhythms in nature—in our casting, as in everything we do, there is a rhythm, and we need to find our own brand of it. We need our actions to co-mingle naturally, without being forced. That means being at the right place at the right time, and in the here and now. No stopping in the past or jumping ahead to the future. You need to tune in to your own here and now or you'll lose your rhythm and miss your chances."

A flashback to the seminar in New Orleans interrupted my reverie. And how did I happen to meet Tim at the golf course the next day? Was it by chance, or was it fate that ultimately led to me being here on this boat with Joe Burlington and finally beginning to see the big picture and how I fit into it? Was there a plan, and all I needed to do was go along?

I needed to let this play out and to stay on my journey with him—that much I knew. It was fascinating, though puzzling at the same time. "Joe, I think I'm beginning to understand your philosophy, but I just needed to experience what you're talking about, and coming out here has opened my eyes and my mind."

"Good, Geoff—that was my purpose in making this trip."

"I have been dedicated and worked hard all my life to improve."

He nodded in understanding. "You just needed a little direction."

"I appreciate that it's you who's providing it."

"A person can have all the energy and dedication in the world, but if.... Let me just say, zeal without awareness is like a runaway horse." That last statement sure rang true. I had worked hard for many years; probably as hard as anyone in golf, but without awareness, what did it get me?

We had a wonderful day on the water. Burlington kept me practicing casting for hours, but we switched when he saw me tiring. He also caught a bonefish and a permit, which with the tarpon, he dubbed the Triple Crown. Not often did that happen, he told me. I couldn't believe I could cast so well with one short lesson and a day of practice. And it was genuinely fun.

The day's true lesson was invaluable. I finally felt I was really getting it. I could go on from here and really, in a sense, begin my golf life again. It was a rebirth and, although it was strange, it was exactly the start I had needed.

When we got back to the dock, Otter was still under the truck, content, but ready to go. We put everything away and secured the boat onto the trailer. Burlington gave the dog some food and fresh water, then we were off. It was getting dark now and the drive back was quiet. We were both exhausted from the day, but it was a good tiredness.

By the time we arrived at the golf center, it was late and everyone had gone. I jumped into my car and headed back to the B&B. I devoured my leftovers ravenously and went to bed. Joe and I had planned to meet at ten the next morning, so I could sleep in a little.

Claire still hadn't called me back.

15

WHY GOLFERS SLICE

I arrived at the golf center and made my way to the maintenance area. Joe was seated at the table in the barn.

"Good morning," we greeted each other simultaneously as I entered. Hot tea and warm breakfast bread awaited me: everything to begin a conversation. I sat down and thought about how I wanted to begin today's inquiry.

Feeling more comfortable now, I had some questions about chronic problems and general tendencies that so many golfers encounter, so I got right down to business. "Why do so many players slice the ball? I've heard some people say it's because the golf swing is like nothing else we do in our lives, so that we have never formed the right habits athletically. There are a host of theories, for that matter."

Burlington smiled and then shifted to a more serious look. "I think it goes deeper than athletic habits or actions that students never practice otherwise. It's a combination of factors that afflict the greater golfing population, factors that inhibit them from sustaining positive change and getting out of the dreaded slice. If teachers had hit on the real cause, players wouldn't continue to have chronic problems with slicing."

"What do you mean?"

"Well, anyone who's tried to stop slicing and has accurately identified what's physically causing it—by that I mean the path-face relationships at impact—should be able to rid themselves of the problem, right? And of course there is a psychological component to it too. Yet somehow most golfers never seem to get out of the problem and execute the solution. They feel helpless and hopeless. So when a large percentage of golfers feel this way, more than likely we have not yet arrived at the source of the problem, wouldn't you agree?"

"That makes sense, but how do you know you've hit on the real cause?"

"Because none of my students are chronic slicers after we work it out. Mind you, I had a hell of a time figuring it out myself, but once it came to me, the most difficult part was imparting a strategy in a manner that allowed students to believe in it."

"So what is the problem?"

"First, there is the overriding psychological challenge of fearing that the ball will fly off to the right when the golf club is on a sound path from here." He demonstrated the club coming from an inside path. "This needs to be addressed first. After that, often centrifugal force contributes to the problem—assuming aiming is in order."

"What? How so? I thought centrifugal force was a good thing."

"Only when it occurs at a certain time during the swing. At the wrong time it can actually create the swing path of the slice. In a sound golf swing, the whole downswing needs to oppose C-force until it's triggered in the release fairly late in the downswing." He looked up toward the sky and continued. I sensed that this last bit was a peek into his deep understanding, although he spoke as though it were an afterthought. But I was on the edge of my seat again. I knew so many people who wanted this question answered—I had asked the question many times myself, yet had not found one adequate answer. I was hoping for a definitive one from Joe.

Otter was sitting up as though he wanted to know the answer too. His ears were alert. He had been delicately licking a rawhide chew that sat between his huge paws, but he stopped even that, seemingly for this pivotal revelation. "As I said, at the heart of the problem is the psychological anticipation of the results relative to the target. There is conflict both physically and psychologically."

"What do you mean?"

"Look, the target is forward, isn't it? But the release needs to be backward and downward. Almost every instinct a golfer uses to get the ball to fly toward the target is exactly what flies the ball away from it."

"How so?"

He didn't bother to answer my question. "The target for these golfers has become the obstacle. Let me tell you a little history of my discovering the truth about it."

"The *target* is the problem?" I wanted to be sure I had heard him right.

"Yes, the target." Now we were into the meat. "It was frustration that got me going. I could fairly easily get a golfer to become rhythmic and get them on a pretty good path pattern. Remember our equation. However, as soon as we progressed in the lesson to learning to square the face to consistently fly the ball toward the target, all those good swing qualities would dissolve. It would blow my mind. Their rhythm would deteriorate and their swing path would return to the dreaded out-to-in pattern. It was difficult to accept.

"On top of that, even when a golfer would improve with me, they would invariably go out onto the course and return to their old way of handling the club, and the slice would return. For years I was frustrated with these temporary results. What irritated me was that I knew it wasn't the students, it was my lack of understanding of how people respond and perceive, much of it on an subconscious level. I dissected my own brain trying to figure it out.

"Then one day it came to me. The culprit was the target and the effect it had on the player. It was the students' subconscious response to the target that dissolved the good swing qualities we had worked on."

"What did you do?"

"I simply changed the target. I asked my students, after aiming, to mentally let go of the target out in the field."

"That seems strange to me."

"Of course it does and that's exactly why the answer has eluded most of us for so long, but if you don't change the target for a chronic slicer, it's doubtful they'll ever get rid of their problem." What he was describing rang true in my lessons too. I have always been confused about the fact that a student can make the perfect practice swing, but when you add a ball and target to the equation, all the old bad habits make a return visit.

Joe continued. "Of course they consciously know the path and face they want through impact but when they place the ball in front of them with a target out in the field, the subconscious mind takes over and changes the swing back to its skewed pattern. The only way I've found to overcome this is to change the target. I knew my students needed something radical that could overcome this unconscious effect, but it had to be worked out with the physics of C-force during a swing too!" His voice demonstrated his enthusiasm for his discovery.

"And you did this."

"That's right. It all boils down to one point of reference. If a golfer is willing, it surely works, and he or she will consistently deliver the club with high energy and directional control of the ball flight."

"What did you change the target to?" He got a piece of paper and a pen and drew a diagram showing a golfer's swing pattern when he or she focused on the ball's target. He drew another that showed a golfer's delivery into impact when they focused on the new hand target. "I kind of understand that, but how do you get them out of their old belief?"

"Geoff, when someone is deep into this problem you must get them to change the habit and then the belief will change with sound physical exercises, just as a matter of course."

"But how do you get them to change the habit and the belief?"

"Therein lies another problem. The action of the hands and arms to create the improved action is totally counterintuitive. That's why teachers and golfers alike rarely touch on it." I sat there with my mouth open, waiting for him to continue, finding it all hard to grasp. "Be patient, Geoff. As I said, I simply change the target. It is no longer out in the distance, forward near the flag on the green. It's now in the area where the golfer is standing and backward. Give them a back hand target near the impact zone that relates to the face angle. The beauty of this target is it comprises all three dynamics. They'll all be in order: path, face, and angle. I've found it to be the most effective way to get golfers to sustain the change. When the brain registers—actually sees—the downward delofting closing face angle, it completely rejects the old habit of an out-to-in path pattern."

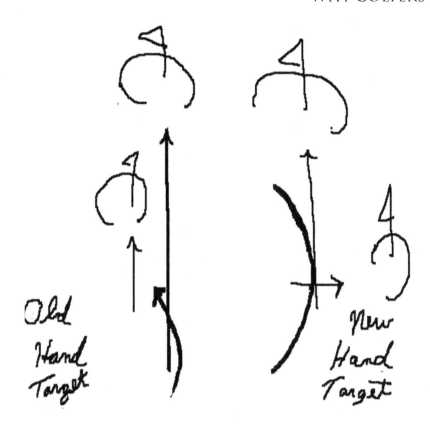

Old Hand Target

New Hand Target

"That's the level we need to get to for the change to be sustained. When the brain sees the face angle of this release trigger, it totally rejects the old pattern of path. And then, when you get to the point of hitting a shot to a target, the subconscious brain doesn't switch the swing path back. It was a real epiphany for me, and I no longer get frustrated by people who arrive with a slice; it can be dissolved forever in short order."

"So when they have path and face problems, you work on the face first?" I asked.

"That's right. If they can't fix the path by working on it, then their subconscious may be driving the imbalance and has a false impression of how to flight the ball to the flag. You see, Geoff, that's the trick of it all. When you work on adjusting the face angle to improve their swing pattern with this back hand/face target, it produces an improved path. The brain can then trust in the new path with the new hand and wrist action that flexes inward and backward to produce this face. Essentially, what I've done is change the picture and hand action of the timing. Get the face first with this crazy-looking hand target, and then it's likely their brains will *not* reject the improved path.

"The inside path becomes not just a desire but a need, mentally! The brain, on every level, will never accept an outside path with this hand and wrist action. So you've not only solved the physical swing problem, but also the psychological problem the golfer has about the inside path, too."

"So to improve the path and swing, you must first develop trust in the hand/face action?"

"Exactly. When the sound path has not been sustained, you have to take a different tack to address the golfer's subconscious disbelief. You must get them to commit to this change, the inward/backward hand and wrist action, in the delivery zone or near impact. After a little while, it's very likely that their brain, subconsciously and consciously, will process an acceptance and trust of an improved path, especially once the brain knows the golf ball has no chance of flying to the right."

"Can you show me?"

"Sure. Turn the face downward, like this...." He got up to demonstrate. Here's the new target; it's a hand target. I call it a curl. You literally back the club into the impact with the action of your lead hand, wrist and arm. Like this." He showed me. Just as Tim had said, it looked like a hockey player swinging at a puck. It was strange the way Joe's wrist flexed and hand faced, because the direction of the action was not toward the target. I could certainly understand how it would be difficult to believe.

"Of course, the face could close a lot too, if not done in balance," he told me. "Give your students this impression of the delivery and they'll be making progress very soon. Let me show you." He took two clubs and had me help him form a triangle between the face of the club, the ball, and the direction of the back of his left hand. "This is basically what it looks like at this point in the downswing. This reference more than any other practically guarantees a solid impact toward the actual target. As I said, it combines all three dynamics of a sound delivery: face, path, and angle. This discovery enabled me to combine those three dynamics in one point!"

Path, face, and angle.

GB

"Can your hands and wrists really do this in the swing?" I asked.

"If you begin slowly and relax the muscles you can begin to get it. When I curl way down I'm exaggerating a bit, but if you try to achieve it, just coming close, you will improve and become consistent. The C-force during the swing will probably not allow you to get this much curl, but just get the impression and I guarantee you'll improve. As I've been saying all along, your hands and wrists are the most influential part of your body when it comes to club control. This method maximizes control over their action and therefore the club. The impact and wrist action is very stable when you use them this way.

"Too often, when the hands are mentioned in golf instruction, it's assumed that they're inherently unstable. When I speak about the hands I'm not talking about being slap happy with them! There's a duality to the process too. The swing action is fluid to make the impact solid. Fluid and solid are not mutually exclusive."

He winked at me and continued explaining how to gain maximum energy and control over the impact. "Mind you, as you learn, you may have to modify where, when, and how much you do this. At first, learn it to the extreme and teach it to the extreme, especially when a golfer has the so-called incurable slice. Remember, nothing in golf is really incurable. The average golfer really needs to learn the release this way, and once they get it, frankly, they hardly need golf lessons. When they see this closing and de-lofting face, they get a clear picture of the ball flight going straight or curving to the left. Then and only then do they trust in the path coming from what's commonly called inside. In fact, their brains will refuse to let them strike the impact from an outward swing path. And now you have the brain on your side. A great advantage, wouldn't you agree?"

"I was under the impression that the action of the hands and wrists had little to do with squaring the face to the target physically."

He looked at me incredulously. "How did you plan on getting your students to strike the ball squarely?"

"I thought it would happen naturally, if everything else was in order."

"Well, did it?" He didn't wait for me to say no. "Really, I won't delve into what you call 'everything else'."

So here we are playing a target game and the way to get the ball to the target is to *not* concentrate on it. It still seemed crazy. I was still puzzled. Then I mimicked with my own hand and wrist the angle he prescribed. The back of my left hand was facing downward slightly to the right of the ball when my hand passed in front of my right thigh. It was a good 90 to 110 degrees away from the actual target. "If you're going to do this with your hand and wrist, why not just leave it that way all the time?" I asked.

I could tell he had heard this question before; he responded without hesitation. "This question highlights one of the reasons I teach the whole swing first before dynamically adjusting the delivery. As the club orbits, it's building up energy based on its design, mass, speed, and pattern of movement. Too often, golf teachers—and club makers—attempt to design a swing and club without appreciating the dynamics of the swing and how the mind works in conjunction with it! They assume a lot and try to preset what they ultimately want at impact. It simply can't be done that way.

"The swing itself is inherently dynamic. It's alive, always going somewhere. The club face, the path, and the angles in a swing are patterns of energy that depend on each other; they cannot be achieved statically. You cannot superimpose a static position onto that energy and be accurate and successful in balancing it. To find balance in an energy system you must recognize the Yin and Yang of it. You must account for this dynamic energy when adjusting how the delivery is created. There is a sequence and pace to it, too.

"Geoff, the square contact is achieved dynamically. All we can really do is pass through square. You've got to take the chance. The club is flying, whirling through the impact zone. There are no guarantees. You can't aim the club for square as you swing. The curling just provides a great opportunity for square and solid contact."

"That seems confusing."

Joe seemed to be trying to put himself in my shoes and patiently continued. "Well, Geoff, the club is traveling way out here, on a much greater orbit" He got up again and demonstrated the arc of the club head and how much larger it was than the handle arc, and then the difference in the speed and distance between the handle and the head as the downswing progressed. He then pointed to the action of the club head when he triggered the release with his curl. "This action is just a trigger, so the natural forces of momentum and C-force finish off the release so that the club face is looking toward the target through impact. The C- force can now be an advantage, instead of ruining your swing path and impact into the ball."

"You let it go from there?"

"Most of the time; sometimes I turn it more, and the more I let it go from there the higher I fly it," he said with a smile. "There are a couple of rules that must be adhered too, though."

It all seemed weird to me, but I was willing to listen because I had yet to find a release reliable under pressure. Maybe that's why I got so anxious when I played. I knew deep down that I didn't know how to feel or create the impact reliably. "Tell me," I said, "what those rules are."

"Well, first, it must be done by the lead hand, wrist, and forearm so that the hinge is supported when the change occurs, and, of course, there is a guaranteed positive effect on path when it has been done with the lead hand this way."

"That sounds like you're manipulating the club, which is unnatural, isn't it?"

"I guess you could call it manipulation, but it's a very valuable manipulation that's necessary in developing the release, especially when someone's hand action is that out of balance. What's natural at this point is not serving them well, but so many good things can happen when you do it this way.

"I recall a lesson some time ago with a fellow from Austria." He looked skyward, trying to remember his name. "Ah: Fischer," he said, pleased that his memory hadn't failed him. "Fischer was a fine student, extremely focused. He had learned the golf swing mostly by position and complex analysis, rather than dynamics and feel. He had a good swing and he was a good player, but intuitively had come to the conclusion that where he was would be as far as his approach could take him. Like many golfers, his game had hit a plateau. He came to me because he knew analysis was not getting him to his full potential.

"I was impressed with his perseverance but concerned about his seriousness. I thought that if he could couple his work ethic in feel with a lightness of mind, it would be a truly successful combination. I chuckle when I think of him, because he so enjoyed my simple approach. That is, the first two days of it. Our lessons up till then were only dealing with flow and path—you know, Da, Daaa, Daa—and then we worked with the Pathfinder for his orbit. It made perfect sense to him."

"What happened then?"

"I introduced the 'curl' timing, and an alarm went off in his head. His first reaction was to protest that it was too technical and ask what happened to simplicity. I told him that I was sorry that I couldn't make it more basic. I really believed we were at the bare bones, Geoff. You can only make it as simple as it is, and if your students are going to really see their potential, they need to learn timing. The wind-up is, Fischer trusted me and soon accepted my timing trigger and learned it well. He returned to Europe with the whole enchilada, and I believe he should be able to coach himself extremely well for the rest of his life. Sorry for the..." He apologized for getting away from my question.

I waved him off. "No, it's great."

"Where were we?"

"Back to the path?" I reminded him.

"Yes, the path has a much better chance of being fundamentally maintained from the lead side."

"How do you mean?"

"Well, picture this. It's like with a wagon. You can't control where a wagon is going if you push the handle. It won't steer well because there's no directional control. That's what pushing to get the delivery from the trailing hand during the delivery would be like. The link, the front of the wrist, collapses or flexes backward when pressure is applied from behind and the sound path is destroyed. That's why so often in golf past champions call the swing a left-side dominant swing—because the only way to control the hinge is by not applying pressure from behind."

"If you don't use your right hand, wouldn't you lose power?"

"Absolutely not. You don't add speed by pushing on the hinge; that only reduces energy."

"Are you saying that all these current great golfers are wrong about unloading the right side or hitting the ball with the right hand dominating the delivery?"

"I'm just saying it's neither pressure nor force from the right hand that they're really feeling. It's the flex-reflex action resulting from the club head weight and velocity orbiting, rotating, and accelerating. In other words, it's a result of allowing centrifugal force to take place in the delivery. That's where centrifugal force is useful! What those experts say they're feeling is what they're feeling, but I don't think it's the physics of it. Is it possible that they feel the right hand because they're right handed and that the hands and wrists are really flexed, a contracted position when entering the release zone?

"Let me put it simply because this is getting way too complicated. The feeling of the trailing hand releasing in the delivery is really the effect of the centrifugal force of the club head. It's an effect. I know from experience that if you describe the release from the trailing hand, you're in for a heap of trouble, confusing your students and making it more complicated than it needs to be.

"We also need to be careful about confusing golfers when we're talking about feelings versus fundamentals. Again, 'feel' statements in teaching can be very misleading, for several reasons. Mainly, golfers so often confuse a personal feeling with the physics and fundamentals of the club. I repeat myself at the risk of being pedantic: If the physical properties of the club are OK, then what you feel is OK. It's this interchange of personal feel with fundamentals that's confusing to many." Burlington was upping the velocity of his lecture with an infusion of passion.

"If someone feels that they deliver the club with the force of the right hand or side, that's their business, Geoff, but to misinform a golfer trying to apply true fundamentals makes it an unfortunate and misleading approach. You can't increase the centrifugal force of the delivery by pushing on the handle end from the trailing hand. Centrifugal force is an outward-pulling force. It's this misrepresentation of fundamentals that has set the average person's game back too far for too long. People end up feeling they have no talent or ability. It robs them of the pleasure they could be getting from golf. We as teachers need to improve far more than our students."

I saw Joe take a deep look at me—probably seeing that I was getting close to over-load territory—and he said, "Let's have a snack break."

Burlington went inside to get us something to eat. Otter was asleep, his snout resting on the rawhide. Burlington came back with a tray bearing grapes, a box of muffins, lemonade, paper cups and plates, and napkins. He broke the bunch of grapes and gave us each some. I poured the lemonade and opened the muffin box. We were quiet for a few minutes, just enjoying the ambiance before continuing our discussion.

"Joe, I'm kind of getting the picture of the release you're describing. What can you tell me about drawing the ball or curving the ball from right to left for a right-handed player?"

"I'll give you the dynamic formula for a consistent draw, and I would bet it's the opposite of what you think. Tell me, what do you imagine needs to happen in the delivery for the ball to curve right to left?"

I thought about it for just a second and described today's golf teacher's common assessment of why a golfer's club face is open at impact. "I believe the club head is stuck behind the golfer at impact and that causes the face to be open."

"Really?"

"That's what I hear players on the tour say all the time, especially when they hit a drive way to the right."

Joe began to shake his head. I hoped he wasn't going to dispute the great tour golfers; surely they must understand what's happening with the club when they lose control? Joe began, "Obviously, they're some of the most talented golfers in the world. But I believe they too have fallen prey to misinformation. I'll make this simple. The reason tour players mishit it to the right has nothing to do with the club being stuck behind them. If that were the case, and the other dynamics were in order, they should only strike the shot lower, not to the right! You do not draw or strike the ball straight and solid by slinging the club head forward during the delivery."

"Why do they constantly refer to the hand action as something negative?"

"I have a theory about that too," he said with a grin. "I believe one reason they so often ignore timing is because they always had an unconscious sense of it. I mean, it functioned well without them having to go through the process that most people have to go through to develop it. Most golfers are fairly incompetent with their timing at first, but through proper hand and wrist exercises they can become proficient consciously, and that leads them to an unconscious competence. That's where you want to end up, like signing your name or riding a bike.

"But these fine golfers haven't had to go through the process. I believe that's one reason they get all confused when they try to learn about their swing once on tour. It's easy for them to get lost because they're great athletes with great feel, but no program."

"So, how do you work on timing?"

"As I said earlier about the curl, you simply turn it downward while the club head is still behind, exactly as I showed you a few minutes ago. You curl it back there."

"You mean you want the club behind you?"

"Absolutely." He pointed to a spot well to the right of the golf ball during the downswing.

I raised my hand to interrupt politely. "It looks as though the ball would be smothered with that action."

Another head shake. "You don't continue to turn it down, you just trigger it downward and let it fly forward toward the ball from there."

"But the ball is on a tee. Wouldn't the club strike too downward a blow when you turn it down that way?"

GARY BATTERSBY

I saw the first hint of Joe getting seriously impatient. He took my driver out of my bag and swung back and around behind him and then downward and forward to the point in his downswing when his left hand was near his right hip. Then he curled it down and stopped. It was revolutionary to me. I had never heard the release described as a curl.

He continued. "Now with a driver, from here you let the club head fly forward to impact the ball." He walked into the ball on the tee, made a curl and stopped, in slow motion so I could see it, then swung back up again and this time curled it down and let it fly at full speed. It sailed high, long, and straight, and he remarked, "That's how you drive it. When you time it here, you have no urgency to square the face near impact either. This delivery is very easy on the mind too." Again in slow motion, he curled it downward and then let the club head swing forward as his hands passed in front of him. The angle had leveled off and was now ascending into the impact. The release trigger had done its job and would surely launch the ball as high as he wanted.

"I thought it would be popped up or smothered to the left when you turn it over like that."

"Geoff, I never said turn it over." I was surprised by his look, his eyes squinted and his nose crinkled up as though disapproving of my description of his release trigger. "I said turn it down, not turn it over. I showed you."

"What's the difference?"

"There's a big difference." He seemed exasperated. "When you curl it down you maintain path, whereas when a golfer is told to turn it over, the path circles about to the far side of the ball. That's why I showed you the reference with the curling. Curling is turning it downward, not over. The point I showed you is critical to the timing."

"So I won't duck hook it if I turn the driver down like this?" I pointed my left hand downward as it approached my right thigh in my downswing. The club head was way behind me.

Joe's patience returned. "If you let it fly from there, you'll launch it, and if you're concerned about hooking it, after curling it downward try to launch it as high as you can. It all depends on when you do it. If done at the proper time, when the club head arrives, it will be a perfect launch angle and square. I once heard a great golfer describing his swing while playing well. I knew he

180

was in for trouble because of his belief about timing. He seemed to believe that timing was some sort of recovery, not a fundamental, that it's unreliable and unstable. In my opinion that couldn't be farther from the truth. This timing trigger creates total stability of the hand and wrist action. You can't get it by eliminating the hand action from the swing; you must develop it and learn to trust it."

Joe had just taken the mystery out of what so many golfers are afraid of: the delivery. When I thought about it, I knew that's why we lacked confidence. Why should we all be afraid of the hand action? Maybe only because we hadn't worked it out. I tried to pretend my hands didn't exist and hoped they would behave.

Joe was shaking his head again. "Moe Norman once gave a friend of mine some of the best advice I've ever heard: When it comes to swinging a golf club, whatever you decide, stick with it! These great golfers should take a page from Roger Federer's tennis playbook. He travels the world solo, with his game, never doubting his technique. He knows it's within him because he developed it when he was very young. He has settled on how he plays and sticks with it. I'm sure he doesn't reinvent his technique every three or four years. He just elevates his awareness and sharpens his strategy. You know the paradigm shift isn't just 'the whole creates the parts;' it also encompasses the elimination of the unhealthy dependence golfers have on their coaches and teachers."

I was mesmerized by his assessment of the modern tour players. I wished everyone could hear his perspective. On the other hand, I was glad to be his private audience. We sat silently for a few moments before he continued.

"The issue, in my opinion, is that these great golfers are looking in the wrong places to regain their awareness. It's like fishing. My friend Lowell once told me of the time he met a fisherman on Big Laurel Creek in the mountains in North Carolina. This fisherman was not familiar with the stream but Lowell knew it like the back of his hand—he knew where every fish lay. Of course the fish lie where food is passing by and where they don't have to expend a lot of energy resisting the current. Lowell stopped to watch for a while as the fisherman cast time and again. No hits; the fisherman looked perplexed. He said he'd been working this section of the creek all afternoon without a single hit, though he was casting the fly perfectly and it dropped softly on the riffle in the stream.

"Lowell said to him, 'you'll never catch a fish here.' The fisherman asked him why not. 'Because there are no fish there. You can tie the best fly in the world, make the most beautiful cast, but you'll never catch one. You need to cast where there are fish. Throw your fly above that rock over there. Let it float down and around that swirl and let's see what happens.' No sooner had the fisherman cast where instructed than wham! A trout hit his fly like there was nothing to it.

"But there was something to it! You must look in a place that provides possibility. I know the story seems obvious, but all golfers, no matter what skill level, are often looking in the wrong places for the answers to their problems. No one is exempt. The answer to awareness is in the action of the club, which lies in the hands, right? These golfers need to identify the accurate swing keys, go there, and work on them. If they're looking in the wrong place, then they'll have to just wait for their talent to overcome their lack of awareness. Sometimes it never comes back."

I decided to continue my inquiry about novice golfers. "Why do so many people have trouble getting the ball airborne?"

"Precisely because they're trying to get it airborne! But it isn't hard to teach. The average golfer has the impression that one needs to get under the ball to get it airborne. They can do this when the ball is sitting on a tee above the ground. As soon as the ball lies on the ground, it's another story. They end up trying all kinds of ways to get it airborne, most of which are exactly what keeps it on the ground."

"The classic approach is trying hard not to lift their heads!" I interjected. "Can you believe some teachers actually teach that as a technique? And they tell students to concentrate on the ball."

Joe was shaking his head again. "Golfers need to concentrate on the club and its relationship in terms of angle of descent through the delivery, or where on the arc they want to impact the ball. That dynamic really has the greatest effect for getting the ball airborne. If I had my druthers, once a golfer has a swinging orbit of the club, I'd have them practice with a lofted club off a downhill lie or in front of a divot, not on grass. In a downhill lie the primary cause of flight is angle, not loft. Golfers would learn very fast that the angle of descent down the hill is the way to get the ball in the air."

"You mean you'd put a beginner on a downhill lie without a tee and expect them to get it airborne?"

"It may take some time, but they'd never get the wrong impression of what consistently gets a ball in the air. They wouldn't be making the error of trying to get the ball up from underneath. Did you ever wonder why novice golfers love an uphill lie? Well, there you have it—the upslope is appealing to the eye, and they're comfortable! They can see and feel loft from the slope. On the other hand, more experienced players will always favor a tight level or slightly downhill lie to one that's uphill and grassy, because they control the ball better and use the ground to their advantage with their angle of descent, not to mention the added head speed.

"If the novice golfer can get it airborne from the downhill, the level lie will never pose a problem. If they only get it to fly off the tee, we've set them up for a real negative shock when the ball is on the ground, and trying hard will most likely get in the way of everything. Golfers have been under the false impression that they could get the ball up from loft and a lifting angle, not from a descending one. So, when you put someone on a slight downslope, he learns naturally without trying hard to get the ball airborne.

"The bonus is that the slope acts like a magnet, especially for their legs. They can feel their lower body move down the slope in a sort of shift to support the angle of the delivery, so they'll really be getting the right impression in their whole body. They'll naturally learn to impact the ball at the best part of the club's arc, at the end of the downward section."

"Would you place the ball farther back in their stance, too?"

"In normal conditions, yes, but for learning purposes, leave the ball as though they're still on a level lie and that will make them move down the hill to strike the ball on the downward side of the arc. This is a good time to make it more challenging, like me using my one iron."

"I never imagined teaching someone to play off a downhill lie. I always thought it was so much harder that way."

"Well, yes, it seems so at first, but after a few minutes, they usually get the hang of it. Their mind-body system processes what it needs to do naturally, if you let it. They are well served by never again having the chronic problem of trying to get the ball airborne by lift."

"Do you believe in sticking with the short irons to learn the swing and then gradually lengthening to the woods?"

"In most cases, no. I'll tell you why: Especially with people who lack club head speed, the longer club provides more swing potential, not to mention the fact that the swing lends itself to improved timing. One cannot get away with being forceful. I often like to have my students begin with a three wood or driver. The key is to get them to swing at Tai Chi speed first, very slowly. Get them feeling a swinging force that comes from something other than their own strength. Have them swing about one-quarter speed with a full range of motion."

He looked at me and smiled. "Grab your clubs, Geoff. Let's have a look."

"Now?" I asked with surprise.

"Yes. I thought it would be a good idea to check out your swing."

I could feel an expression of shock spreading over my face and noted his grin in response. I knew this was an invitation I couldn't refuse.

16

MY SWING—
AND MY BRAIN

Joe smiled his quiet smile as he said, "I'd like to give you a lesson so you can have the perspective of a student again. It's good to appreciate how your students learn and what they feel like while they're learning. It's especially good to try something new that you've never done before. If you let the process take place and don't interfere with judgments (yours or theirs) the transformation is usually quick and easy. I mean, how awkward does a beginner feel when he first picks up a club? We tend to forget because it's so natural to us, but the novice can feel so out of sorts, as though parts of his body won't take direction or aren't part of him. Do you know what I mean?"

"I think so," I said cautiously.

"Go fetch your clubs."

I went back to the rental car and got my clubs. I had had no idea Joe was going to work with my swing today. I could feel my blood pressure rising. I didn't know why I was nervous. I'd gotten very comfortable with Joe Burlington, so why didn't I feel easy now? I guess I still lacked confidence.

At his direction, I took out a wedge and hit some shots. Burlington relaxed in his chair. Otter, nearby in the shade, was again sound asleep, snoring in the background. There was just a whisper of a breeze, and it was a little chilly. The cloud cover indicated rain would be coming by afternoon.

Burlington didn't say anything while I swung with my wedge. I wondered what he thought about my swing. The doubt was rising and with it my insecurity. After a few shots, he asked, "So what would you like to work on, Geoff?" I told him that when I played, I often had difficulty getting the distance accurate, especially with a less-than-full wedge shot, just like the first wedge shot I'd played with Tim and the guys at Pompano. He nodded. "OK. Is there anything else?"

"Well, yes. I've had a lot of trouble driving the ball with good accuracy and distance. If we could deal with that, I think that with my other observations this week, I'll be OK. I'm sure it could really improve my scoring."

"OK then; let's begin." His face looked very intent—a little more serious than usual. "May I ask you, before you play the partial wedge shot, are you surprised at the result? Or is your play something entirely different from the practice?"

"Most of the time, when I play the shot, I think it's perfect, but then it invariably ends up short."

"OK, let's try this. We can do a simple exercise to determine whether you have a concentration problem or an awareness problem."

"I don't understand the difference." I responded, puzzled.

"A concentration problem means you have the awareness or the feel to produce the shot maybe in practice, but when you do it for real, something else happens. Awareness, on the other hand, means that you practice a certain swing—in this case, one for the energy of a three-quarter wedge—and you play it exactly as you practice, but then it ends up short and is not accurate. Let's find out which problem we're dealing with. What is going through your mind before you hit the shot, Geoff? How do you prepare?"

"I make a few practice swings, trying to determine the distance."

"Do you try to determine the distance with the length of your swing?"

"Yes, I try to visualize the length of swing for the length of the shot."

"OK, let's begin there. Are you aware that that may not be a good way to go?"

"What do you mean? I've always heard that it's a good criterion for gauging distance."

"But Geoff, what you're doing isn't working, is it? In my experience, there isn't necessarily a correlation between length of swing and energy of impact. You could have a short swing with a lot of speed at impact or a long swing with very little speed. The way to go is to feel the energy of impact to determine the length of the shot and then let the length of swing be a function of the energy. You also need to feel for, or take into consideration, the dynamic loft at impact, so you can picture and feel the flight pattern and the ball's response when it lands.

"I would suggest you use the Three Bears approach: the middle-of-the-road exercise."

"Three Bears? How does that work?"

"First pick a target, then make a swing feeling the energy for going too far. Make another swing for too short, and then make another one just right. Just like Goldilocks, remember?"

I nodded, rolling my eyes. "Yes, that much I remember."

He continued. "If you need to, just guess! Picture the flight pattern, high or low, etcetera, depending on what you're feeling with the particular club in hand. Make your actual swing and see what happens. If your actual swing matches your practice swing, and if it's not the right distance, then you have an awareness problem. If you don't play the practice swing, then you have a concentration or a confidence problem. There's a formula for this: *performance equals your potential minus your interference!*[7]

"Playing an instrument in an ensemble is a good analogy," Joe explained. "Let's say all the instruments—like the muscle groups of your body—are playing together nicely, and then someone gets out of synch. But no one stops playing. They just keep going. Honestly, no one cares that you made a mistake. If you're to be present, you need to continue playing or you'll miss what's happening in the next phrase. The process doesn't stop for you to correct yourself. Conversely, if a difficult passage is coming up and you start anticipating the mechanics of it in an effort to get it right, you rob yourself of the moment you're in. It's a state of mind thing, but it can be learned.

"If there's something bothering you, concern over the result usually, your potential is what you felt and saw in your practice swing, and the interference is what you felt and saw in your actual swing. If this is the case, then you don't have a swing or awareness problem. You then must work on developing your confidence and trust and you must do it on fundamental ground. Develop confidence in your ability to feel the impact energy. If things don't work out, just say 'cancel' to yourself. Do not, I repeat, do not spend a moment on what didn't work. To figure out on each occasion what went wrong is a total waste of time."

"But if I don't figure out what went wrong with my swing, then how can I avoid it in the future?"

"Your swing did not misfire before your brain did, Geoff, it did it after! But because you're so preoccupied with feeling in a physical way, you don't realize that you misfired in an emotional and psychological way. Your approach needs to address that aspect first."

"What do you mean? What does my brain have to do with it?"

"Sit down. Let me define it in a little more detail. Only part of your brain interferes, the doubting and logical part. Brain science, like quantum physics, is constantly changing, but there are some basics we can rely on. Your brain has two sides, or lobes, each designated for particular tasks and functions. We can personify the left brain and the right brain as though they were two different people in one body, which is exactly how they act a lot of the time.

"Now if we agree that the golf swing is a task best performed in the environment of the sensory system—feeling, and the imagination—that is, when it comes to instantaneous performance, then the right brain is the natural leader. The right brain can synthesize things and put them together quickly. It can do things in a complete fashion and it's intuitive. The left brain is inadequate for rapid complex synthesis, which is what's needed for athletics and such. The left brain is simply not designed for these types of tasks; it's just not the proper tool. The left brain is good at intellectual work, slow methodical analysis, categorizing, ordering, and breaking things down into pieces. If the sides of the brain could talk, and they do communicate in their own language, the right side would volunteer that it's dying to do the task. But the left brain attempts to block it, if given half an opportunity. There is a competition going on between them, going all the way back to when you were a child."

"Uh-huh."

"Before you could speak, Geoff, you were a total sensor. All your body's movements were based on how they felt—balance, speed, and so on—totally right-brain oriented. However, when you went off to school to get 'educated,' the left brain began exercising heavily, working out at the brain gym they call school. You got graded according to how well you understood or memorized material analytically, intellectually. You rarely got an A because you were intuitive about something, right? That's because in general, Western education doesn't seem to value intuitiveness. That's why more and more, our school systems are eliminating music, art, and athletics. The powers that be seem to only believe in math and science, even though modern science proves the value of—and pleads for more—art, music, and sports. The brain needs those developmental exercises to blossom fully and function to its potential. The fact is, students who exercise their brains in music or art are more likely to be able to cope creatively within our complex society later on. Anyway, that's a topic for a whole other time.

"The left brain likes to sort things out, get them down on paper, and plan for the near future. So the left brain has been active and the right brain has for all intents and purposes been on a long vacation."

He took a long swallow of lemonade and broke off a wedge of muffin top. I refreshed both our glasses before taking a slug. I had worked up a thirst, swinging and listening, and we finished off the gallon container and four muffins before he resumed speaking. "Did you ever wonder why intellectuals have such difficulty getting better at golf or other athletic endeavors, Geoff? Or why the golfer who practices a lot often gets worse? It happens so often you'd think we'd have figured it out by now! The golf swing certainly is not so complex that it can't be known. We were meant to *play* it, not comprehend it! So I think, no pun intended, it's of no value to comprehend the golf swing; however, it's of great value to feel and trust the golf swing—which the right brain is just dying to do anyway.

"So the trick is," he said, "don't give the left brain an opening. Do things in a manner in which the left brain will simply surrender and allow the intuitive self to operate freely."

"Is there a method to doing this? Are there steps to get me to that point?"

"There are many strategies. A typical response to a golf task from the left brain is slow, as if you had a lifetime, and then it will give you the impression that you have a lot of figuring to do before you try to play this shot. It will try to list all the do's and don'ts about the swing and the shot. It could give you a detailed list of problems lurking. You can imagine the trouble this will create.

"The right brain, on the other hand, is like a kid at the front of a classroom with his hand in the air: 'Give it to me, I can do it now!' The right brain really believes. Your imagination and your feel are in right-brain central, which never questions the outcome and just takes chances. It has an optimistic bias, which is a good thing even when it's unrealistic. It will take a giant leap based on this optimism. That's the let-go mode, which great performers so often call being in the zone. They're in a zone, all right—the right-brain zone that allows all their potential to come out.

"We need to get our students started this way on day one, and get them into the habit of relying on feel. And we need to develop practice habits that turn it on rather than shut it down."

I conjured up visions of times when I had been in the zone and tried to recall how I'd gotten there. I couldn't tie my zone moments to any period when I had been taking instruction or trying on one of the new-and-improved methodologies.

"Don't be impressed with golfers who can recite great volumes on the so called mechanics of the swing, Geoff." He had read my mind again. I wanted him to elaborate, but he continued on his own track. "Take concentration; what is it? All you need to do is be aware of the space you're in and what's happening in that space. Avoid attempting to control things in other spaces."

I smiled, aware I was gaining another nugget of wisdom. "I'd like to learn more about the left-brain/right-brain relationship in golf." Although I was getting a sense of the connection, I needed it articulated more.

"Sure," he said. "How *does* it pertain to golf? OK, I'll give you a little scenario of what happens in your head between the brain's two halves when you knock a ball into trouble. It's a good example of the right brain winning the competition over the left brain.

"Knowing that the left brain is analytical and the right brain is about feeling sensing will help you understand the conflict that can cause trouble when they have to work things out. Take a typical golf shot from out of the trees. Let's say there's a very narrow opening and the ball has to fly through the hole and then curve to the right to get onto the green 150 yards away. The left brain will say, 'I can't do this. This shot is impossible.' At the same time, the right brain is dying to get involved. The left brain's got an attitude like a spoiled child because it knows it can't do such complex tasks expediently. It needs time to figure out how to program the action. If you give it a job that it doesn't accept for one reason or another, or if it gets lost while analyzing all the variables, it cedes to the right brain, and the 'feel' side takes over."

"Which is what you want, right?"

"Yes, but it happened here by accident. You need to learn to do this intentionally. There are many exercises you could do, and I'll show you some as we work with my students. If you looked to apply this idea to any other sport, it's easier, because most are very reactive, full of fast action, and, of course, the ball is always moving. Those performers are naturally in an athletic frame of mind—meaning, naturally trusting their feeling and employing their right brains.

"Golf, on the other hand, is such a slow sport, so it lends itself to interference from the analytical left brain. When you miss a shot and you're walking down the fairway trying to figure out what happened, you're just programming in another problem. Analysis of why things don't work is not conducive to good golfing." He took out a pack of gum and offered me a stick. I declined and he continued. "The subconscious mind does not know the don'ts. We need, as teachers, to create tasks that get our students to be into the feeling, tasks that are so sensory and intuitive that they cause analysis to shut down. When you do that, students have no choice but to trust their experience and their intuition."

"So you need to create tasks that cause the left brain to shut down?"

"That's right. Or at least, it has to shift out of the way."

"Does it shift because of the time frame you have to complete the task?" I asked.

"Exactly!" He clapped his hands. "That's one strategy I've found to be very reliable. I suggest you be creative and teach your students different things to keep their sense of feel awake and operational so they don't fall asleep—especially while playing. The analytical brain will, by its very nature, try to take over the tasks as if it were the best tool for performance. It has a greedy attitude toward tasks, so you have to keep it in check as much as possible. In putting, the left brain is especially obvious. That's generally where the most interference occurs.

"The real precision tool is the right brain, the sensor. Any athlete, even those with limited experience, will tell you analysis is the wrong tool for making instant adjustments. But your right brain is well suited to the task. It's specially designed for the delicate tactile action of a golf swing—it pares things down to their essentials. While doing the exercises, you can actually feel this brain shift from left to right if you pay attention.

"The right brain believes in itself, so to speak, so you must be creative when you teach a student to nurture it. You'll need to be able to demonstrate your own feel as an example of what you're teaching. There is nothing like a little live-action demonstration to make a believer out of a skeptic."

"You make this sound so simple. Can you give me an example of how you go about convincing a student to trust that feel is the only way to go?"

"Give them minimal time for preparation and have them hit shots through little openings in trees. Or have them swing five shots in succession without stopping to think about alignment, setup, or anything else. Then make them swing five shots in eight seconds. As they're doing this, ask them to pay attention to their rhythm. You can even ask them to swing with their eyes closed, which is a quick way to wake up feel. Ask them to be super precise with a shot—let's say, a nine iron shot flying through a three-foot hole between branches of a tree, with only a few seconds of preparation. I guarantee their analytical brain will shut down and the brain shift will create some amazing results."

This was solid information I could use. Just then, an errant range ball came flying and bounced between us, forcing us to pick up our chairs and clubs and move to a more secluded area, with Otter trailing behind. When we got settled in our new spot, guarded by a large pine against any more wayward shots, Burlington continued. "Geoff, what I'm talking about is keeping your focus on the task at hand, disciplining your mind, and not allowing yourself to transfer your thoughts outside the place or task at hand. It's simply a matter of being present…"

"Huh?"

"You, as a golfer and a teacher of golf, need to be in this mode too—it's not just for students. Create strategies so your students will naturally change their minds. The changes must occur without force because they need to surrender their way of going about it! Demonstrate your awareness by executing golf shots that require super-awareness, like flying shots through little openings in trees." Burlington picked up a four iron and demonstrated just that. The shot flew through a narrow opening in the pine tree in front of us. There was obviously no time to figure it out.

He continued without missing a beat. "Show them you possess the skills to perform with super-awareness. There's no time to waste on swing debates and resistance. Everyone who's learning to swing needs to get into habits that shut down the interference of the left brain. It's a real test to learn how to do that, Geoff. I call the right brain the 'let-go present mode' and the left brain the 'try-hard mode,' which operates in the past and future. To be primarily right-brain functioning, you need to be present in the golf task at hand, especially because the right brain trusts itself. It does not question, so it fits neatly into our program of concentration, doesn't it? It's the perfect tool for performing because it has confidence in its ability to get the job done."

"Isn't what you're saying contrary to what we hear today about being methodical and deliberate?"

"Yes, it is. I think being methodical to the point of stalling is extremely counter-productive. It causes tension to rise and that's dangerous to any sensory performance like a golf swing—it basically opens a Pandora's Box of doubt. Slow and steady lends itself to switching on the left brain. I'm not saying you can split your brain and function totally right brained. The lateral connection between the brain lobes keeps each side communicating and behaving as a whole.

"But just like in school, almost all golfers who practice increase the use of their left brain rather than their right brain because golf instruction has become scholastic, very complex and analytical. Don't you hear all the time, 'the harder I practice, the worse I get'? The left brain is the primary reason. Golfers simply don't know how to practice. They end up training with the wrong strategy often not only from the physical side, but the psychological side too. They never improve their golf self-image either. And that negative image will limit their success substantially."

"Wait, what do you mean?"

"Let me explain that later." I relented and he continued.

"Then they go out on the golf course with great expectations, but with only one ball and a few seconds. What happens next? Paralysis! That's followed by the next mistake, which is the one that befuddles me most: They go back to the practice tee to analyze more and dig themselves an even deeper hole.

"No wonder the average practicing golfer is frustrated. I would be too—and I have been! But this is where modern technical instruction has led us. The increase in analysis is inversely proportional to confidence. But we can talk more about this later. Let's take a look at that driver swing you mentioned."

17
SWING STYLES

"**B**efore I begin, Joe, I was wondering, is there a difference in swings from the driver to the irons? I've always been a superior iron player, but at best, I'm average with my tee shots. And I often have students who say they can hit the woods and not the irons and vice versa."

"Yes, I know. I've seen that a lot."

"Are the swings the same, though?" I repeated.

"They are and they aren't."

"What do you mean?" He seemed to enjoy confusing me.

"Well, Geoff, just as you said, some people hit irons well and others are better with the woods. In most cases, their natural swing is connected to one of the releases. I basically teach three releases of energy into the impact. One is more passive, with centrifugal force. We talked about it earlier. That approach lends itself better to the tee shots. If you really become aware, you can actually feel the handle slow down to let the club head accelerate and act on your hands and arms. The centrifugal force of the head pulls on the handle and, given that the path is still intact, the face rotates and accelerates from this action. You must get the ratios of speed and distance right for it to occur.

"Now let's talk about your driver swing."

"I remember when I first started having trouble with the driver. One summer I began working on retaining the angle, like this." I showed him what I meant.

Joe shook his head, as if he'd heard this many times. "That fad of trying hard to retain angle became popular years ago when golfers became aware of the tremendous left wrist angle that Ben Hogan had late into his downswing. Unfortunately, these golfers made a grave assumption, and it destroyed many good golfers' swings."

195

"What did they assume?"

"They didn't realize that Hogan's wrist angle was a natural function of the synchronization of the club and his body's action during his swing—not to mention the extraordinary degree of flexibility he possessed. Too many golfers tried to isolate that strong angle by holding it with pressure and tension. But angle must be a natural result of sequence, direction and the desired shot pattern. Trying to artificially retain it will inevitably disrupt the release of the club into impact. I can tell you more later, but for now, just avoid that approach."

Like a kid, I still wanted to tell him what had happened to me. He listened patiently. "I could retain the angle when the ball wasn't there. I took videos and people observed me. But my angle with a driver or longer iron would always dissipate when the ball was there. The pictures show that in the practice swing without a ball, the angle was great. The odd thing is I knew what I wanted, but when I saw pictures of my downswing, they showed I had lost angle prematurely, even though it was in my mind to retain it. The result was that I lost club head speed and distance."

Joe understood. "Yes, I know what you mean. There was obviously something going on in your head that caused you to lose angle when the ball was in front of you, ready to be put into play. It happens to a lot of golfers. What happened the first time you worked on retaining the angle, Geoff?"

"With the driver, I hit the ball way to the right."

"Did that happen when you played?"

"Yes. I had a chronic block or push slice. The swing after that would be this weak hook as I tried to adjust. I got to the point that I would drive with a three wood, which worked for a while, then I had to go to the one iron. Again, I was OK for a time, but then it got so bad I hated to play any hole except a par three. Even that got bad! It was as if whenever I was on the tee, I had zero confidence and my swing would prove it."

"I see. When you say 'chronic,' how long did it go on?"

"It has gone on for years now, and I've given up trying to get more energy from angle. I drive the ball OK, but very short for my size, strength, and flexibility. I know it was the mental side affecting the physical, but it was like this negative obsession was controlling me, the image deep inside, as you say, and I just couldn't seem to get out of my funk."

Burlington considered, then said, "I understand. I've been there and there is a way out. Let's first deal with the physics problem, if indeed there is one. Let me see you make a few swings with your driver."

I took a couple of practice swings and they felt like I had very good angle. Then I went to hit the tee shot and wham—way right.

"Go ahead," he said calmly. "Another swing." The ball flew off to the right, but not as far. "Did you feel as though you had good angle? Is this a typical result when you work on getting a strong angle of attack?"

"Yes, it is."

"And you did achieve the angle you desired?"

"Yes."

"When you try to increase your angle in the tee shot, you lose control over the recovery of the face to square. When you try to get the face square, you lose speed and angle, resulting in a weak shot to the left."

"I would say that's an accurate assessment."

"OK, Geoff. This is very simple." There he goes with that 'simple' again. "There are two ways to solve the imbalance. If this takes more than five minutes, I'll be surprised." As Tim had said, for Joe, everything took five minutes. He continued. "Your problem begins in your head and you support it with an imbalance in the delivery. May I make an educated guess about what's going on in your head on a subconscious level? Deep down, you have a negative self-image. You believe your swing is weak and the ball is going to fly way right if you have angle and so unconsciously your mind-body system gives up the angle to strike the ball squarer toward the target."

I considered his answer. "That makes sense, Joe, but how do I adjust?"

"Very easily. The physics in the swing that you relate to is the shape, or position—the geometry only. The problem with that is you end up missing the synchronization or the dynamic properties of the action from the good angle. It's part of timing, or the speeds and distances that things travel— more precisely, the speed and distance ratios of the handle and the club head needed to deliver it squarely from the strong angle that you want."

"What exactly do you mean?"

"Well, if you want that much angle, you must consider the speed and distance the handle is traveling in the delivery zone so that the club face has a chance to balance out for square contact. When the club travels in the pattern of an oblique ellipse (plane and path) the face will likely rotate to square with the speed/distance ratios balanced."

"That sounds good, I guess, but this is really getting confusing."

"I know. Let me tell you the first strategy I would share with most of my students who want to let the club square by centrifugal force alone—the ones who aren't yet ready to trigger the release physically with the curl." I wondered if he figured I was too dense or untalented to try the advanced release. I could feel my insecurity rising triumphantly.

Joe continued. "As your swing progresses toward the impact zone and you feel that strong angle in the wrists—just before the impact, imagine the handle slowing down—it's commonly felt in your lead arm speed; feel it in your lead hand and lower arm. And attempt to stay in the phone boot too, after impact!" I looked at him out of the corner of my eye and saw his smile but I didn't bother to address 'phone boot.'

"That way," he continued, "the club head can recover its rotation and travel the necessary distance for a square impact. Major centrifugal force at the right time is imperative for this swing timing to work consistently. Take the club again and swing like this." Burlington demonstrated a strong angle, but when his hands got down near his right leg, he slowed the handle down and the club head flew by. It must have rotated, because the ball launched off the club face squarely and flew a long way. "Here, take the club," he offered. "Now this time, get your strong angle by your swing sequence and as your hands and arms approach the impact zone, purposely slow down the forward speed of the handle."

I couldn't believe what he was saying. "Slow down?" I repeated.

"That's right."

"I've always heard you must accelerate through the ball to the finish and extend!"

"Yes, I know, Geoff, but just do the opposite this time and you may be surprised at what begins to accelerate." He pointed to the club head and smiled. I tried a practice swing while Burlington advised. "Slow down the handle." He got up, grabbed my driver, and demonstrated again. "Like this," he said. Then he took a full swing and swung down faster. During the second half of his downswing, he exaggerated the slowdown and the handle almost came to a stop and literally reversed directions near impact. The club head went right by the handle, fast, and rotated. The handle was pointing backwards.

I didn't realize that was the balance in timing. "Wow, just like that?" I admired.

"That's right. You can get the face rotation when you're on a good path, but you need to time the speed and distance of the handle-head relationship. That's essential in timing."

"But again, it seems so manipulative," I protested.

"I know, Geoff, but you may need to consciously develop the hand and arm action to change the dynamics of your delivery for the better."

"But everything is happening so fast, how can I do something that late and get it done?"

"Good point; you'll probably have to swing Tai Chi speed at first. On the other hand, if you rely on feeling the action, you can achieve precise tactile action beyond your wildest dreams at incredible speeds late into your downswing. Your mind-body awareness is quite capable of that." Then he added, "But not your intellect! Once you can do this rote, I'll show you other possibilities in timing too. For now, I suggest you spend time experimenting with the speeds, purposely slowing the handle and then maybe accelerating it and then balancing it out. You have to go through the process to get a balance and develop your confidence. I think it's exactly what you need for your mind to accept a strong angle into the impact with a driver. Otherwise, I don't believe you'll ever sustain a strong angle for a high energy at impact."

"Let me try again."

He gave me back my driver. I teed up about six balls and swung trying to slow the handle. The first few swings were consistently drop-kicked as I slowed the handle with my left hand and arm—not a very good feeling. I looked back at Joe, who was smiling, unfazed by my apparent mistakes. "Can you show me the other way to get it to square?"

"Not yet; you're just beginning. Be patient; keep going. Just stay with the speed-distance ratios."

I wondered what he was getting at. Could I begin curling the driver release? My mind began jumping in and out of old swing thoughts, but I was able to quiet it down even though I felt lost now. Neither my old way nor this new way seemed to be working. I was frustrated but had no choice except to surrender and follow Joe's direction.

Left: The hands traveling faster in the downswing. Right:
The hands traveling slower in the downswing.

GB

He reassured me. "I will be responsible for the results; you just attempt to feel."

I relaxed a bit. I realized I was still concerned about the results and how my swing might look to others. But if I didn't need to care about the results, I could begin feeling more accurately. I began to swing again, this time carefree. I drop-kicked a few more and ducked several balls to the left.

"Good," he said.

I looked back with half a grin and said, "It's your fault!"

"I know," he said. "Keep going."

And then, just like that, something happened. I could actually feel the action of the club, its speed and rotation, and the slowing lead arm as it rotated and folded right against my left side. That must be the 'phone boot,' my left arm against my left side, and the forward swing feeling abbreviated, but now the results were there. It didn't seem right, but it worked! I began to get the hang of it. It felt like I wasn't even swinging. I mean, there was no resistance, no effort, yet I struck the ball with a lot of energy. I really could believe in a strong angle and hit it square now.

"Wow, I don't think I've felt that impact since I was a kid!" I was beginning to see how much my focus on outcome had been interfering with the changes Joe had proposed.

"It's a wonderful feeling, isn't it?" he agreed.

I teed up six more balls and experimented with this newfound idea of release. The balls began to fly straighter and farther. I could feel the energy and its release as though the club head had a life of its own. I stopped for a moment to catch my breath. I hadn't hit tees shots like that in years. "This is amazing, Joe. You really think that's all I had to do to get on track?"

"It's a start. We can go deeper into the release, like really backing it in with your lead hand, slowing it down and curling, but this is a beginning." Again he left me dangling like a participle. There was more to it, but he wasn't going into it now. "Let's just discuss this problem for now. You see, Geoff, you weren't allowing your mind-body system to function fundamentally, because you failed to realize the synchronization of the whole system and your negative self-image contributed too, but I will discuss that later. While you were trying to gain angle and energy through tension and accelerating the handle, you were sapping energy from the head, which is the type of release that feels like a drag. It probably felt like a heavy log, very sluggish, and the harder you tried the less impact energy you had. This approach is, again, very oriented toward shape and parts." Joe emphasized his disdain for golf teachers positioning the body parts of their students during the swing as though they were not already connected and ready to work as a team.

I made another swing during his dissertation. "Good! That's it!" he said. It did seem slow to me, but the energy felt great! But was it slower? Certainly not the club head! Lacking timing made me feel weak and I knew I was stronger than most of the guys I played against.

I blurted out, "I just felt weak at impact because of this imbalance."

"Precisely!"

Burlington was right. It took about five minutes. For years I had been thinking that I just didn't have it, or that I'd lost it. I immediately felt confident again. We had truly solved one of my problems. Now I believed I could repeat it forever.

18
THE CURL AGAIN

"Is there anything else you'd like to work on, Geoff?"

"Well, since you mention it, Joe, there is. In my iron play, I've been having difficulty gauging distance."

"Go on," he said, encouraging me.

"Is the release the same as with a driver?"

"No, not at all. Because of the angle you'd like the club to strike and the length of the club, the release is more active and aggressive. Some call it an offensive release. You achieve that with lead arm and hand action. Remember the curl. You can learn it by hitting punch shots. You can develop a keen sense of trajectory and distance with all your irons, and, of course, you will spin the heck out of it. Watch me; I'll show you the release just like before."

He picked up a club and began to swing in slow motion. "Allow your swing to take its natural course until here," his hands followed the natural shift of his feet and legs down and forward. "Now make your swing in slow-mo and stop right here." His hand stopped in front of his left thigh. "It's a general reference for triggering this release. With your left hand, your lead hand, curl downward in this direction." I didn't move. "Your left hand and wrist," he repeated.

I didn't realize my hands were so accustomed to being firm and that this stiffened my wrists. There was no way I could get that flex with all that pressure. Before I could think, he said, "You need to lighten up first!" His voice was slightly elevated and I think he was surprised at how tightly I was holding the club. "Your wrist flexes inward like this when your hand gets to this point."

He showed me. His left hand was in front of his left thigh and the back of his left hand was pointing downward, which created a flex in his left wrist:

the curl. As he demonstrated, his right hand came off the club with just the ends of his fingers still on the grip. Just then he stopped to place a golf tee into a small grommet he had placed in the Velcro flap of his glove for this purpose. "Here's your reference." The tee was pointing downward, indicating the direction and angle of his hand and therefore his club.

"That seems so radical," I said.

"Yes, it seems that way at first, but it's the only way to combine all the delivery dynamics into one."

"What do you mean?"

"This action will give you the best path, face, and delivery angle for consistent ball striking, and once you begin swinging rhythmically in an orbit, this can become your singular goal for consistency. This is the release trigger I've developed to cover all bases of impact. It affords golfers the ability to deliver the club as a tour player, and on top of that, I've discovered that practically anyone can learn it."

I questioned this in my mind; what a claim! "It seems so weird, though," I commented weakly. "I've never seen anything like it. Why point in this direction when the target is over there?" I wanted him to confirm this point of reference, this angle. I pointed down the fairway to the flag where I was aiming.

"Good question, Geoff, but you're making the same mistake most people do. You relate to the club as though it's not moving and as though you were physically attached to the club head. You are at the *handle* end. The weight and action at the other end is another story. Often when golfers try to square the face toward the ball's target like that, both the path and the delivery are seriously compromised. What seems a logical way for golfers to strike the ball to the target won't work. The target is forward, but the release needs to be backward, so to speak. You have to balance your physical action with the club's energy. You see, by this point in the swing, the club has built up a potential to rotate and the angle is compressed and wants to expand.

"As the club head travels on its orbit there's an energy that has to be accounted for in the delivery. So the physical action has to be congruent with this potential energy to strike the ball to the target. This is why the hand and wrist angle has to be in this direction—so that it's congruent with the energy built up in the club head, ready to be released into impact. Mentally, you need to let go of the target out there." He pointed to the flag in the distance. "To get to it, point the back of your left hand down toward *this* target," he pointed at his spot about 110 degrees away from the actual target. "This is exactly why golfers have such difficulty: They never let go of the target off in the distance. If you're having trouble, this is the best and fastest way to get the ball to fly to the target—by first releasing the ball's target from your mind."

"But it still seems way too complicated and strange."

"It's not, it's just different. All golfers are capable of this release as long as they aren't bogged down with the minutia of typical modern golf swing techniques."

I looked closely at the curled wrist angle again. "The club seems like it will arrive closed."

"It could, but if you commit to this angle you'll adjust what comes after naturally. This release takes all the urgency out of trying to impact the ball squarely, because it sets up a beautiful centrifugally released square contact. And the added value of this release technique allows your mind to trust in the inside path. That's the heart of it. When you commit to this face-downward trigger, your brain will want to swing the club from the inside all the time, and from this comes a sustainable fundamentally sound swing.

"This is exactly how your students will believe in the improved path and ultimately get the results they're looking for. This is what's missing when a golfer's best swing dissolves as he goes to play a shot. This is the basis for growing confidence."

I had never heard such an explanation of the release, but it made sense, even though it looked weird. How would I remember all this? Joe seemed to see that I really needed to know, so he explained how he arrived at such a radical approach to building a swing that flights the ball toward the target with incredible consistency. "Let me give you a bit of the history of my teaching this aspect of the golf swing. In the past, I was generally able, through swing exercises, to get a student to become more rhythmic. I could also help students improve their path—mind you, this was while they weren't caring about the ball flight. As soon as I asked them to feel the club face square at impact, the path would typically dissolve into an outward orbit that destroyed the energy and ball flight toward the target. In other words, if a golfer tried to feel the face rotation toward the target, the swing path would be off again.

"I've thought long and hard about this problem, Geoff. Surely they knew what swing path they wanted, but something changed once the target was added to the equation. You know most golfers suffer with the dreaded pull slice. The question is, why? I realized that a golfer could not trust in that swing path and, at the same time, try to get the ball to fly toward the target. That was the conflict. The very way a golfer typically tries to square the face toward the target destroys the path. A paradox, eh?"

I thought there wasn't much I didn't know about golf, but I had never heard things explained this way.

"The ball's target is the 800 pound gorilla in the way of their success. So I had to come up with a way for the average golfer to get the release into impact without losing the path and angle of delivery. I had to bring them around to a whole different way of knowing and believing. The target out in the field became insignificant. The target on the ground in front of them that they could see clearly as they swung was most important. The crazy-looking angle for the back of the left hand and wrist in motion achieves exactly the angle for the club face for the target in the field. The curl achieves this." He took out his pencil and drew a top view of how a golfer had to picture and feel the hand and wrist action to achieve a consistent square impact from a sound swing path.

"But I don't see the tour players doing this."

"Oh, but they do. In most cases it's blended in so well that you can't distinguish it from what you thought you saw. And it's not really apparent to golfers because these parts of your body are small and moving very fast. It's hard to see, unless you're looking for it."

Left: (Top) Backhand/face target. Right: Downswing: backhand/clubface target during the delivery.

GB

"Other parts of your body are much easier to see, but they don't mean anything to the fundamentals of impact. Of course you must adjust according to your unique physical abilities and reactions, but that's basically it.

"Let's go back to your earlier question about different releases. They are similar but are not the same for all the clubs. You see, you have different-length clubs that have a smidgeon of difference in releases, based on the angle you desire for the impact and the club in your hand. I'm not going to confuse you with the formula, because you can work it out by feel." My nature was to be more precise. I would have loved to see his formula, but thought it better not to ask.

"When you trigger the release," Joe explained, "how much you activate the curl, the degree, and the time all change according to the club and shot you desire."

"Could you give me some parameters for the different clubs?"

"Sure. The driver is the earliest and least curl, while the wedge is the latest, with the most curl. However, in most cases, golfers adjust naturally to the different clubs and shots. Essentially this is a universal release."

He showed me again. "All you do is swing the club downward and curl your lead hand and wrist, like so. Here's your target for your hand." He demonstrated with the tee in his glove pointing again. Placing a ball about six inches before the impact of the ball and a few inches to the far side of it, he said, "Now with the momentum of the downward force and the curl in this direction, you've set up or triggered the centrifugal release of the club head into the ball and toward the target. You then simply let it go." I watched as he demonstrated.

View of back/hand and club face targets
during delivery.

GB

"The beauty of this method is that you'll never lose the path pattern relative to the target. In the past, we had to qualify our instruction by saying that if you worked on the path, you could lose the timing, or vice versa—if you worked on the face you'd probably lose the path. No more; the curl combines the two.

"With a driver, you do everything the same, except let the club practically fly out of your hands. It's amazing. Now the target isn't a barrier to your ability to swing the way you'd like!"

I was awed. "So I don't have to worry about the real target down the fairway as I swing? Wow!" I exclaimed. "Does it really work?"

"You can try it and see."

"Are there any problems associated with this action?"

"Golfers can always get off track when trying anything. The only two problems I have found is that the golfer often begins to pressure the grip too much and gets tight working with their hands and wrists. The other tendency is for golfers to begin curling on the way back, unconsciously. Of course that would make it impossible to curl on the way down and at the same time strike the ball squarely, so I remind them that it's an opening and closing club face action that creates the balance. Other than that, it works incredibly well."

I couldn't resist. I picked up a club and began to swing, going through the sequence step by step. Swing down, curl, and let go—release! I was getting it with just a short pitch and executing it in pieces. I couldn't believe my control. Then Burlington showed me how to do an exercise without a club in hand. "Open your fingers, Geoff, and follow me."

He set up with his left fingers a little forward and down, then swung his left hand and arm back and said, "Sky." Then he swung downward and said, "Thigh." He used his fingertips as pointers and his fingers and wrist flexed forward as he whispered, "Fly."

"Sky, thigh, fly," Burlington repeated, "That's it. Do it a thousand times and you won't believe the control you'll gain. I know this is an exaggeration, but it's a great way to feel the hand and wrist action throughout the swing."

I followed his example a couple of times, then asked, "But what about the differences you just mentioned, like for various clubs or angles of attack?"

Top left: Begin with fingers pointing down and forward at address. Top right: During the backswing, fingertips are toward the sky. Bottom left: Fingertips are toward the right thigh during curling. Bottom right: Fingertips forward in the fly zone.

GB

"You may need to adjust the ball position for angle, but all you need to know is at what portion of the let-go arc you want to impact the ball." I must have looked confused. "Here's the arc of the let-go." Burlington let the club swing freely back and forth in two fingers. The club swung down and forward and then up and forward. "Now you must determine at what point of the arc you'd like the club to make contact. For an iron on the ground, I'd guess a little bit on the downward side of the arc. And with a driver when the ball is on a tee, you want it level or a little bit on the upward side," he explained. "However, you still curl and let go—just adjust at what point you want to make contact relative to the let-go arc."

I started to do as Burlington said, even though it seemed weird and contrary. But it began to work and I was pleasantly surprised at the results.

"Release is a very misunderstood idea in the golf swing," Burlington commented. "Obviously in the timing fundamental of my program, it varies."

"Tell me more about how you teach it. You said there were three variations of the release of energy from the handle to the head and into the ball."

"I've already talked about the centrifugal force release in the driver and longer clubs. If the student is advanced enough, I'll teach the curling release. Sometimes with the centrifugal force, we add in a little 'double-secret probation rotation' with the lead hand and forearm. We'll skip explaining that for now, Geoff. It really requires a little more awareness, so you have to be judicious about whom you teach it to. Once a student is very good at pacing, and the path of his or her swing is sound, it's the last progression in my awareness program.

"So the swings are definitely different when it comes to timing and release. The general tempo and shape are similar, but the release is different, especially in terms of angle of attack in the timing. The picture most golfers have of the swing path is the same back and through. But actually, there are definite arc and angle changes. They don't have this vision. Therefore, it's difficult for them to deliver with this timed energy that I just showed you."

19
ARCS AND SWING LENGTH

"Could you show me the arcs you've been talking about?" Joe sketched them out for me. I reacted to his drawings with puzzlement.

He noticed my expression and nodded, saying, "Yes, this illustration may look different because in the past, the arc was over-simplified to be identical for the downswing and the backswing. Remember those big PVC circles that were so popular few years back? They gave the wrong picture."

"Is that why some golfers are better with the irons and others better with the woods?" I asked.

"That's exactly what I am talking about. All psychological aspects aside, often players with more hand and arm strength are generally better with the iron shots, and weaker-handed players are more centrifugally oriented and play tee shots better."

"What about swing length? I so often hear that too long a swing is where you lose control."

"Length is a very misunderstood aspect of the swing. It's not a fundamental, you know."

"What about extension through the ball? I hear all the time you must extend."

"Another fallacy," he said with disdain.

"How so?"

"The expansion of the swing arc through the impact zone, or extension as you say, is an effect of centrifugal force. If you attempt to manufacture it, you'll likely slow the club down and wreck the path too. It must be a natural consequence of letting go, the 'fly' aspect of the timing fundamental." His statement surprised me, but he continued without a blink. "Back to swing length. It's a very personal thing. Once you've checked out that the hand control over the grip and the swing arc are fundamentally sound, the range of motion really depends on the unique attributes of the golfer's physique and their internal rhythms. In most cases, if you start fooling around with a golfer's swing length without first checking the hands on the grip and the arc, you're on the wrong track and you'll likely destroy the golfer's natural rhythm and timing, which would not be a good thing, would it? The length is arbitrary, not fundamental."

The different arcs from the backswing to the downswing.

FT

He changed gears. "But first let me see you hit a few more wedges, working on the middle-of-the-road exercise for distance, and then we can combine what you need to say to yourself—your personal mind talk—and what you need to ask of yourself in terms of the impact action."

We practiced for about forty-five minutes and I was really beginning to get the feeling of my wedge shots. Making swings, imagining them flying too far, then too short, and then just right, I was surprised how accurate I was getting. My feel was definitely improving. I tried the curl at the same time and began to get some real control over direction and angle, too. As Joe had told me, I just needed a strategy that gave me fundamental awakening to my feel. How much time I had wasted, obsessing about the golf swing and the mechanics, rather than just feeling it!

Our lesson was over for the day. Burlington had to chip some of the dead branches and a huge pile of palm fronds he had picked up after the most recent storm. He told me he didn't need any help and left me there so I could continue to practice. Again I tried to pay him, but he waved me off, telling me in no uncertain terms that the time and experience he was sharing with me was not for money. He seemed uncomfortable with money, so I decided I would get him a special parting gift instead.

I really felt confident. I had never been able to figure out why I couldn't combine what I wanted in my swing with my driver. It made so much sense now. I could believe the club was going to square now that I had adjusted the delivery speed of my hands swinging forward through the impact. In the back of my mind I wondered if I would be able to curl a driver release too. When I used to think 'accelerate,' all I had moving fast was the handle. It had created so much resistance in my hands and wrists at impact and it always felt heavy and forceful.

Now I had a way to be energized and effortless. This was an absolute golf epiphany for me. I realized that I never really understood the physics of an effortlessly powerful swing. Burlington had three adjustable releases of the energy, and all centered on the action of his lead hand, wrist, and forearm. If I was going to be somewhere in my swing mentally, that was the place to be. What a luxury it was, having one place to put my mind!

I practiced for about an hour longer without tiring. Very pleased with myself, I felt I could now understand and teach this centrifugal release to my students. But the curl might be another story. I could wait on that for now; it was certainly something to look forward to.

My confidence in teaching was growing. More than that, my confidence in myself was growing. My image of myself was transforming too. I was beginning to see myself as strong and my swing formidable. I loved the track I was on. I knew I could continue and help myself, just as Joe Burlington had said. I was ready to go forward and see where this new road took me. I hoped somehow it would even take me back to Claire.

I drove back to the B&B. It had been a momentous day and very encouraging. My doubts about Joe's style had evaporated. There was concrete reasoning and a history to his method. The fact that he had helped me with my driver was a miracle to me. I'd taken countless lessons on it with no success. I was thrilled that it had finally happened.

I needed to call Claire, but again I had to be content with the machine. If she could only see what was happening to me now! How I looked at things was really changing. I knew that if we got back together, I surely would be a better partner. I was ready for it, for her. Just one more opportunity, that's all I needed. We had been like Harry and Sally, two good people with lousy timing. I felt like now we could get on the same page at the same time. Really, I'd just needed to be able to see myself as I truly was; surely she could understand that. She'd told me the same thing, but somehow I'd needed to learn it for myself.

This evening's message was two short words of optimism: "It's happening!" I was hoping that would pique her curiosity.

PART TWO

20

LARRY FINDS HIS PATH AND
WALT FEELS THE ENERGY

When I arrived at the golf center the next morning, we set up again behind the barn. "Today is going to be different," Joe told me. "It's important for you to see how the method works with a variety of students, from beginner to advanced. I've scheduled the next two days with clients."

I'd been waiting for this! Observing a full day of teaching would be great. I wondered how Joe's approach for each student would differ from my lessons. I was grateful to be just an observer again. Out of the spotlight, I could get a better perspective.

Larry's smile arrived several seconds before the rest of him. He was tall, about six foot two. He looked fit and had a full head of curly blond hair. He also had enormous feet. I couldn't help but think how difficult it must have been for him to find the very expensive and obviously brand new golf shoes he was sporting at this, his first session with Joe. He set up his clubs on the bag stand and we all shook hands and introduced ourselves. "You found the place OK?"

"Yes," Larry replied, "it was very easy, although at first I thought I was going wrong. But I followed your directions and here I am." I recalled exactly the second-guessing Larry was talking about and smiled inwardly.

"Good, I love a student who can follow directions," Joe said with a wink. Then he got right down to business. "So, do you play much?"

"Yes," Larry said, "I love to play the game. But I think I could be a lot better. I can play to a twelve handicap on a course with a 128 slope rating and I've only been playing for three years."

Joe's face puzzled. Maybe he didn't know the new way of rating courses by slope, but suffice it to say, a 128 slope was a challenging course. "Well, do you have a story for me?" he prompted. It was now Larry's turn to look puzzled. "I mean, could you give me a brief history of your golf game?"

Larry repeated himself. "Oh yes, sure. I've been playing for just three years and, as I said, I carry a twelve handicap."

"Very impressive." Joe nodded in approval and waited for Larry to continue.

"I really enjoy playing, but I've run into problems with my path. When I get really bad, I take a lesson and it seems to straighten me out for the short run. But after a while, the same problems seem to crop up again."

"Have you come to any conclusions about your lessons or your corrections?"

"Well, yes, I have an analogy. I feel like it's putting a piece of duct tape on a leak. Eventually, it begins to leak again, since it really wasn't fixed properly."

"Oh, I like that," Joe told him. "So you're looking for a fix for the leaks in your game and you're willing to refit the plumbing, so to speak?"

"Yes. Why else would I have come?"

"Oh, you'd be surprised. I once read a story from eastern philosophy. To a distressed person who came to him for help, a Master said, 'Do you really want a cure?' And the patient said, 'If I did not, would I bother to come to you?' 'Oh, yes,' the Master sighed. 'Many people do.' 'What for?' asked the puzzled visitor. 'Not for a cure. That's too painful,' said the Master. 'For relief. But,' the Master explained, 'people who want a cure without any pain are like those who favor progress without change.'[8]

"You can substitute the word *process* for pain in the story. A lot of the time," Joe explained, "we're unwilling to persevere through what's necessary to sustain a positive change. It takes time to process a change, to refit the plumbing the right way. Learning this program is a process," he emphasized. "It is not an event, a quick fix." Larry looked at me, trying to read my reaction. I ignored him, trying to appear nonchalant, if not invisible.

"OK," Joe said, relieving Larry's awkwardness. "Why don't you hit a few so I can see your swing."

Larry lined up a few balls and sent them off the tee.

"Now see what it feels like to swing as though the ball was going to fly to the right."

"Over there?" Larry asked, pointed some thirty yards right of the intended target.

"Yes," Joe nodded. He then stepped back toward me and whispered, "Now watch his swing path change."

"Why would I want to do that?" Larry interrupted.

"Just trust me," said Joe.

"OK," Larry hesitantly agreed. He swung what he thought was to the right, but the ball flew right at the target. Larry looked back at us and grinned. Then, a bit perplexed, he asked, "How did that happen?"

"Just keep feeling like you're going to hit the ball to the right, and do it until it flies way right," Joe answered. "You want the swing path of the club to feel like it's going to the right of the target line before contact and you want to get the path consistently from the inside during the delivery into the ball."

"Why are we doing this?" Larry asked.

"Well," Joe said patiently, obviously unfazed that Larry couldn't just trust him, "We are attempting to develop a constant on the club's approach to the ball relative to the target. If the club can come from the same angle or path, then your mind-body system can begin to settle in on a particular delivery of the face angle for square, if that's your goal. This is just one strategy. The path constant then becomes part of the timing for golf shots. On the other hand, if the path is a variable, then the mind-body system gives a variety of signals for what to do differently with the club face to get to the target. In other words, Larry, there is a need for a recovery based on the path variable. So if you get a path constant, it's likely that you'll develop a timing constant for impact."

Larry attempted to process this information. "But why don't I just try to hit the ball toward the target?"

"Simply because your baseline path—the path you arrived with—is not what you think it is. You came here trying to hit the ball toward the target with a path that you thought was directed toward the target, but most of the time the club was traveling unknowingly to the left of the target well before impact, right?"

Larry nodded in agreement. Burlington demonstrated to Larry the difference between his perceptions and his reality. His first shot nailed

Larry's desired swing path. Burlington then showed him what the reality was. There was a disparity of about thirty degrees. "Oh. I get it," Larry said with assurance. "What I thought I was doing was not what I was doing at all."

"That's right. I just want you to realize where you want to go, so you can be in reality—and that reality is what will give you your best performance. To be perfectly honest, Larry, we could have chosen another strategy, but I think this one is best for you at this moment." Joe offered Larry's club back to him, but Larry's face still registered doubt. Burlington continued, "I don't want to confuse you so I'll explain as succinctly as I can. You have had a major path imbalance and the habits you've formed don't serve you, so we need to go through this process. I have no doubt that you will hit shots that will be beyond your wildest dreams, if you stick with it. Trust me, you will see." He coaxed the man to take some shots, again holding the club out to him.

Larry took the club and got started. The balls began to fly to the right. Then, all the way to the right. Larry was nervous.

"Just keep swinging, Larry," Joe encouraged him.

"B-but...it'll be OK, right?" Larry stammered.

"Trust me, Lare," Burlington told him. Then he whispered to me that Larry was almost ready to add in the timing component. I was taking it all in, fascinated, only regretting that this wasn't being videotaped.

"OK, Larry, now this time, see if you can notice when the club head flies by the handle."

"What do you mean?" Larry didn't appear to be nearly as fascinated as I was.

Joe took the club from him and began from his finish. "Notice the relationship between the club head and the handle when they reverse relative to the target. When do they convert from forward to backward, relative to the target?" He handed Larry back the club and stood back while Larry started the experiment. The man swung once. "Can you feel it?" Joe asked.

"Yes, I can."

"Now notice when they convert."

"OK."

"Keep swinging and noticing, Larry."

"I think I have it," Larry mumbled tentatively minutes later, more to himself than to Burlington. He took a few more practice shots.

"Good, OK. Now, see if it changes the same way back as forward."

Larry almost closed his eyes on the last two swings. I could see he was in a totally different zone than when he'd arrived. "OK, yes, about the same place. Yes!"

"This is the beginning of sensing and knowing the timing ratio in your impact, Larry. Now let's make some more swings. I want you to notice the club and handle relationship to see if you can feel the face rotation as the handle and head convert."

"Yes, I feel it."

"Good. Where do you feel it?"

"In my hands."

"Great, now let's add golf balls. Walk right through them, no pauses between shots," Joe instructed.

Larry began to walk and the balls began to fly long and straight. His smile had returned and he told us excitedly, "I've never hit four irons like this before."

Burlington whispered to me, "Geoff, this is a bit oversimplified, but we need to go this way because of Larry's level of awareness. Down the road, I'm sure, you'll see another one of my strategies for club face and path control." I wondered what he meant, but returned to being an unobtrusive observer as I watched Larry continue the exercise.

Burlington turned to Larry. "Now here's the kicker, Larry. We have been here about twenty minutes and your golf swing is in good balance. So if you didn't already possess that ability or talent or whatever you want to call it, do you think I could have given it to you in twenty minutes?" He paused to let Larry consider this, but didn't let him respond. "Of course not. It was always in you, fellow, and you just needed a program to draw it out. I just showed you how to access it. You just needed to focus on what would serve you better. Now isn't that a confidence builder? So make a few more swings now and keep noticing."

Larry's smile dominated his face. He continued and hit most of his shots well. When his path returned to its old direction, his awareness kicked in and he made the adjustment readily. Larry was clearly enjoying his success.

I was so impressed with Burlington. He'd made it especially clear what the basis for Larry's newfound awareness and subsequent success was— Larry's own talent. Burlington had only helped him to notice it.

While Larry was practicing, Joe explained to me that for Larry to leave here on solid ground, he'd need to use the exercises he'd learned. But he'd also need to ask good questions that would allow his talent to emerge. I could see now how an ego-driven instructor could sabotage a student. I realized what Joe meant about not taking credit for the success or failure of his students. He said that he only gave them a nudge in the right direction.

Larry's satisfaction seemed to be leveling. "This is fine for off the tee, but what about off the ground?"

"That requires more awareness of timing." Joe gave me a look as if to say 'there's the other strategy,' but answered Larry directly. "Just let yourself digest what we've done so far today. No overload. You go ahead and practice just as we have done here. That's really enough to keep you busy. Next time I'll go deeper into the release to address control over the angle off the ground." Joe seemed to have a feel for what a student could handle at one time. We all want more, I thought, and most of the time it probably isn't good for us. The dosage of a cure is critical.

So Larry shook hands and said goodbye. I thanked Joe and told him I'd be back in time for his next lesson, then made my way to the campus cafeteria across the street from the golf center. The time had flown and I was hungry for lunch. The cafeteria was full of college kids, all doing their own important thing. I picked out a chicken salad sandwich, found a seat and slowly ate my lunch. I tried to review what I had witnessed in Larry's lesson, how Joe had asked the questions. I needed to remember things as they were said, exactly.

So many things Joe had said and done were beginning to make sense to me. Yet I was unsure of my ability to impart what seemed to be such a passive method to my own students. I wasn't confident in my ability to ask the right questions at the right time. I needed to work on this a lot; that much I knew. What became clear to me was that Burlington believed in a student-teacher relationship that didn't try to fit square pegs into round holes, but rather seemed to find the right hole for each individual student. He really didn't say very much, but what he did say was so simple and made so much sense. I wondered why the answers seem so out of reach when we try to find them ourselves.

I had a lot to learn in not much time. I'd been through so many teachers and different theories that had fallen short over the years, but I felt I was inching closer to the right path, though I was still a little skeptical about which fork to take. After all, I had been gung-ho before. And I had been let down before. It took a little time for the honeymoon to end and for me to see the wrinkles in a new approach. Despite the fact that I had just seen amazing success, I decided to check my excitement so I wouldn't be disappointed yet again.

I did realize, as I sat surrounded by students, that my teaching had been all about me. I noticed that Joe Burlington never spoke about himself during a lesson. In contrast, I had spent lesson time on self-promotion; convincing students that I was the right teacher for them—and something of a golf wizard—was my primary goal. As perceptive as he was, Burlington probably knew where I was coming from, and knew that *he* was exactly where *I* wanted to be, but he was too polite to point this out.

Today with Larry, Burlington proved that the best teacher was actually within oneself. An instructor's job was to draw that master teacher out of every student and to make them aware of the gifts they possessed. A teacher really can't give them anything except a push in the right direction, which was all the job should be—that's what I'd gotten from watching Joe with Larry. Coaching is really just guiding students, getting them to wake up and do the work themselves so that, in the end, they became confident and enjoyed playing. Students need to be coached about what is deep within to recover qualities that have been misplaced, drowned or buried by the very instruction that was supposed to bring those qualities to the surface.

Over the years, I'd had some experience with this type of teaching, usually when I taught children. I'd always taught them differently from adults. Less instructing, more standing back and observing, looking for strengths to focus on. As Joe did, I just guided them, pointing out their abilities and offering very little remediation. It felt right with kids and it had worked. They learned so naturally, I didn't need to say much.

I don't know why it never occurred to me to try it with adults; I guess I just didn't think they would accept this approach. Adults wanted meat, I'd assumed. They needed to hear their name-brand teacher tell them things— not to ask what it feels like and then expect them to figure it out for themselves. Burlington had turned the dynamics of an adult lesson upside down for me, inverting the student-teacher relationship. Children didn't care about my credentials or want to copy my style. They were in it for the fun. It was a great joy for me to teach children. The realization of how I taught children and adults differently was enlightening. I had a lot to think about.

I awakened from my mesmerized state; I had been in the cafeteria for over an hour. I cleared my table and raced back to Joe's teaching area. He hadn't arrived yet so I took a seat and waited.

Joe soon came around the corner of the maintenance building. We fell into talking about students and I told him I would love to see him give a lesson to the type of student who always seems to get in their own way, the kind who keeps recycling the same problems and can't get out of the web. I asked Burlington, "What happens when you teach a person the awareness method yet they still can't seem to sustain an improved swing?"

"You mean they don't get it?"

"That's right," I said.

Just then, an older man ambled around the corner. "Well, you're in luck, Geoff. Here's a perfect example of what you're talking about. I don't think Walt would mind if you watch his lesson." Joe introduced me as a golf pro from up north and asked Walt's permission for me to observe his lesson. Walt was OK with it and set his clubs down on the turf so he could stretch his muscles before the lesson.

I was high with anticipation, and curious about how Joe would proceed. Walt told us that he'd been up late watching the basketball game and hadn't got much sleep. He was sniffling as well and said his sinuses were bothering him. Joe just listened. Then Walt pulled out a piece of paper. "I have a few questions before we begin, Joe. Joe nodded for Walt to proceed.

"First, I don't know if I should take the club back straight, or inside, like this." Walt demonstrated with his wedge. Joe just nodded. "Well, which is it?" Walt asked.

"That's personal, Walt."

"I knew you were going to say that. How can it be personal?"

"Well, it really doesn't matter because whatever will satisfy what you want to do on the downswing creates the backswing, and there are a lot of different routes to get there."

"You mean it really doesn't matter?"

"That's right."

"OK, but what about my weight shift?"

Joe asked Walt to come nearer and said, "Seems fine to me."

"I mean, when I swing." Walt said, seeming flustered.

"I know, Walt. I was joking."

"Last question," Walt said. "Shouldn't the club square itself without any manipulation from my hands?"

"Good question. It depends."

"You never have a definite answer, do you, Joe Burlington?" Walt teased back.

"I think so, but your questions seem to be more personal than fundamental."

"Well, what *is* fundamental?"

I was wondering the same thing myself when Joe answered, "Fundamental is anything to do with the club at impact. Everything else deals with margins. It's like statistics. There are no definite answers when it comes to style. It's quantum—the uncertainty principle. It depends on how you look at it." Now I was getting his point about the physics. "That's why there are so many different swings. All your questions deal with dynamic patterns of energy and nothing in this realm is set in stone. These patterns form according to the unique attributes of the wielder. Each swing is unique until the point of no return—that is, the impact zone—but I agree there are margins that increase your possibility of achieving a more consistent fundamental impact. Margins of speed, shape and timing..."

"Flow, path, and timing. I know, Joe."

"I would be glad to help you find a strategy to get what you want. It only takes a few minutes. I'll show you a couple of exercises to make it very simple." Good—I was finally going to see something. But Joe just let Walt go.

Walt took out a club and began to swing, and then he began to hit some shots. He was a little stiff to begin with, as if he were a robot with differing angles of swing. He definitely manipulated the club as he tried to swing it. It was the opposite of smooth. Obviously, in his mind, he had a lot to do in one swing.

Joe gave Walt some time to warm up, but Walt was getting less effective as he practiced. Balls were flying in every direction and I was wondering when Joe would intervene. I was sure I would have done something by now.

Just then, Joe asked Walt for his club. Joe began to swing from his finish. His swing was super fluid. It had a natural orbit and there seemed to be no effort in it. His whole body seemed to be in harmony and the orbit formed a perfect path for his club head. Joe and the club looked like partners who had danced together for a long, long time.

Then his swing began to pick up speed. Burlington seemed so relaxed as the club squared beautifully to his target through the impact zone. This went on until the last swing, when he let the club lower to the ball's level and *wham*! It flew straight, high, and long,

Walt stood there and smiled. "I'll never be able to do that."

"Yes you will, Walt. One day soon, in your own way, you will." Joe gave the club back to Walt and asked him to mimic what he had just seen as best he could.

Walt set up and swung the club forward from in front. His body complied, but his head was shaking no. He looked uncomfortable and remarked that he had no control over that much motion. Joe reassured him, "Just trust me."

Walt might have trusted Joe, but he didn't trust the exercise. "I have to tell you, Joe, this feels pretty awkward to me. There's just too much movement for me to control." He swung anyway.

Joe ignored the statement. "Oh, that's good, Walt." Walt shook his head a few more times in disagreement as he continued to swing.

As far as I could see, Walt's swing shape, coming from the finish and back, created the most beautiful blend of actions, and his tight manipulation of his swing was dissolving. He looked coordinated and fluid. Then Joe said, "The most important thing is to know where you want to go and use the momentum and centrifugal force of the swinging club to get you there. All you need to do is cooperate with these forces. This exercise will help you develop a repeating swing path—with no concern for the beginning of your backswing."

Walt stopped swinging and whined, "But I can't do that with a ball there."

"Of course you can. I heard that Jack Nicklaus practices with this very exercise. He's a master of flow and sequence. I believe it would be a great benefit to you too." Joe set him up to do the exercise again, this time without a ball. Walt began to swing and Joe coached him to allow his body to be free to support wherever the club wanted to go. "Just go with it," he urged him.

Walt was getting the hang of it. Burlington continued to coach. "That's right, Walt, just let it swing and allow your body to do whatever it wants to support the speed and direction of the swing. Then allow the swing to finish the forward motion, like so." Joe showed him the relationship between the grip end of the club and the target. Walt kept swinging and redirecting his finish. Joe tried a new approach. "We'll call this home base, Walt. Always go to home."

"OK." Walt was beginning to trust in his motion and swinging the club naturally. The form of his swing seemed to shape automatically, without positioning him in the step-by-step method I was so accustomed to. Walt's body just seemed to move in perfect harmony with the club now. It was a beautiful orbit and path. "Is that a good backswing?" Joe didn't answer the question. He just asked Walt what it felt like. "It feels good to me."

"Then it is." And it was. Walt's body was cooperating with the swinging force.

"What a great lesson!" I exclaimed quietly.

"The lesson is just beginning, Geoff. We need to get Walt in tune with the feeling now. Walt, what picture does your swing remind you of right now? What does the feeling tell you?"

"It feels like a circle."

"Good. Notice how the circle relates to the ground and the target?"

"Yes, I see what you're talking about."

"The circle is at an angle; good. Can you feel the path the club takes as it passes over the impact zone?"

"Yes, it feels like a pathway moving around toward me, then up into the air again."

"Good, now notice how your whole body responds to knowing where you want to go with the club." Burlington had placed two small pieces of his Pathfinder foam on the ground that formed a corridor for the club to pass through on line with the target. Walt was still swinging. "See if you can get the club to brush the grass as it passes through the corridor going forward." Walt performed it with ease. "Now Walt, notice all the feeling in your body. Pay particular attention to how your hands and arms feel." Joe slipped a ball inside the corridor on the ground, but Walt didn't seem to notice. On his next downswing, *wham!*—the ball flew into the air and straight toward the target. "OK, now stop."

Walt was out of breath. I guessed he was in his late seventies, but I was impressed with his stamina. "Wow, that felt like I wasn't even swinging," Walt exclaimed. "The ball felt weightless."

"Walt, that to me is swinging. I think what you meant to say is you didn't feel any resistance as you swung."

"That's it—no resistance! It felt effortless," Walt confirmed as joy lit up his face.

"I had one more question for you. Every time I take a lesson with you, I feel like I'm hitting the shot with my right hand. It feels great, but I know you always talk about the lead hand, so I'm a little confused."

"That's a good question. Many of my students have asked about this. Let me explain." Burlington turned to me, smiled, and said, "You knew we'd revisit centrifugal force, didn't you?" To Walt he said, "The feeling of the right hand releasing is only the centrifugal force of the club head in disguise. I will leave it at that." I was fascinated by his explanation. Essentially he had told us the right hand had nothing to do with the release. I would have liked a more detailed answer, but Burlington stopped short.

Walt moved on. "I've never been able to figure out why so many golfers, myself included, feel a need to be so forceful with the swing—to rip the cover off the ball with so much effort, even though it's counterproductive most of the time. You know, making the perfect rhythmic practice swing and then when the ball is there, swinging recklessly and completely different from the practice. What causes that?"

"Well, it's fairly obvious something is going on inside, right?" Joe pointed to his head to confirm. "But let's begin with those golfers who swing recklessly both in practice and on actual swings with the ball. They just don't understand that timing is power. The golf club is an instrument that needs to be handled with a deft touch and coordination. You see, gentlemen," Burlington addressed us both, "those golfers equate might with power and don't realize precision is an integral part of power. They try to muscle the ball with the force of their weight and the strength of the massive parts of their body. If I were you, I'd do a lot of hand and wrist exercises with the club and practice your swing exercises, with the bulk of your weight and body quiet during the swing. You can still hit it very far and toward your target. You know, feet together shots, etcetera."

"OK," Walt said, "I understand that, but what about the times my swing seems to change completely from one second to the next, from the practice swing to the actual."

"I'm getting to that." I had a couple of theories about this, too. Of course I, like a lot of my students, had experienced overworking the swing to get more energy at impact, only to find that it rarely worked. I wanted to hear what Burlington had to say about this. He cleared his throat. "The main problem is that golfers are insecure about their swing's strength—the power of the club into the impact. They aren't necessarily weak, but their swings feel that way to them. Something deep down inside, on a subconscious level—their self-image—believes the impact is going to be weak. Many golfers also think they're not going to get the ball to the target through timing.

"Let's say it's a long par four into the wind, which is the classic situation when this occurs."

"Exactly," Walt agreed.

"Our mind-body reaction becomes forceful—you know, 'heave-ho.' Of course, we get the opposite result. The more forceful we become, the less speed we generate and so the ball flies weakly and inaccurately. This compounds the problem, because as hard as we try, the results confirm our belief in our swing's weakness."

"Looks like we're back to the belief system again, aren't we?"

"Yes. We have to begin believing, deep down, that power and speed are not functions of brute strength. We need to learn how to generate speed through the shape, synchronization, and timing of our swing and to really have faith in it. We need to feel powerful and energetic without being forceful. Again, you can begin with the mind talk and visualization and then support it with exercises of timing, which generate club head speed, rather than forcing it, which diminishes club head speed."

"So then, it's this insecurity that causes the change from smooth to out of balance and forceful?"

"Yep."

I offered up my two cents' worth. "That makes sense. How else could a swing change so dramatically in a second or two? On a conscious level, we know what we want and feel, but subconsciously something else is operating."

"I see, I see," mumbled Walt. "What else can I do to get rid of the insecurity?"

"You need to do the mind talk and feel what real power is, Walt. Practice into a gale and try the different timing exercises I've shown you. Don't allow the wind to influence your timing. Get those angles and speeds organized and, after a while, you'll see the potential. But you need to do the mind talk and concentrate fully on the timing. Most people need to make an effort to feel a slower swing to get the club head to accelerate."

"That doesn't make a whole lot of sense to me," said Walt. "I have never seen anyone teach club head acceleration by slowing down."

"What I mean is to get in balance and usually this means for students to get less forceful. You see, Walt, you need a little lesson in centrifugal force generation in your swing, too. And allow it to occur at the right time during your downswing. Most golfers don't understand centrifugal force. They only relate to their own force and centrifugal force is the opposite of them working near impact. In a sense, you need to accelerate to a slowdown to get optimum centrifugal force in the swing, which is the most reliable timing force in the golf swing. It's a function of the sequence and direction of the swing, and it occurs when your hands are below your waist in the downswing. That's as much of a hint as I'm going to give you today, Walt."

I interjected. "Is that why, when I made my best swings, everyone said I didn't even swing?"

"That's right. Most golfers describe an effortless swing as not swinging. I'm always amused at those remarks, as it's obvious they don't know what a real swing feels like when it's effortless. What they mean is that it's a swing without resistance and to me, that is effortless. Let me try something that may make a stronger impression for you."

Joe's friend George and another friend, Billy, were sitting a ways off. Joe went over and enlisted them to help him create a human model of C-force. Billy, the largest of the three, gave Joe his hand, as did George. It was obvious that Billy and George had done this before. Joe explained that Billy was the golfer and the grip, Joe was the shaft and George, the smallest, was the club head. Billy took a couple of steps and began to make a turn. Joe was pulled along behind him and George followed. The three of them looked like a train going around a bend, simulating the path of the downswing.

Then Billy pulled a little more and made a quick turn to the left; he was now going in the opposite direction. There seemed to be a rippling and whirling effect. Joe's arms were stretching. George, the caboose, was picking up speed as he swung wide. About halfway through the turn, Billy let go of Joe and then Joe let go of George. And off George went, flying away. They had just cracked the whip. It was a perfect human model of centrifugal force.

"Get it?" Burlington asked.

"Yes," I said, "I get it." Just like he'd said, Billy had slowed down and gone in the other direction, exactly like the grip end after impact. Joe was the middle link and he let George (the club head) fly past both of them. Smiling, George remarked how fast he'd run without trying to run; he was accelerated by Joe and Billy's action. "It wasn't coming from me. What an awesome feeling!"

I looked at Walt and saw that the demonstration had hit home for him, too. Walt smiled with appreciation and said, "I finally understand the release. That's why when I really swing, I feel as though I didn't do anything. What I actually did was finally swing!" Billy and George went back to their bench in the shade.

Joe was pleased with Walt's epiphany. "OK, Walt, that's it for today. Keep practicing the front-end exercise and you'll really feel the power of the swinging club." I was impressed. Burlington had solidified his point with this last demonstration.

As Walt packed up, Joe said, "Listen, I see the UPS guy delivering a spreader I ordered. I need to go show him where to drop it off. Practice, if you wish. I'll be back in ten minutes." He started to walk away, but turned to me and winked. "Kind of neat, eh?"

21
JUDY: A NEW GOLFER GETS A GRIP

Burlington returned a little later with two bottles of spring water and a plastic bag filled with cold, cut-up vegetables. He offered me a bottle and held the bag out to me. I took a couple of carrots and savored the cool crunchiness. My senses were awakened by the euphoria of understanding. Walt had just left with a spring in his step, his confidence buoyed by his lesson. Soon after Walt's car had pulled away, a young woman walked toward to us from the parking lot.

"OK, Geoff. I thought that since you haven't seen me work with a raw beginner, it might be useful for you to observe a lesson with someone who has never swung a club or taken a lesson before. Earlier this month, we had a raffle and only beginners could participate. The winner got a lesson with me. Some grand prize, eh?" He joked. "Anyway, this young lady, Judy, won the draw."

As the winner approached, I thought that Joe's method would be really difficult for a beginner, since there were no real concrete rules a person could sink their teeth into. Judy was in her mid-twenties and obviously athletic. She arrived with a look of optimism; she was bubbly, pleasant, and wholesome. She didn't have golf clubs, but knowing she was a beginner, Burlington had brought a few out. We introduced ourselves and the lesson began.

Joe started by asking Judy what she would like to happen in the time they spent together. Did she have any goals? Had she ever thought about the golf swing? She sheepishly told us, "I've only made a few swings before at a driving range. I quickly concluded that my boyfriend couldn't help me. That's when I decided to enter your raffle. I thought maybe I would get lucky, and here I am!" She went on to explain that she had become interested in golf watching it on television with her boyfriend, who was an avid golfer and played to a scratch handicap. "On TV it looks so easy and fun, yet my friends tell me it's very hard to play. I'd like to see if I can do it."

"OK, Judy, then let's begin," Burlington matched her enthusiasm with renewed energy. "Take hold of the club any way that seems natural to you." Judy took the club he offered and placed her hands with the club against her wrist and across her palm. This is going to be difficult, I thought. Judy had the club positioned diagonally across her palm and up toward her wrist. The pressure she applied looked like a white-knuckled death grip. Her grip position would make for a rigid swing with little or no wrist or hand action. This would be interesting to watch.

"OK," Joe said, "now go ahead and make a swing." Judy began to almost carry the club back and up into the air. Then her move took on a curve, sideways, with the club face terribly closed. She went back and forth like this a few times. She stopped and asked Joe, "Should I try to hit one?" She placed a ball on a tee and got ready to swing. Again the swing took on a sort of slow carry as though the club weighed five pounds, and she pushed the club downward and whiffed it. She looked up at Joe and he said, "Very good; let's begin."

I know I'd have said something like, 'we have a lot of work to do and it may take a while.' Burlington's response was the antithesis of that. He just asked her to take her right hand off the club and look at the grip in her left. Then he took hold of the club down the shaft and positioned the grip of the club in her left hand so her hold on the grip was down toward her finger channel, as he called it. He placed her thumb on top of the shaft, applying pressure to her thumb tip, thumb pad, and the heel of her left hand. The grip looked perpendicular to her fingers and the pressure points were now in order.

"There now," Burlington said, "you have leverage on the club. Can you feel it?"

She nodded and smiled at him. "That's what the position of the lead hand is for," he instructed, "control for the angle of swing and feel for the club face. Good! Now notice how the back of your left hand relates to the club face." He placed a tee in her glove between the Velcro strap and the leather backhand portion. It pointed basically at the target in the same direction as the club face.

He paused so she could see that. "OK. Now lift the club up and down with your left hand, letting your left wrist flex and allowing the weight of the club head to act on your wrist." Judy looked at him tentatively, so he demonstrated what he wanted her to do. "Now, Judy, with this newfound leverage in your left hand, you don't need so much pressure. In fact, the left hand position is for leverage and face control. Pressure is for generating speed. If you think about it, if there's a lot of pressure or tension placed on the grip, then what possibility is there to generate speed? I suggest much less pressure without letting go," he advised her. "Have you heard about timing?" Burlington asked.

"No," she said.

He gave her a reassuring smile and explained, "It's necessary to have it to swing with effortless power and consistency. Timing depends on flexibility and flow. We need to hold lighter." He included himself in her swing; now they were a team working together. What a great tactic! She seemed confident with his support.

Judy told him, "Before, I couldn't hold lightly; I had to hold on for dear life so I wouldn't lose the club out of my hand!"

"That's exactly right: When there's no leverage over the grip you would naturally pressure it heavily to feel secure," Joe confirmed. "Now let's get your right hand on the grip. Bring your right hand below the left and against the 'life line,' like this. Now close the fingertips around the shaft and allow the life line of your right hand to lie against your left thumb."

"So the club is really in the fingers of my right hand, but it feels like I have no control of the club with my right hand."

"Exactly. The club lies like this in your right fingers." He demonstrated the right-hand grip position. The club lay way down in his fingertips, straight across the ends of his fingers and far away from his palm. The life line down the center of his right palm was against his left thumb and his right thumb was lying over the other side of the shaft and it seemed to not even be touching the grip. His right thumb and first finger covered his left thumb on top of the shaft. His right palm was also facing his left palm, basically in the same direction as the club face.

He continued to show Judy. "Now cover your left thumb with your right thumb and first finger like a crab claw." He had the meat of his thumb together with the first finger and they did look like a crab claw. She followed his lead exactly. Her right hand was now pacified on the club, instead of dominant.

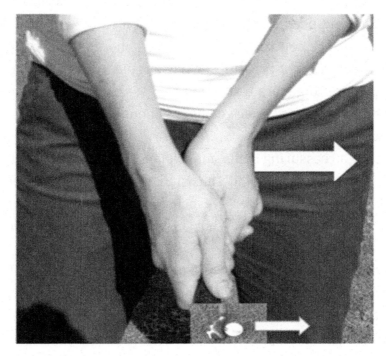

Neutral grip matching the direction of the clubface.

JW

"I have to say," Judy said, "it feels weird to me—my right hand can't really do much. But now it feels like I have control over the club with my left hand and I can still feel the weight of the head at the other end. I couldn't have light pressure and control without this position, could I?" She seemed surprised.

"Right" Burlington said. "If you lightened the pressure without a sound position of leverage over the club, it would be difficult to control and it would be swimming in your hand! You would get a lot of slippage. How does it feel now?"

"I'm feeling pretty confident that I can lighten the pressure and not lose control."

"Good. Let's begin swinging again," he said.

I had never heard the grip position detailed so thoroughly. Her hands looked perfect on the club now. It was often difficult for me to get my students to lighten the pressure over the grip of the club. Burlington was right on target when he said that when you have leverage over something, you have control without the need for pressure. It was pretty clear to me now. Even if I got my students to grip it well, I would move on to the bigger parts of the swing and let the grip fend for itself. Burlington was obviously not moving forward until her grip was optimized and I suspected that if she had changed it back, he would begin again. I knew how important the grip position was, yet I wasn't this much of a stickler about it.

"This time," Joe said, "let me show you how to start the swing from the finish." There was no effort in her motion this time. The starting place made it that easy. Gravity and momentum were put into play from the beginning with this exercise from the front end. Judy's attention naturally shifted from hitting the ball to swinging the club. This technique of starting from the finish seemed to be the perfect beginning for swing motion, perhaps because there really is no effort involved in beginning the motion from the finish. Gravity and momentum are at work rather than physical exertion through one's muscle.

With the new grip position and pressure and new starting place, the shape and flow of Judy's swing began to emerge like magic. Burlington turned to me, smiled, and said, "Pretty cool, eh Geoff?" Then he turned back to Judy. "Now let's try the grip again, this time with your eyes closed, and I'd like to place it for you." He took the club and lifted it into the air so her grip was low and the club head was high. The grip went right into her finger channel. "Now, can you feel the leverage you have on the club again?"

"Yes, I feel it better with my eyes closed." Now he held her club horizontal and supported it for her while she gripped it. Still with her eyes closed, he asked her to turn the face of the club toward the ground. "How do I do that?" she asked him.

"Make a guess," he replied. She turned her hand, and the face of the club went right toward the ground. "Now turn the face toward the sky," he instructed. This time, no question. She just did it. She still had her eyes closed, but she had felt and already pictured what the club face did when her hand moved in each direction. He took out a ball. "Keep your eyes closed. First, turn the face toward the sky." After she did this, Burlington began to bounce the ball off the club face. He asked her, "Which direction did the ball bounce?"

She said, "Up."

He lowered the club head to the ground. "Keep your eyes closed. Do you remember where the flag is?"

"Yes."

"Now turn the face toward the target," he instructed. She did. He bounced the ball again and she responded, "I felt it bounce toward the target."

"What tells you that?" he asked.

"My hand. I can feel it in my left hand."

"Good," he said. Burlington turned to me. "You see, Geoff, the first step is to familiarize your student with the feel of the club. Get them to feel that the face of the club and the club head itself is just an extension of their hands. Judy can now feel where the ball may fly, based on the feeling in her hands."

This all took only a few minutes, and yet I knew Judy was more in touch with the club than even my students who had taken many lessons. "Let's take a break, Judy." When she opened her eyes, she was smiling. She had just had her first success experience. Joe found his drink and took a long swallow. Judy went over to his table and grabbed a water, too. They rested for a few minutes.

"Now, Judy, do you think you can find your new grip again?"

"I think so," she said.

"OK, swing the club as though you were going to let it strike a ball toward that target." He pointed in the direction of a flag about fifteen yards out. Judy took hold of the club again, placed it behind the ball, this time with her new levered grip. She made a swing that again did not remotely resemble a good swing as I knew it. I wondered what Burlington would do.

Judy had begun her swing from the ground again and that starting place returned her to the swing pattern she had arrived with. The club went up into the air immediately and she seemed to be carrying it again instead of letting it swing. Then, as she lifted the club back and up, it began to circle very low around behind her. The face was very shut. As she moved it forward, it whirled around the ball way to the left and she almost lost her balance. Judy had completely missed the ball. Her smile and look of optimism vanished.

However, Burlington just smiled and said, "That's OK, Judy. Are you ready to begin again?"

"I guess," she said softly. "But how could that have been OK?" she asked, at the same moment I'd thought it.

"Well," Burlington said, "it's good because number one, we don't care about the results. During this lesson, I'm responsible for the outcome. You're responsible only for sensing and feeling. Anyway, I have seen where you are and, with your cooperation, I believe I can coach you to get where you need to be—in just a few minutes—if you just trust me." Looking much less burdened, Judy answered, "I like the sound of that. I'm all yours."

I had to see this happen—and in 'just a few minutes.' Yeah, right! I did notice one thing right away, though: In the lessons I had observed so far, Burlington had put people at ease. He exuded the feeling that he was in complete control and wherever their feel would take them, it was OK with him. Nothing to be concerned about! It was as if he were on the journey with them, an experienced guide helping them get where they wanted to go. Cooperate with him and he'd take you there. Nothing fazed him, either—not whiffing or shanking; none of the initial clumsiness a new golfer might exhibit seemed to give him pause. It was simply a matter of feeling the physics and, since he knew the physics inside and out, everyone could relax. Problems were not problems, just awareness challenges with Burlington. I couldn't wait to see more of his strategy with this first-time player. If Judy's awareness could make that quantum leap in only a few minutes, then I'd be a total believer too.

"OK, let's begin again," he said. He brought out a club that had the flex of a fishing rod. He called it a whippy. "Here, let's use this club." Judy looked at him with a baffled expression. Everything going through her mind at each moment was inscribed on her face just as soon as she felt it.

"What's this?" she asked. "It was hard enough with the other one."

Again, Burlington said, "Just trust me, Judy. Hold the club in the air in front of your face with your new grip. Notice the pressure with which you're holding it. Between one and ten, attempt to be about a five. Flex and unflex your wrists so the club head moves up and down. Can you feel it?" When she nodded, he said, "Now be a one. Got it?"

"Yes," she responded. "The club is almost loose in my hand."

"Good. Now be a ten. Can you feel it?"

"Yes, that's the pressure I used in my first swing."

"OK. Now when you're a ten, what part of the club do you feel?"

"Only the grip."

"Not any weight at the head end?" he queried.

"No."

"Now slowly reduce the pressure. What are you feeling now?"

"The weight at the other end."

"Good. Now find a pressure where you can still feel the weight at the other end."

She experimented. "It seems comfortable at about a five."

"Good. Let me help you. We're going to begin this swing with the club in the air over here again." It was similar to Walt's exercise, from the finish; Joe called it point B. Burlington positioned the club over Judy's left shoulder with the grip end pointing toward the target. "Now," he said, "begin swinging by letting the club pick up speed. As it swings back, down, and around through the air, allow your whole body to respond to the swinging club. Now here behind you is point A." Burlington pointed to a lamppost behind us at the end of the practice area. "You can watch the club as you swing, so you know that you're swinging in this pattern. Simply swing the club around you in a circular pattern from point B to point A."

Judy made a few swings this time, very vertical like a Ferris wheel. Joe told her it was good. He instructed her to continue swinging while he stepped away to set up his Pathfinder so the pattern of path could be improved. He set up his virtual wall and the curved path through the delivery zone, just as he had with Walt; no ball yet. He instructed Judy to swing from point B to the far side of the virtual wall; this gave her a flatter swing around on the way back to point A, and then through the center of the corridor of the two pieces of foam while brushing the grass on her way back to point B.

"You mean I don't have to concentrate on the ball?" Interesting question, considering there was no ball there yet. I guess she imagined one.

"Just the club."

"OK. It seems like a loop."

"Yes, it is. A good loop." Judy was puzzled but complied, and her eyes followed the club from B down and around the foam to point A and then back downward and through the corridor on her way back to B. It was amazing to watch her body learn as she concentrated on swinging her club through the corridor to the two endpoints. Like magic, her swing was morphing into a classic shape.

"Let all your muscles and joints give way to the swinging club, as though they were not strong enough to support it." Judy's arms were no longer rigid and her wrist action began to occur naturally. The club face was rotating too. The fundamental dynamics were coming alive right before my eyes. "Allow your whole body to be free to support the swinging club," Joe urged. Judy's feet and legs began to move in harmony with her arms swinging, and her torso began to pivot naturally as the club head's path took on a beautiful curve.

I noticed all this action, while Judy was only aware of the club. It was all happening just as Joe said it would—as a function of the club being OK. Judy's swing was smooth and natural. "She has a swing!" I exclaimed.

He gently, quietly corrected me. "She always had a swing. If she didn't, do you think we could have accomplished this in five minutes?"

Next Joe stopped Judy and asked, "Hey Jude, how does that feel?"

Judy was vibrant and said resoundingly, "Like a golf swing!"

"OK, take a break," he said. She was exuberant and clearly proud, but winded.

"That's real aerobics, isn't it?"

"Yes—and they say golf isn't exercise!"

I was almost a believer, but I wanted to see her swing with a ball in place.

"Let's begin again, Judy; you ready? As before, start your swing from in front, pointing at point A. On the way back, let the club swing on the far side of the foam and on the way through, brush the grass between the foam without touching the foam. Can you feel the flex, feel the pressure against your left thumb when your wrists flex near point A?" he quizzed her as the club changed directions. "Are you feeling a freedom in the motion? Let it swing," he coaxed her. All his discovery questions described a balanced hand and wrist action and a sound swing path.

Swinging from B to A and back to B.

KT

Judy responded, and her swing took on that perfect form again through the super-fluid quality of the motion. "Now this time," Burlington said, "I'm going to put a tee on the ground between the foam boundaries. Just knock it out of the ground as the club passes through." She did so with ease. "OK, are you ready now?"

"Yes," she said eagerly.

"This time let the club pass through and, on the way, notice the brush of the grass." Again, he knelt down near the foam but slipped a ball onto the tee as she was swinging, just as he had with Walt. It seemed to be a fun thing he challenged himself to do, getting his hand out of the way before he got nicked by a club. *Wham!* The club struck the ball up into the air and it flew about fifty yards. Judy was amazed, as was I—both of us inspired by Burlington's magic. But he just smiled and said, "Lucky again?"

All Joe had done was get Judy to focus on the right things without interference. Fifteen minutes into her first lesson, she had developed a beautiful swing! The ball flew toward her target and she was ecstatic. She had not gotten a ball in the air before and yet this time, she was exclaiming about how easy it seemed.

I was much closer to drinking Burlington's lemonade, but I still wasn't sure how he did it. Maybe Judy was just uncommonly talented. But remembering her first carries of the club, I didn't think that was the case. It would have taken me ten lessons to get what he got out of Judy in minutes. It was miraculous. I didn't need to see more; I was a believer!

Burlington had more lessons in store for me and I was determined to learn all I could through observation. Besides his experience in golf swing physics and his mindset about learning and performing, Joe had a knack, a gift. He obviously loved to see students grow and was willing to take responsibility for all the poor results to get his students to relax. I realized it was also his way of getting them to let go psychologically. When students could give up responsibility for the results, all their 'trying hard' dissolved. And then they could really see results. Sometimes he seemed more like a psychologist than a golf pro—he knew those boundaries he talked about.

The physics and his sensory questions shaped the swing and synchronized it perfectly, if the learner was at all in touch with his or her body. I could see from my own experience what he drove at with his questions, but I noticed he didn't explain much to his students. He never answered them directly about why he asked certain questions. He shaped their swings without much explanation. Students' swings changed naturally according to his questions. I was beginning to get the method and his style, but I knew it took talent, experience—the complete package. No one could synthesize all that overnight.

Joe Burlington was more than the sum of his experience and talent. It struck me how easy it was to be blinded by someone's talent but miss small, but equally important, things: Joe had compassion. He really cared about his students and he wanted success for them as much as they did for themselves. The difference was in what he considered success. His view of success was a student being able to stand on solid ground and grow confidently on their own. It wasn't about hitting one good shot, it was about helping themselves. In my case, I believed I could take his message and improve my game. He'd already started to transform me—all of me.

Judy was well on her way to improving her swing and he had left her alone to practice. She stayed with the program. I watched her club start at point B, swing down and around to point A, and then through the corridor to B again. She was enthusiastic about her new beginning and very thankful.

"You keep doing that exercise," he told her. Joe and Judy hugged, and she waltzed away with a bounce in her step as though the ground were flexible.

"Only two more left for today. Can you handle that?" I thought he was talking to me, but he had addressed Otter. The dog wagged his tail, as if giving his consent.

22
WALLY: SLIMMING DOWN THE FAT SHOT

Joe looked toward a couple approaching from about 200 yards away. "You will enjoy Wally and Kay, Geoff. They really suit each other, but they are very different. Wally has been Indianwood club champion more than once. I always work with him on letting go of his seriousness. It's not because I want him to be in la-la land, but because his seriousness gets in the way of his improvement. It leads to a demand for results. At the same time, what matters to him is his shot quality. He isn't so into his score, although he would not accept shooting in the eighties. I can relate to him very well because I was just that serious when I was learning. I also used to let poor shots get me down a lot." The man and woman drew closer.

"Anyway, Wally and I have been friends for many years and I enjoy working with him. We used to play a lot and I like to see him play well. Lately, I've worked on him getting more energy at impact and improving his angle of attack when the ball is in a tight lie, especially with a fairway wood or long iron. Since we've known each other so long we've developed a kind of lingo all our own.

"Kay's a fairly new golfer. She's demanding of herself and competitive, but seems more patient with the learning process than Wally is, although I've heard she can get pretty frustrated when she practices. But we're just working with Wally today."

Burlington gestured for the couple to come over. He gave them both bear hugs. After we were all introduced, Kay installed herself, her book and her latte in a lawn chair, and Joe and Wally got right into what was bugging Wally about his swing. He complained of hitting shots fat and drop-kicking his long irons and fairway woods again. He asked Burlington why that was happening.

"Beats me," said Joe. Wally just smiled. He knew Joe could tell him why it was occurring from a physics standpoint, but Joe said, "All those impacts need to be placed under the umbrella of non-awareness while you're trying to pull off the shot."

"What do you mean, Joe?" Wally questioned.

"Well, who knows what was firing through your mind at the moment you swung? You may have been thinking of what a tight lie it was. You may have been insecure about it and overreacted. We can't begin to really know the source of the imbalance. All we really see are the symptoms. The only place to put your mind, then, is on your goal. I have another idea. Get out your fairway wood."

"How about I warm up with some wedges first?"

"No, just get the spoon. Oh, and show me that fat shot you mentioned."

"What?" Wally asked, incredulous.

"I want you to attempt to fat the shot. Hit the shot you despise, purposely."

Wally took the club and made a swing. Attempting to hit it fat, he caught the ball just right, not fat at all. How does that work? Joe just smiled. He obviously knew Wally didn't just have a swing problem independent of a psychological one with the longer clubs. "Wally, have you noticed your pace change when you have a longer club in your hands?"

"Yeah, you know my swing becomes Flash von Rash. I get totally discombobulated with a long club—very little loft, and a tight lie." Joe turned to smile at me. "But Joe, tell me why I would practice what I want to get rid of?"

"Simply because as you play the shot you're trying to rid yourself of, you are becoming present mentally. If you really feel it, you may have a shot at getting rid of it. When you have difficulty hitting shots fat, one strategy is to intentionally hit the shot you're trying to eliminate. Identify it. Then, at least it's not happening because you're trying hard to prevent it.

"Very often, from a psychological standpoint, the problem persists precisely because you're trying hard to avoid it. You know, 'don't go right,' and you hit the ball to the right, or on a putt, 'don't be short' and of course you're short. The subconscious can't isolate the 'don't.' Once you can perform an imbalance on purpose, it's likely you'll know what to do to reverse the pattern. At least then you're aware of it!

"Here's another strategy. Place the ball way forward in your stance, and see how your mind and body respond to that," Joe suggested.

"But I'm making contact way back here; won't it be even fatter?" Wally asked as he pointed to a spot well before the ball.

"Just put it forward and see what happens."

I was curious too.

"Just give it a try, Wall. You may make a shift McRift. Just be aware of your tempo when you attempt a swing to get to this ball."

Wally was becoming frustrated. "How do you come up with this stuff?"

Joe smiled his enigmatic smile. "I don't know. I just think about it, and the answer comes to me. But really, besides the insecurity, it comes down to the action of your hand, wrist, and forearm. They are the most volatile parts of a golf swing and we can't expect them to become balanced without getting involved. Your wrists and hands must be fluid-like and stable at the same time. They can provide great consistency or total inconsistency based on your adeptness. To get this you must be proactive in the delivery, but I will show you later what I mean. For now just see if you can identify the release angle of the club for the shot at hand. Let's just set up a purpose that opposes your imbalance. In this case, we set up for the timing of the delivery in terms of angle. We can adjust this in about five minutes."

Joe continued. "First, let's get a picture of the swing arcs that will likely produce the angle you want." Joe took the club and demonstrated. Then he pulled a scratch pad from his pocket and began drawing. I couldn't clearly see what he was drawing but it looked like two intertwined circles. Joe explained, "Wally, all you need to do is know where on the arc relative to the ground you want to impact the ball. Here, I can show you a way to do it with the Pathfinder." He seemed to be able to make any impact adjustment using his device. His students seemed to get the picture and feeling immediately with this thing.

"But just a second, Joe." Wally looked puzzled. "You mean the arc in the backswing is different from the arc in the downswing?"

"Absolutely. The bottom of the arc on the backswing is naturally behind the ball and the bottom of the arc on the downswing for impacting the ball on the ground is in front of the ball." Joe pointed with his club some four inches in front of the ball.

Wally looked intrigued. "How can I achieve that?"

"First you have to know about it and then practice your swing and allow your body to get the club to go there. Beyond that I'll show you how to use the Pathfinder to achieve what you want." He had used it earlier with Walt and Judy, but this time he set it up in an L shape at the back along the ground and then bent it up to form a virtual wall for Wally's path to be maintained on the downswing. So going back, Wally would have to start the swing above the ground to get past the foam as the club swung back and around. I smiled. Wally's lesson was just like Tim had told me his lesson with Joe had been.

Then Joe asked him to swing the club well above the foam, swinging downward through the impact zone. "Now place the club here as though there were a ball and make a few swings. Can you feel the differences in the two arcs?" Wally caught on right away and realized it was impossible to hit the shot fat or drop-kick the ball when he swung over the foam into impact. "Is this the path and angle I want?" he asked.

It's pretty close, Wally, though a little extreme. The action I'm describing is really just an impression, but if you get near that angle of attack with the club in the impact zone, you'll never have chronically fat or drop-kicked shots." Wally seemed pleased. Joe continued, "Most golfers don't realize the difference in arc and angle between the backswing and the downswing. They've been led to believe that they are the same paths, but they need to be very different. Isn't your picture of them different now?"

"Very." Wally made a few more swings and noticed how far his lower body shifted to get the club over the foam coming down and to get the club head to the ball. It was way out in front of his left foot. "I feel like I'm shifting a lot."

"That's right! Your mind-body system has the built-in intelligence to automatically make a shift because it knows the club has got to get over the foam to reach to the ball far ahead of your previous impact zone."

The backswing under the foam, then the downswing over the
foam.

TC2

"I haven't felt a shift like that in a long time. And I did it without thinking; I
just knew where I wanted to get to with the club."

Joe looked back at me and smiled. His expression said, 'if the club is OK,
the shift is OK.' It was a real lesson in natural learning, and not just for Wally.

"Just remember the purpose: Get the club to swing in good patterns. In
this case, relative to the angle—though you must be wary. This strategy tends

to elongate the forward arc of the handle too much and get out of balance on the other side of impact. So you must stay in the phone boot. Attempt to swing within the boot and play the flute with your grip pressure."

"OK Joe, I like the phone boot." Wally seemed to know what Joe was talking about. Joe's silly side helped everyone around him lighten up and relax, including himself. I was really enjoying this lesson.

"Now take a few balls out front of the tee and hit some shots, Wall," Burlington instructed his friend. Wally went out in front to a slight down slope of the main tee a few yards and began hitting shots. They were not solid, though they weren't fat either. He started to reprimand himself. He seemed disgusted with the flight of the balls, which were now all surprisingly thin. Joe was pleased and this seemed to puzzle Wally, too. "Why are they thin now?"

"Just keep swinging as if you were in the Pathfinder."

Joe stepped back and whispered to me, "Wally isn't aware of the process his mind-body system has to go through to learn a balanced angle of attack. His feel conditioned him to find the golf ball at a very shallow angle, and the only place he probably felt secure was with a short iron on a fluffy lie. Actually, a fat shot and a thin one are similar even though they feel like the opposite. It's all a matter of arc and angle. Now that he has a lot of angle, he's still not gotten proficient at letting the club release downward in balance with the surface of the ground. You see, Geoff, Wally is blinded again by the result not being what he wants it to be. He wants to skip the step of learning the delivery and, if I let him, he'll never get it."

Wally was frustrated by now at the thinness of the impact, but Burlington insisted he keep matching the foam. After about ten minutes, Joe told him, "OK, Wally, I think you're ready for the delivery." Wally gave Joe a look that said 'why did you let me hit so many shots thin?'

"Wally, you needed to ingrain a little feel of the new angle," Burlington said, answering Wally's unvoiced question. "Patience, my boy! OK, let's see how you handle the delivery. You have basically two choices. Let's try one. Picture and feel the swing. Remember, the handle is you. See if once you get over the foam, you slow down the handle and let the club whiz on by down and through the impact. Just let it fly by. Accelerate to a slowdown." That was similar to what I needed to do with my driver, I told myself.

Wally asked, "You really mean I shouldn't try to accelerate?"

"That's right! In your downswing, picture and feel as though you accelerate over the foam to a slowdown."

"That sounds crazy, Joseph!"

"Just trust me."

Wally got back into the Pathfinder and, at first, hit the foam swinging down into the impact. He shook his head in disgust at his performance.

"Just keep at it," Joe encouraged.

Wally kept swinging and before long, he got it. "Unbelievable! That's the feeling I was looking for!" Wally's shots were right on now, and it was obvious he had increased his club head speed dramatically. Now he was grinning—he finally had the visualization and the feeling. The shots took off at incredible speeds and there was no way Wally was going to hit them fat with that much angle and speed. Now he started to punch shots and the club was coming to an abrupt stop just after the impact. He was having a ball.

"Move down to the front of the practice tee and try it from a downhill lie again, Wall." Wally smiled again; Joe was pushing his awareness further. If Wally could strike it solid from this downhill lie, surely he would have enough angle from a flat lie.

He started swinging and at first made contact with the ground a little early, but then the slope took over and his feet and legs drove downward and forward, the angle increased, and *wham*, he smashed it off a downhill lie with a three wood. It flew low, for sure, but the contact was solid. Burlington was having fun with him now and Wally just cracked up. He started walking forward after the swing like Gary Player.

I found the strategy fascinating: Having a golfer do what he doesn't want to do so that he could become aware of it, then reverse engines and see if he can feel the difference. It's amazing to see the body's intelligence when we allow it to learn through a fresh point of view and nothing is wrong or right. It just *is*! I was getting my money's worth now.

Kay was oblivious to it all. She was relaxing in the fresh air and sunshine. Cell phone at her side and book open on her lap, she was paying no attention to the golfing. Otter was asleep at her feet, with his huge head resting partially on her shoe, but she didn't seem to mind.

Joe stopped Wally to wind up his lesson. Quietly he told Wally that he was still concerned about how Wally had responded to what had occurred earlier.

"What do you mean, Joe?" Wally's expression was interested but questioning.

"When things went to the other extreme a few minutes ago, you began to get frustrated again. Something inside you was unwilling to give time for the process to take place. If I weren't here with you, I believe you would have abandoned a good adjustment before you had enough swings to synchronize it. Look, Wally, you have terrific talent, but I'm concerned that you sabotage change with your negative judgments about the results. You make assumptions about the value of the adjustment too soon. It causes discouragement, and there's no way to build confidence from there, right? That's the only thing that may trip you up, and I think it would serve you well to take a look at it."

Wally seemed to take these comments to heart. "You're right, I was frustrated. I'll really try to catch myself next time."

"Good," said Joe, "because it would be criminal if you didn't. With your talent, there's no reason you can't play scratch golf all the time." Wally seemed pleased with that possibility. "Is there anything else?"

"No, I don't think so; just work on this for now. I think you can have fun with it." Then Joe paused with one hand in the air as if trying to remember something. "How's the Auggie Doggie going?"

Wally smiled. "I did it on the first tee at Indianwood and got a few looks from my playing partners, but hit a great drive with a slight draw." Wally grinned as he pulled each foot backward across the grass making scuff marks like a dog claiming his territory. He remarked as he did it, "Auggie...Doggie."

The new approach was one thing, but this new golf lingo was beyond me.

23

FREDDIE: CURING
THE SHANKS

Burlington came over to me when he finished up with Wally. "We have one more and then we can take a break." Joe told me Freddie had just flown in from New York for a sort of emergency lesson. Freddie had been a student for over 25 years and would come down about every other year for a tune up. But this time he was going to play a tournament and had a bad case of the shanks, especially with the wedge.

Freddie was one of his favorite students, Joe said. In addition to Freddie's talent, Joe liked his humble attitude. Burlington explained, "Freddie has more talent than he would lead you to believe, or for that matter, than he believes."

I was glad I wasn't giving this lesson. I had experienced so much difficulty getting students out of the dreaded shanks! It always seemed so psychological. I watched as Freddie approached; he saw Wally and Kay and greeted them first, fellow long-time alumni of the Joe Burlington School. Freddie was a tall, strong man. His long wavy salt-and-pepper hair curled up from under of his pulled-down cap. When he reached us, Freddie gave Joe a hug and asked how things were going; Joe introduced us. Before I knew it Freddie had pulled out a wedge and began swinging. I could tell he had a good swing.

After a few crisp shots, there it was. He shanked it to the right, almost a lateral. He shook it off and made a few more swings; the ball flew nicely to the target and then again, a shank to the right. Joe stopped him and walked in close. Fred's head was down. I could tell the shanks had taken the wind out of his sails. He didn't get excited, just seemed inwardly dejected. It always surprises me how a good player like this can get this far off with his contact. But there it was in living color. Joe said not to worry, that it was "simple, really."

He told Fred, "This time, at address place the club where the shank of the club is, here." Joe pointed to a spot on the far side of the ball. Fred gave Joe a puzzled look, much like Wally had done when Joe instructed him to place the ball forward when he was hitting it fat. But Freddie did as instructed and obviously trusted Joe. As the club swung down, it struck the ball right in the center of the club face. Freddie cracked a little smile.

Then Joe continued, "This time place the club all the way over here,"—a good four inches past the ball—"and try to hit the ball off the toe at impact." Fred looked a little miffed, but followed the instruction. He swung back from the far side of the ball and the club arrived at impact on the toe, as instructed.

Fred looked back and asked, "Where do you come up with this stuff, Joe?"

"What stuff?"

"To get rid of a shank, you need to line the club up on the shank."

"There's a method to it and believe it or not, logic too. Just not the logic you would think. You thought your shank was a result of an open club face from an inside path, right? Because you saw the ball fly way to the right."

Fred chuckled and nodded. "Mind reader," he muttered.

"So you tried to close the face more and the path traveled farther out, just adding to the problem. Freddie, it was easy to delude yourself about the face angle and path. Actually your path was outside and the club face was closed even though the ball flew to the right. The inside shank was not your shank. Your swing, although very athletic, was slightly out of balance regarding the path near impact. It was a blind spot for you. I'm sure you weren't feeling it.

"So the adjustment was to allow your athleticism to work out the improved path by forcing you to feel the path from over here." He pointed to the spot on the far side of the ball. "It really required you to change your path for the better if you were to even remotely find the ball on the face at impact. Did you notice that you've been setting up with the club face toward the toe at address and forward in your stance?"

"Now that you mention it, yes, a little."

"That's typical of a shanker and only exacerbates the problem. Your brain, on a subconscious level, then created an even greater path imbalance from way out here and still found the ball on the face, for a short while anyway." Joe pointed to a spot where the path would come from way outside the line of play. "You were actually accommodating the problem, not solving it. And it only takes a few swings to get back on track. Now as you go through this exercise, attempt to feel your whole hand path, especially near the impact zone."

"I can, Joe—it feels as though my hands are very near my side before impacting the ball, and after too. Very different from before."

"Great. You're waking up and dissolving the blind spot."

Freddie continued to practice and didn't even come close to the shank. He said he felt liberated and no longer tentative with a wedge in hand.

"Lastly, curl it to the end, like this." Joe's wrist looked odd at the end of his swing, still curled. He never let his wrist flex forward; it remained curled to the end. "Like Gary Player, Fred." Joe walked back a few feet from Fred, turned to me and elaborated. "Player has more talent than you can imagine. He's as entertaining a man as any who has ever swung a club, too. The things he does with a club and ball are an art form. And he's the king of positive attitude! My friend Allan knows him up close and personal, and he proclaims that when it comes to Gary, what you see is what you get."

Swing path from beyond the ball on the
backswing to develop an inside approach.

FT

257

Then Joe was back to Freddie, who had been adjusting his swing with his new path.

"Curling to the end is so weird, Joe. I don't know if I can do that."

"It's just an exercise and with that goal, I doubt you'll ever shank it again, especially if you stay in the phone boot." Fred shook his head and smiled.

"I'll do it!" Freddie tried it and the shot was super solid with a little draw on it. "Feels weird, but the impact is phenomenous!" Like Wally, Freddie had a little Burlingtonism in his lingo, too.

"Freddie, that's it! You can stay and practice, but really, you have it now; have fun at the tournament." Joe and Freddie gave each other a friendly hug.

Joe turned to me. "I need a break, Geoff. Let's go get something good to eat." I couldn't have agreed more. I was famished.

Otter followed us around the corner. Joe gave him a bowl of fresh water and tied him to a big pine so he could enjoy another snooze in the shade. Joe and I got into his truck and set off to the Farmer's Market truck stop to get some lunch.

24
PERSONALITY TYPES

W e found a booth and sat down. Burlington said he wasn't that hungry and after glancing at the menu said he was just going to have a bowl of soup. I was ravenous, so I ordered a turkey sandwich with my soup. While we waited, I brought up a subject that had been on my mind as we drove. "I noticed, as I watched you work with your students, that you teach everybody differently."

"Yes, in a sense I do. I can never predict how a lesson is going to go. Oh, I have my program, but I never know how the student will respond. It's totally up to them—how their experiences and their perceptions shape things. Of course, we're all headed in the same direction and hope to end up in the same place, but you as a teacher always need to consider the talent, experience, and personality types that you're working with. That makes it a different route every time.

"Remember when I spoke to you about perception? That's the whole key to getting right to the heart of change. You need to know how a student processes things, how he or she sees things. Get a feel for it right at your first meeting. Find out how students perceive themselves. Find out if their self-perception is accurate. You can discern some things right away and then you can choose a tactic that will get them going in the right direction quickly. I can discern personality types fairly quickly. Knowing a student's personality type is the key to relating to them. You can determine whether a student needs to change or whether their personality serves them well. It's exactly what makes teaching interesting and never boring for me. You can learn a lot from the myriad of personalities, even though some students may need to adopt a new one to get the most out of their golf game."

Our food arrived. The soup smelled wonderful and was obviously homemade.

"Could you give me an example?" I asked.

"I'll tell you what I've found to be the most challenging. Let's say you have a type-A personality businesswoman. Let's call her Misty. Misty is very competitive; her job requires that quality for her to be successful. Maybe she has to fight the good ol' boy culture every day. She arrives for a golf lesson and naturally enters it with a confrontational attitude. Misty knows that learning the facts, competing against herself, pushing herself, being driven, and basically having a bottom line mentality is what she needs to succeed. On top of this, Misty is a perfectionist-realist, which is an oxymoron in itself, right? She doesn't like fiction or any type of fantasy. Misty will tell you she lives in the real world. She bundles all these personality traits up into a package she calls success.

"Misty enters the lesson with the illusion that those are positive qualities because they made her successful in an unfair, highly competitive business arena. What she doesn't realize is those 'reality' qualities may not work well in learning to swing a golf club or play the game well. In fact, they become a stumbling block. Since she hasn't acquired any skills with a golf club yet, she will probably swing without perfect contact a lot of the time, right? She lacks optimism. Therefore, when she begins to make her usual bottom-line judgments, she will probably tell herself this is very hard—another stumbling block. Remember, from the belief comes the action!

"Well, Misty is so focused on the results that she misses the process. Throughout her practice, she moves in the direction opposite to awareness. She gets farther from her goal rather than closer because of her mind's conditioning and perception. Getting the picture?" he asked. "Now here's the kicker—*knowledge versus trust!*"

"We're back to the knowledge versus trust conflict again!" I interjected.

"That's right," Joe agreed. "That's why I called her Misty: Mistrust! The one trait that will allow her to see her potential the fastest, she has not developed, nor does she have an interest in developing it. She has no trust! In her business life, Misty has learned not to trust, and since she spends most of her day in this environment, it's ingrained very deeply. So if you begin the lesson by telling her something about trust based on feeling, you're likely to lose her.

She just wants to know how to do it and see results! If she finds out how, then she can do it—or at least at this point, believes she can.

"Misty will tell you she just doesn't feel any faith or trust, but the beginning of the development of trust is not a feeling, it's a decision. She must commit herself to acting on faith and trusting. That's the beginning of it. The decision is the key to opening the door. Misty must first believe and trust that you are leading her to the best place, and then believe she can get there on her own after a little coaching from you."

Burlington had raised his voice a bit. He had obviously had a lot of experience with this type of personality. "Don't get me wrong, Geoff, type-A men are just as challenging. It's confusing because again what makes them successful in other arenas is of no value in learning golf. These are not easy traits for an instructor to work with. I have to admit, it is frustrating for me when I think of the barriers these bottom-liners erect for themselves, and then assume there is something wrong with your teaching method. The only thing they don't look at is their own trust level—at themselves. Sometimes during these lessons, I think to myself, 'just take a look, will you?' "

Burlington paused to eat his soup. "I'll tell you about another strong personality I especially remember. Matt used to fly down from New York once in a while to see me. Just to give you an idea of where he was when we started, he used to say things like 'what's good about it?' when I said good morning to him. Very demanding, arrogant, aggressive type. Liked to throw things around.

"He came to me because he figured he didn't have a swing. I didn't buy this, but it was a challenge even to get him to show me what he had. And as I'm sure you've heard from your students, he said he was fine until he had a ball to hit. I explained that this meant the problem was actually how he felt about his swing—he was so negative. He essentially demanded that I tell him what to do to fix it.

"I explained that there was actually nothing I could do until he took a long hard look at his own attitude and asked himself some important questions. He didn't think that had anything to do with it and had no patience for that line of inquiry. He demanded—lots of demands, our Matt—that I get to the point and look at his swing.

"So I cut to the chase and told him he had internal problems that were manifesting in his golf swing."

I could imagine how well that went over.

"This type of hyper-aggressive personality is actually pretty common, so I keep a big mirror around. I pulled it out of the workshop and asked Matt to take a good look in the mirror and tell me what he saw. He refused, he blustered, he threatened to leave, but instead stormed back to the practice tee and started whacking balls and complaining about his shot and complaining about the lesson. I just let him blow off steam. When he'd had enough and packed up his things, I reminded him to settle up for the lesson at the pro shop. I knew he wasn't really going to leave.

"Matt confronted me. He didn't think he should have to pay since he figured I hadn't given him anything."

I knew that by now I'd have been screaming at this guy.

"So I laid it out for him. I described his own behavior back to him. He'd begun by disturbing my previous lesson with his loud self-complaints and diminishing any positive energy at the practice tee. He'd behaved as if his negative attitude were acceptable and become confrontational when I'd refused to subsidize that belief.

"I also told him I'd be happy to accept the challenge of guiding him to a better place, but that he wasn't ready, as demonstrated by his refusal to tell me what he saw in the mirror. I explained that the reason he complained out loud so everyone could hear was that deep down he was deeply insecure. His damaged ego wanted people to think he was better than his swing revealed and that his time was worth more than anyone else's. I told him it wasn't just his swing he didn't like, but himself. And because he didn't like himself, it was impossible for him to have any compassion for himself or anyone else, never mind play better golf. Because golf required humility and appreciation, and his attitude just didn't fit. That got his attention."

I would think so.

"I told him he needed to leave his familiar zone of conditioned misery. Getting to a healthy place by finding out why he was so unhappy with his game would be uncomfortable but I assured him it would provide him with endless appreciation and enjoyment.

"That, I told him, was my lesson for that day. If he wasn't going to examine himself, and begin at the beginning by fundamentally changing his approach, there was nothing more I could do for him. As you know, Geoff, I don't 'fix problems.' He didn't know what to say. I said that the universe is a big place."

I wondered where he was going with this one!

"It's my opinion that we all need to become aware of how we fit into it. We need to be mindful of our significance—and our insignificance. Balancing behavior between those points is necessary to develop a well-balanced perspective, not only in golf but in life itself.[9]

"I let Matt think about all that for a while. I explained that I had to remain true to myself and my way of teaching, and so could not just give him the quick fix he sought. I pointed out that many golfers had gone through the attitude adjustment I was asking him to undertake—and that they had been pleased with the results. I told him he had a real chance here, because so many golfers never recognize their problem and therefore can do nothing to solve it."

"So what did he do?" I figured the guy had to have been either ready to blow his top or deeply embarrassed at this point.

"First, I think I'll get some dessert—how about you?"

"I thought you weren't hungry."

"Dessert has nothing to do with hunger." He smirked mischievously.

Joe tried to get the attention of our waitress. He caught her eye and she brought over the menu again so we could order some dessert. Joe was silent as he perused the options.

"To his credit, Matt actually took what I said to heart. He actually started to laugh!"

"Really?" That's not how I imagined it playing out.

"Yes. I told him a man named Charles Swindoll said, 'I am convinced that life is 10% what happens to me and 90% how I react to it...we are in charge of our attitudes.' Swindoll's got a lot to say about attitude, Geoff; look him up.

"We all have to deal with things that don't go the way we think they should. Matt and his golf are an example. How we respond is critical. The Buddhists have a way of dealing with conflict that to me is the most effective way to solve a problem."

"Which is?"

"They imagine being shot by an arrow. What's the first thing you'd do if you were shot by an arrow? Would you wonder who shot it or where it came from? Would you notice the smoothness of the shaft or the beauty of the feathers? Would you ask why you had been shot?"

"I'd pull the thing out as fast as I could!"

"Exactly, Geoff," he acknowledged. "You pull it out. That's the most effective way to deal with the arrows coming at us in life. In golf, often when we have problems, it's because we're shooting arrows at ourselves. We begin asking questions about why we got into the situation we're in. We reprimand ourselves for not being smarter or we feel sorry for ourselves. We do anything except pull out the arrow, which is the only right action. If we plan on playing this game for the long term, we must make an effort not to shoot ourselves, and if we do, we need to pull those arrows out immediately."

I'd been shooting some arrows of my own. In fact, I'd been my own worst enemy at times. The waitress returned and Joe ordered a slice of apple pie. My own hunger had abated with the soup and sandwich, but I decided to have something sweet to chase it down, and ordered blueberry pie.

"My role is to give my students what they need, which is not always what they desire. Matt needed to integrate a completely new way of looking at things and at himself, and to see how his attitude fit into change. Arrogance is a sign of weakness," Burlington continued, "loud weakness, acting-out weakness. What makes learning and playing golf more like life than any other sport is that no matter how skilled you become, this game will teach you humility. So often folks misconstrue humility. I believe humility is the true sign of strength, yet somehow our culture equates it with weakness. Arrogance masks itself as strength.

"Swindoll's thoughts on attitude hit home for Matt. I literally watched a look of peace come over his face. He thanked me for the lesson."

Joe's story made me determined not to point fingers elsewhere about what was happening to me. I vowed to myself to look in the mirror every day and make a choice to have a positive attitude. It was time to begin living and teaching with this strategy and attitude as my basis for life.

"How did you know Matt wasn't going to leave when you were at the mirror?"

"I just had a feeling, Geoff. I took that chance and frankly didn't care if Matt left. I couldn't abandon my principles just to keep him happy. I've had students leave before and that's their right. If they're not ready to change and accept responsibility, then we're just wasting our time anyway.

"You see, he really wanted to be helped, but he didn't know what he needed or how to ask for it. Relinquishing control is a big step for a student, especially people like Misty and Matt. Without that release, we would have gotten nowhere. It's not my favorite type of lesson, but one I have to give sometimes. But when someone needs a reality check, it takes a lot out of me, Geoff. I would much rather have helped Matt elevate his swing awareness, but that would have been a waste of time without him first changing the way he perceives things. You know, when you change the way you look at things, the things you look at change."[10]

I knew I would have handled the situation rather differently. I would have either kicked Matt off the tee or pleaded with him to try this or that, hoping something would work.

Our dessert arrived and the waitress refilled our coffee. "One thing that's absolutely critical with students like Misty and Matt is to stay calm. It goes back to what I said about being at peace. If you're secure in who you are and what you're doing, you will not respond in an aggressive or defensive way." I looked at the table. I knew this was something I needed to work on, and I knew he knew it too. "Matt has to own his aggressive behavior, not me. When he thought back on it, he might not have liked what he said or the way he said it. If he thought about my response, he wouldn't have seen a reflection of his tone of voice, but something very different. Maybe he realized that the reality check was truly in his own best interest.

"You must always remember that you're still in a student-teacher relationship even if you agree to disagree. I must admit, I work on this daily. It's still one of my biggest hurdles. It's important to keep in mind that so often, 'the eye sees not itself.' Those lessons are the most challenging! Matt's view of himself didn't coincide with how reasonable compassionate people view him."

"Anything else you can tell me about dealing with this kind of personality, Joe?"

"You have to start by not engaging in their game. You must get them to trust in you and then in themselves, Geoff. They must believe that you care. You have to listen and observe them very closely. They need to feel safe with you, not vulnerable. The coaching is very delicate in purpose but strong in boundaries. I have found I just have to be creative to get them out of their own way, with positive mind-talk and right-brain exercises."

"Tell me how..."

"You must set strict ground rules during the lesson. Don't let them get away with even one statement of disbelief. Never let them cross that barrier with statements like 'I can't do this or that' or 'this is hard.' Make them verbally cancel their negativity. Literally make them say 'cancel' to whatever negativities they throw down. This personality type tries to control; in their minds, that's how they succeed. They don't realize that the formula for success in golf is very different. Letting go is control, but they are conditioned to hold on, as though it were control both in the mind and on the club. To succeed in golf, these folks have to be willing to surrender, and that can be uncomfortable. It places them in unfamiliar territory, feeling very vulnerable.

"Most of the time, I've found that they'll try to get you to teach the way they like to learn. If you fall for that, you're no longer teaching. Never, I repeat, never, let them control the lesson with that brand of success! It must be process, process, process!"

Burlington made sense. I had run into students like this myself and found them very frustrating. I would be dissatisfied with my teaching and the negativity was contagious in both directions. These students didn't improve, and I would be left with a sour taste and an empty feeling when the lesson was over.

Joe continued to emphasize his point. "People with this type of personality are usually your most difficult cases. Remember the cure-is-too-painful story? Their greatest challenge is what is most painful: relinquishing control. Ask them, for just that hour, to adopt an attitude that will serve them better. If they're not willing to do that, I'm afraid you cannot help them, because surrender is paramount for this personality type. You can lead a horse to water...." he trailed off and dug into his pie. Mine was delicious—I had almost finished it while he was speaking.

"Sometimes you find that people like Matt have been emotionally injured in their past. Somehow you need to get them to feel safe with you. For example, if you tell them that following their lesson, they can return to their old ways of perceiving and doing, but just not in golf learning, and not with you, it may help. Their golf identities must be different than their identities in business, for instance. You may be able to get them to relive some of the moments in their past that were real positive times of learning and growth. Or, give them a picture of your past, your own failings, and how changing your attitude was the key to beginning your success. Tell them how you found your way.

"Ultimately, however, they need to realize that these personality traits, although possibly useful in the business world and maybe in golf competition, are real barriers to developing their feel for a golf swing, complicating things and making the process slower and more difficult. Once they make the decision, you need to set them up for success. Give them physical tasks that relate to their current state of awareness."

"What do you mean?" I inquired, polishing off the last bite of my dessert.

"If you were learning to play the violin you would not be asked to attempt a Bach partita the first week, right? It would be unachievable and would just put you off. 'Trying hard' would be your modus operandi. You would never see or hear your authentic musical awareness. Don't get me wrong, I love Bach, but if you were a beginner and you were to try some of his solo pieces, you'd find your fingers jammed together!

"Now Mozart, on the other hand, falls into your fingers like soft butter. I have always believed that Mozart better appreciated the limitations of the fingers and hands on the fingerboard of the average fiddle player and composed accordingly.

"So if you were teaching the violin, you could get your students to listen to the sound as they pluck a string. Feel the vibration, then play an easy scale. Their ears and brains would be getting familiar with the tones, and once they developed a finer sense of hearing, you could help them become aware of their fingers pressing a string to the board, each place for a certain tone. Eventually they could begin using the bow, first feeling it slide across the string at the best angle, with just the right friction for the volume you choose. Then you would move on to a simple tune.

"This type of progression is easy for them to pick up. So it goes in sports. Give your students challenging but achievable tasks and be ready to move forward to the next awareness level. They can develop some beliefs based on that beginning success pattern. You must set them up for success. Let them crawl, and then walk, before running. In golf that would be akin to putting and chipping the ball. Or if you begin with a longer club like I do, do everything in super slow motion.

"You need to support their decision to trust with appropriate tasks. They have to realize that this is not hocus-pocus. Try visualization exercises, or you may need to lighten up the lesson with some humor. To put them into the moment, you need to use your whole arsenal to help them to believe and develop. Getting students like this to believe and then to let go of their bottom-line personality will be your greatest challenge. These golfers have to learn the process to be able to stand on their own two feet when they are alone."

Joe stopped short, seeming to sense it was time to go, though I'd never seen him wear a watch. "This waitress needs to make a living and we've hogged this table long enough." Joe went to his pocket, but this time I was the one waving him off.

As we drove back to the golf center, Joe asked me, "Would you like to see a fun lesson? Don't you think we could use one about now?"

"Of course," I responded eagerly.

"Well, tomorrow morning I have a lesson with a young boy who has had some instruction before. As I understand it, he hasn't progressed the way his parents thought he should. I chose to work with him because it can be very fulfilling to see the transformation in a young person. He won my lesson lottery for his age group."

"I look forward to it, Joe. What time do we begin tomorrow?"

"Nine o'clock sharp."

"Sounds good to me." We parked and shook hands. I walked to my car with my mind filled with new thoughts and perspectives. I wrote down two more nuggets that Joe had nonchalantly voiced during our conversation when he described the strategy to helping Matt get out of his own way. The points were based on perspective, as I'd come to realize practically everything is: If you change the way you look at things, the things you look at change; and, The eye sees not itself. Matt had only seen outward at first.

No wonder Joe was so misunderstood. Throughout my career, I had attended many teaching pro workshops, yet never had I heard such insightful descriptions of how people perceive, learn, and perform. It occurred to me that the only way to get this is through experience, dedication, and being an exceptionally open learner. This stuff was wrought from the dirt, no other way. I felt privileged to receive the knowledge.

Golf was so much more than a game. Sure, it required developing the skill in swinging the club and playing, but it also required the development of humility and appreciation. All life lessons. Just watching how Joe Burlington approached each lesson brought that to life for me. How was I ever going to repay him for this?

25

TOMMY: THE KID'S ALRIGHT

I rose early, got down to Lou's Diner in just a few minutes, and ordered my usual. It was a perfect morning. I perused the *Sentinel*, but didn't see much of interest except that the Panthers were playing the Islanders at home again at the end of the week. Maybe Tim and I could catch another game.

I drove over to the golf center and went around the back, where I parked under the pine trees across the road. I could see Joe getting off his fairway tractor. It looked as though he had cut our hitting area, preparing for the day's practice and lessons. Not far away was a youngster making practice swings. It looked as though the boy's mother was watching from the bench behind the hitting area, which was littered with pine cones. It was warm this morning and looked like it was going to be a clear day.

I got to the practice area at the same time as Joe. He made the introductions all around and Tommy's mom told us a little of his golf history. Tommy was a beginner. His dad, whom she described as a fine golfer, thought it would be a good idea to get Tom started with professional lessons. He had taken some at a resort while the family was on vacation. Tommy's mother, Barbara, related that the lessons started out well, but soon became very complicated. Tommy's progress seemed to be slowing down, and after just two days, he was frustrated. He was not normally that way, she told us.

Barbara had gotten into a conversation with a fellow at the resort's practice tee; he knew of Joe and recommended that she not miss the opportunity to have her son work with him, so she entered Tommy in the draw.

Tommy continued swinging during this conversation and didn't hear the story. When Joe called him over, Tommy's ears seemed to prick up like a puppy's and he trotted over. He was slender but seemed sinewy and strong for his age. His dark brown hair complemented his tan. He was polite and respectful; his manner reminded me of Opie from Mayberry RFD. The kid seemed optimistic, too. Joe crouched to face him and asked how he was doing. Tommy had a soft voice, still high-pitched. He was obviously relaxed. Joe demonstrated again that he was able to establish a rapport with whomever he was with in short order.

"Let's get started, Tommy," Joe said. "Show me your swing."

Tommy went over to the practice tee and began by getting his grip in order, then he tried to aim toward the flag nearby. He set up to the ball, arched his back, and stuck out his rear end. A mean look came over his face as he stared down the ball. He took a mighty lash for someone his size and missed the ball completely.

"Try it again," Joe said good-naturedly.

Tommy went through the routine again and this time tipped the ball to the left. His face began to turn a light shade of red. Joe moved in closer to him and spoke very softly. I couldn't hear what he was saying, but Tommy's face relaxed.

Joe then gently took Tommy's left hand and turned it palm up, appearing to draw a pattern with his finger on Tommy's palm and fingers. He seemed to be showing him pressure points on his thumb and thumb pad along with the heal pad of his left hand. Next, Joe closed Tommy's last three fingers around the end of the grip. He then cradled the boy's hand in his own. Somehow it seemed a perfect match, as though Joe's hand was the perfect glove for Tommy's. You could tell Tommy was feeling secure by his new expression.

Next, Burlington took Tommy's right hand and placed it against the left with the life line against his left thumb and his fingers wrapped around the grip with most of his right hand above the grip. Joe was obviously taking great care with how Tommy placed his hands. I noticed this ritual in every lesson. When Joe finished the adjustment, Tommy's hands seemed like they melded together perfectly. The club appeared to be a part of his anatomy. Then Joe took hold of the shaft of the club below the grip and pulled it back and forth, as he looked at Tommy.

Joe asked Tommy to release much of the pressure with which he was holding the club, but not to let it slip—to hold just tight enough that he could move the shaft. Then Joe lifted the club up and down, back and forth, and rotated the shaft so the club faced the sky and then the ground. Everything

272

they did together to change the club face direction matched what their hands did. Tommy's wrists now seemed very flexible.

When Joe felt the pressure was just right, he asked Tommy to move the club in the same manner alone. The boy did. He flexed his wrists and turned his hands in every direction. His flexibility rivaled Gumby's. This new grip gave him the maximum leverage and control over the club and the potential to generate the most speed with the flexibility and rotation. Joe then asked Tommy to put the club down and rest it on his leg and then pick it up and regrip it the way Joe had shown him. Tommy followed his request exactly and looked to Joe for approval. Joe nodded and Tommy rewarded him with a smile, beaming with confidence with his new grip on the club.

Before Joe let him go, he took another wood club from the bag, lined up about five balls, and got on his knees. Joe began swinging, hitting one after the other. Each ball sailed right over the target.

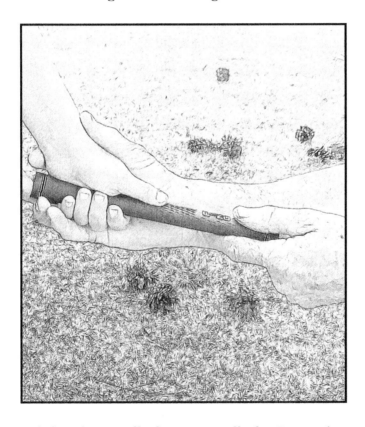

Joe's hand naturally forms a cradle for Tommy's left-hand grip to be sound.

TC3

Tommy was fascinated. "How did you do that, Mr. Burlington?"

Joe smiled and said, "It's really not hard, Tommy. Now you do it."

Tommy took the club again and adjusted his grip just right, but you could see he was anxious. He began swinging and made good contact with two of the balls as he walked through each shot without stopping to stick out his rear or follow any of the swing rules he had been taught before. After this first set, there was a huge grin on the boy's face.

"Would you like to try again, Tommy?"

"Yeah," he said.

Tommy regripped, being careful about the new placement of his hands. Joe lined up the balls and Tommy went after them.

"This time see if you can copy me," Joe said. Burlington swung his arms very rhythmically and super fluid. Tommy started fast at first, but then Joe reminded him to pay attention to his speed. "Watch closely, Tommy."

Tommy's whole body, with his free swinging limbs, became more blended and more rhythmic. He also looked fluid-like. That beautiful circular path pattern was emerging again like clockwork. Maybe the path can be a function of the flow? Burlington went over to his bag and pulled out his famous foam Pathfinder and had Tommy swing the club through it without touching. After a couple of hits to the foam, Tommy's coordination with club in hand improved. It took only thirty seconds for him to swing the club smoothly through the corridor without touching either side. He seemed to be getting familiar with the boundaries. The circular pattern was again becoming ingrained.

Joe then placed some more balls some five feet away from the props in a line so Tommy could keep swinging while moving forward, hitting one after the other. This time Tommy swung very rhythmically. As he walked through, he struck several of the shots perfectly solid toward the target. I looked back at his mother and there was a startled look on her face. Her boy was hitting golf shots she hadn't thought possible without months of lessons! And it was a swing that was beautifully formed in its shape and speed.

Burlington walked over to Tommy's golf bag and picked out a wedge. Then he stood out in front of him. I thought that was awfully brave with this club in this lad's hands, but Joe seemed to know what he was doing. "Swing the club slow enough for me to catch the ball. Make a full swing but only with enough energy to get the ball to me," he instructed.

Tommy responded naturally. His swing became ever so gentle. Then Joe moved over to Tommy's right, about ten yards in front of him. He coached, "Continue to aim at the flag but make a swing so the ball can fly over here to me." Tommy swing's path took on a shape that still resembled a good approach path. Burlington then moved way to the left and said, "Keep aiming toward the flag, but feel the swing go toward me as it makes contact." The swing went around to the left, and then Joe moved directly in line with the flag. "Now swing so that the ball will fly into my hand here." He raised his hand and Tommy's club struck the ball softly with his wedge into Burlington's outstretched hand.

Joe began moving out about ten paces at a time. Tommy kept swinging and remarkably, the balls were going in the same direction. Joe was about thirty-five yards away from the boy now and he called to him, "Take your five wood, Tommy, and sail the ball over my head." Tommy went for his wood club and quickly set up five balls on the tees and began swinging, paying close attention to where he wanted the balls to fly. One after the other, they went sailing in a parabolic arch right over Burlington's head. It was incredible! How beautiful and simple this lesson was! And all Burlington did was get Tommy out of his own way.

The boy obviously trusted Joe now. Once his hands were well placed and the pressure was right, all Burlington did was get him to feel the speed and direction the club was going by getting him to focus on where he wanted the ball to go. He didn't need to let go of the target; it wasn't an obstacle to Tommy. It was attractive to him. And Joe didn't bog him down with instructions about how to do it. Joe came back in to speak to him. He dropped to one knee and put his arm around Tommy's shoulder while they had a short conversation. The kid turned and faced his mother. He was beaming, and Mrs. Tommy seemed happily flabbergasted. I just shook my head at how simple it had all been. Joe got up and came over to us while Tommy resumed practicing. Joe quietly discussed with Barbara what Tommy could do to continue improving on his own.

"That was neat, wasn't it?"

"Very," Tommy's mother said.

"You see, it doesn't take much to get youngsters like Tommy going in the right direction. Most of the time all they really need is to get their hands well placed on the club and establish sound patterns of speed and path with a target."

Joe looked back at me, winked, and whispered, "He doesn't need another target. Tommy's body sets up just like a cat ready to pounce—he's very athletic—especially without all the pre-swing positions and rules he seemed to be tangled up with before. Tommy's focus needs to be on his rhythm and where he wants the shot to go."

Joe turned to include me, "Geoff, in golf development, all you need to do is ask good questions." He looked back at Tommy. "Can you feel the shape of your swing, Tommy?"

The boy smiled and answered, "Yeah, it feels like going from a merry-go-round to a Ferris wheel." Tommy was relating perfectly to his experience in watching the rides at the carnival.

Joe beamed, "Exactly." He turned back to me. "You can ask questions like how fast do you want to go, is it rhythmic, can you feel the path, and where's the flag? Tommy's athleticism will work out any wrinkles as he practices focusing on those fundamentals. It really is that simple."

I believed him. I had seen with my own eyes the magic that can occur when someone is not distracted—when he returns to being athletic and begins to trust. These principles seem so simple, but somehow in my teaching I had forgotten them. I realized that kids, and everyone for that matter, do not need to have so many things to do. I was also beginning to realize that the problem with adults did not lie just in their athleticism, but also with their ability to trust.

A perfectly balanced swing path and club face ready to rip it.

TC3

Tommy's lesson was another example of the trust versus knowledge conflict, the thread that wove its way through every lesson Joe gave. Then, of course, there was Burlington's physics program. He was a master of asking the best questions when it came to the physics of the swing—that was the second part of his expertise, and exactly why his lessons seemed magical. The questions always dealt with the club: what direction it was traveling, what speed it was going, and when. This lesson really let me see the program work.

Tommy and his mother left on cloud nine. When Barbara tried to arrange another lesson, Joe told her it wouldn't be necessary. He suggested they wait a little while and let Tommy absorb this one and really learn it well.

Burlington and I sat on the bench. I could see he was tired this morning—he looked drained. He'd given a lot of lessons in the past few days.

"That kid had the perfect attitude, didn't he, Geoff? He readily let go of all the concepts he'd been working on and trusted quickly. That was the reason everything went so smoothly. He trusted within minutes and after that, it was just a matter of asking the right physics questions."

I was inwardly proud that I had realized what had happened before Burlington had explained it to me. I was getting it. I was beginning to think in a different way and look with a different perspective. With this new vision, I thought back on the lesson. It *was* possible that path can be a function of flow; that idea was like an epiphany for me.

I asked about the way Joe worked with Tommy's hands on the grip at the beginning. He answered without hesitation. "It's important that Tommy realize the critical nature of his hand position and pressure for his golf swing at this point in his golf development. It's an aspect of swing development that's so overlooked. Hopefully, we've made an indelible impression on him. After all, when hands are well placed and pressure is optimum for speed and awareness, it can make the whole action of the swing sound and simple. When teaching the physics of the club, there is no more telling aspect than how a golfer places his hands. That will determine whether the patterns of the swing and club face are in or out of balance. Pay close attention and notice your students' hands before you get into adjusting any other part of their swing.

"That's the only lesson I have today, so let's call it a day. Tomorrow I'm very busy in the morning. We need to verti-cut the green and trim the hedge first thing. If you come down early, you could practice, but the treat is on the course. I have a playing lesson in the afternoon with a very interesting pupil, Geoff. He has a personality totally different from what we've been discussing, but just as challenging. I would say his personality is complex, so it should be a good lesson to observe," he said as he walked me to my car.

I was exhilarated by all I had observed. These lessons were unpredictable. I'd thought I knew about the complexities of the golf swing, but that was the simple part. The real challenge was getting the students to get out of their ruts and their useless habits, and the challenge was inversely proportionate to their willingness to change their attitude if necessary. What was becoming very clear was that Burlington's methodology was entirely based on the student's trust in him first, and then trusting in themselves and the process. Even before the golf swing comes to issue, there should be an evaluation and adjustment of the student's perception and attitude.

As I was driving, I thought of the Swindoll quote Burlington had mentioned: The beautiful thing is we have a choice each and every moment, each and every day, what attitude we adopt. I thought of Claire, of how she seemed to live by that philosophy. Always ready every day with a positive and realistic attitude. Somehow I wished I could let her know that the way she perceived our relationship and how she lived her life were beginning to make sense to me now. In that moment realized I needed to pen a few lines to her.

I arrived at my place and ran upstairs to my room. I found a pad of paper in the nightstand, sat down on my bed, and began to write. I just let my feelings pour out. But mid-thought I realized I had to go: I'd arranged to meet Tim and Jake.

I put the letter aside on the night table; I would finish it later in the evening. Then I freshened up, and in few minutes was on my way to Pompano. I didn't want to be late for the guys.

26
BACK TO POMPANO

With only a few minutes to get to Pompano to meet Tim and Jake, I stepped on the gas. When I arrived at the first tee they were waiting.

We shook hands and I walked to the back tee with my driver. I teed my ball and took a couple of practice swings. Feeling uncharacteristically calm and confident, I looked down the fairway and lashed my tee shot with a slight draw down the right side. I smiled at Tim and Jake as I walked to their tee a good twenty yards ahead. Jake teed off next. He looked a little nervous and was muttering to himself while he made his practice swings. Tim told him to be quiet and swing. He proceeded to sail the ball down the center of the fairway. Tim was last up. He made his usual Snead waggle and kick start and struck the ball solidly down the middle.

We walked onward, our Sunday bags slung over our shoulders. We reached Jake's ball first. He pulled out a mid-iron and faded it into the right greenside bunker. He shook his head, called himself stupid and slammed his club into the ground. "I do that all the time, Geoff. You think that was bad, now you get to see my sand game." I knew exactly how he felt, but also found myself thinking that his reaction wouldn't help him play better or more enjoyable golf. When we reached Tim's ball, he looked at me and asked, "What do you think?"

"A medium punch eight should do the job." He pulled out his eight iron, took a couple of practice swings, walked in, and just as before, with no hesitation, looked toward the target, waggled, kick started, and swung. He struck the ball crisply and it landed some thirty feet from the hole. Tim was a confident golfer, steady and smooth. He believed in his swing and used it. I felt good that he respected my experience as a golf pro and had relied on my suggestion.

Here were two close friends with fairly equal golf talent, but one seemed to trust and enjoy and the other was cynical about his performance. I noticed that Tim was smiling as he strode to my ball down the right side of the fairway just in the rough. I had a three-quarter pitching wedge, which I punched low under the crosswind blowing from the west, landing it a few feet to the right of the pin. It was gratifying to play the shot I was capable of. Burlington's magic was working. I felt authentic as a teacher and a player.

As we approached the green, Jake took his sand wedge into the bunker, muttering again. I went over to inspect the situation. His ball lay in a footprint. He complained about the lie as he entered the bunker. After a couple of practice swings, he proceeded to skull the wedge shot across the green all the way to the fence bordering the little Pompano airport. He cursed as he walked to his ball. Before Jake even reached his ball, Tim played his putt to within a couple of inches. They didn't play by honors or who was away; they hit when ready. That was fine with me—it made for a fast pace of play. Jake picked up and waved at me to finish since he was done.

We all played the next couple of holes hitting the fairways and greens. No birdies, but easy pars. As we played, Jake kind of went off on his own, appearing disgusted as he walked to his ball, even though he had some good shots. I was a little uncomfortable. I've always found it difficult to play with a too-serious golfer. The other golfers are afraid to even say 'good shot' because someone like Jake would 'correct' them and say it wasn't. But now, I saw my former self in Jake, too. I needed to apologize to a lot of folks for acting this way.

We came to a long par three. Jake landed his tee shot in the front bunker. Tim and I hit the green. As we walked down the path toward the green, Jake asked, "Could you give me some help out of the bunker? I haven't a clue how to get out consistently."

"Sure, Jake." I jumped at the opportunity to help. "Before we begin, I have to have your word that you won't judge the technique or the result before it has been well tested."

"What do you mean?"

"I mean it could take a little time for your mind-body system to coordinate and integrate a different swing pattern. You need to adopt an open, non-judgmental attitude."

"But I'm not judgmental."

"OK, just do me the favor of not drawing any conclusions before you give it a fair trial period."

"OK, OK, I will."

"Are you sure?"

"Yes, just tell me what to do."

At that point I felt like Joe, setting the ground rules for his lessons with students like Jake. "How do you usually get out of the sand?"

"I don't," he said with a smile. "Really. I've had so many lessons that I don't know what to do now. But I've been taught by everyone to put the ball back a little, and aim for a spot a couple of inches behind the ball, then I open the club face and my stance, and swing the club a little out-to-in and try to cut the ball out of the bunker. What do you think?"

"I think you're in for trouble."

"Why?"

"First off, this technique has very little margin for error and too many things to do. If you don't strike the sand just right, you could easily find yourself in a big mess. The shot you're trying for is really best suited for a downhill or buried lie."

"What would you suggest, then?"

"If you have a normal lie, I would suggest you attempt to make a sweeping hook swing to get the ball out." Jake looked at me as though I were crazy. What I'd said contradicted the typical style of the pros. At once I knew how Joe must feel most of the time.

"Could you fill me in a little more?" he asked skeptically.

"You've been attempting to strike the shot with a sharp angle to spin the ball out of the bunker. I favor lobbing it out with a full swing that doesn't require so much precision. Also, I never aim for a spot. My wedge splashes a rather general swath of sand before, beneath, and after the ball naturally. You need to get a feel for the speed, length, and depth of the club passing through the sand. You don't have to be so precise. I would rather use the sand to absorb the club's energy and release the energy of the club with a long shallow splash. Go ahead, try it."

Jake walked down into the bunker. The shot was medium in length and needed to get up in the air to clear the lip. "Go ahead," I encouraged him, "close your stance too, so you can swing in a circular pattern." Jake continued to shake his head, not believing it could work. He made a practice swing. It was still too vertical for the technique. "Pretend you have a driver in your hand. That bunker swing is the closest swing to the driver."

"What?"

"It's the closest swing path and angle to a driver release."

The short game shots, especially the bunker, were an aspect of the game I had never lost. When I was growing up, I had learned to get out of the bunker with a nine iron. I was forced to hit soft shots by adding loft in my release and sweeping the ball out in a lobbing fashion. Finally, Jake gave it a try, exclaiming that he had nothing to lose since he hadn't had any consistency in years. Fear and tension had been his M.O. in the bunker. He closed his stance and took a long swing like a drive and skulled the shot again. "That doesn't work!" he yelled.

I shook my head. "In one swing you're gonna tell me whether it works or not? You're breaking our agreement. Try again. This time ground the club and sweep the sand back in a nice circular pattern."

"But touching the sand is against the rules."

"Not today."

"OK, but I still don't understand."

"Grounding the club will give you a better feel for the depth and texture of the sand. Eventually we'll play by the rules, but for now, just do it." I had raised my voice unintentionally and made a conscious effort to cool it. Golfers like Jake frustrated me, debating when they couldn't achieve even minor success with their own technique.

Then Joe came to mind; this was my lesson, too. Teaching is always learning twice. I reminded myself to be patient so that I could help Jake even though he resisted my strategy. I also knew I needed to be firm. I had to be the leader.

"For the next five minutes you need to let go of what you think you know and just learn as though you were a curious five year old, Jake."

He put his head down and checked himself. "OK, just show me, then."

I got down in the bunker, threw three balls down, and made three driver-type swings with my wedge in slow motion, lifting each ball out with the sand softly onto the putting surface. I turned around and looked at him.

He was smiling. "That's so much motion—I don't know if I can do that."

I returned his smile. "Jake, you have nothing to lose. What you've been doing is not working. Why not try something totally different?" I looked over to Tim, who had a grin on his face and had come over from the other side of the green to watch. After a moment's hesitation, Jake agreed he had nothing to lose in trying something new. I laid out three more balls in a row and asked him to swing without stopping. "Just walk through them and keep swinging."

He surrendered and did as I suggested. He struck the first ball too cleanly and it flew too far onto the back of the green. But the last two floated out like Trevino's butterflies with 'soar' feet. I threw some more balls down to Jake and he made more long swings, sweeping the sand under the ball. Each one rode out of the bunker on a cushion of sand. With this technique Jake was using the sand to his advantage. A grin began to creep over his face as he realized there were alternatives to what he had been taught. He lobbed the balls out with very little spin. The look on his face had changed to curiosity and joy. He was elated. So was I. But I wasn't finished yet. "This time, let go with your right hand after impact."

"Are you kidding?"

"No, try it."

Jake shook his head incredulously but tried it. He swung the club and let go with his right hand, soon remarking, "That one was the smoothest through the sand," as the sand and the ball flew beautifully onto the green. He tried several more shots, releasing his right hand and finishing with only his left hand on the club. His swing and his consistency were uncanny. He lofted the balls with perfect energy for the distance of the shot. "OK, I admit it works, but why would I do that?"

"It can really free up your swing and allow you to purify your hand and wrist action. According to Joe Burlington it could be the future of the golf swing."

As I observed Jake at that moment, I noticed him turn away from me slightly and glance out over the course; he clearly had a bias against Joe.

Based on what Tim had intimated, Jake couldn't handle Joe's demand for an attitude adjustment during his lesson. But Jake was soon present again and remarked, "I always believed the sand shot was an explosion. I thought it required brute strength, but I can see your technique requires touch."

"Exactly. It requires light hand pressure and a smooth rhythm. Toss a couple more balls down in the bunker and try to really hook them out and let go."

Jake seemed liberated once he felt free to make his normal swing path and make a swing with a hooking feel in the release through the sand. I left Jake in the bunker to practice while Tim waited patiently for me to finish putting. Jake picked up the balls from the green and followed us to the next tee.

Luckily it was near dark and no one was playing behind us. We all hit good tee shots and then all hit the green. Tim and I headed down the fairway together. Jake was just ahead of us, practicing his hook release with his left hand. When we reached the green, Jake picked his ball up and tossed it into the bunker. As Jake was practicing, Tim and I hit good putts, but didn't make them. Across the green, Jake was making long, slow lob swings, sweeping the sand and balls out of the bunker easily. It was satisfying to witness his success.

Tim turned to me, "I really have confidence in my long game, but my short game is another story. Do you think there's a big difference between the two?"

"It depends on your purpose. To take a line from Joe Burlington, it's all connected, but in your long game, driving for instance, your purpose is usually to create as much energy as you can in the club head to energize the ball accurately. In the short game you're usually trying to take energy off the ball, especially with your wedge shots around these high mounded hard Bermuda greens."

"I don't get it. You can take energy off the ball?"

"In a sense you can."

"Could you show me the technique?"

"Sure. I developed one that's right down Joe's alley. I mean, you'll think it's radical."

"I'm open to it, Geoff; my short game could use it. Most of the time, I hit shots that are rolling to the hole, but when I can't run it there, I'm at the mercy of the greens."

"Tim, really it's simple. Remember the hockey game the other night, when you told me about the similarity between the slap shot and Joe's curl release?"

"Of course, that's his timing release for high energy."

"Right. If high energy is to let the club circle, rotate, and time the curl downward, can you guess what would create lower energy?" Tim looked at me, still puzzled. "Simply do the opposite! Reverse the face."

"What?"

"That's right, reverse the face. Shut it going back, then open it and lay it back going through." Tim looked at me as though I were from outer space.

"You've been hanging around Joe Burlington too long!" he laughed. "That's radical!"

"Here, let me show you." I took Tim over to the other side of the green. We both dropped several balls onto the grass. I took out my sand wedge and showed him the reverse face. "This is limited to fairly short wedge shots, but it works wonderfully when you need to stop the ball. It's especially good in long grass around the green."

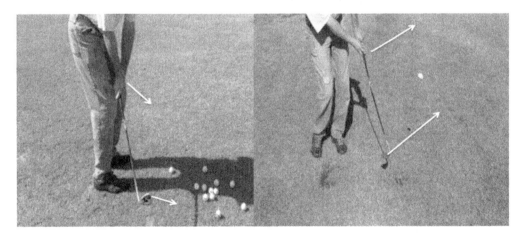

The reverse face, shut and delofted back and opening with loft through impact.

GB

"You mean you can spin the ball in long grass, too?"

"Definitely. If you get good at rotating the face in reverse right at impact, you'll stop the ball very well."

"Let me see you do it again." I took my wedge, shut the face going back, and as I neared impact, reversed it open. The ball flew softly onto the green and came to an abrupt stop. "Wow. I'd never have thought of that, Geoff. Let me try."

I retrieved the balls from the green and tossed them to him. "Be sure to close it going back so you can really open it as you strike the ball. It's the action at impact that does the trick." Tim did it beautifully. His ball came to an abrupt stop. "Now try it over here." I took him to the other side of the green where the grass was long. "Pretend the pin is right here. I pointed to a spot only eight feet onto the green. Tim made a mini-swing and reversed the face perfectly. The ball hopped over the long grass and stopped quickly again. Tim smiled broadly. He had just learned a shot he didn't even know existed. I knew it would be very useful on these hard greens when he had a short-sided shot. I was happy to have shown him.

"Geoff, what about short putting? Do you have any tricks there?" he asked with a smirk and a wink. "I suffer a little shake once in a while. I know it's mental, but I haven't been able to overcome it."

"Actually, yes, there is an easy strategy for that and it works most of the time."

"Tell me."

"When you get ready to hit the putt," I explained, "first aim it off line, purposely."

"Really! What does that do?"

"It gets your brain to see the correct path of the ball into the hole."

"Is that it?"

"Well, no. Next look toward the hole as you putt and feel the energy."

"You mean not look at the ball?"

"That's right. Look where you would like the ball to go, not at the ball." I tossed a few balls near the hole and asked Tim to try it.

"This seems so weird. You're morphing into Joe Burlington!"

"Thank you."

Tim was a good student. He tried it and couldn't believe he made almost every putt without looking at the ball. And as he looked toward the hole the energy on the ball was excellent. "I can't believe this, Geoff—my stroke is beginning to feel smooth, like when I was young and my nerves were fresh. I never would have come up with this; I always thought I should concentrate harder with my eye on the ball."

"Yes, I know, and you watch the putter move and you try hard to hit is square and so on." Tim nodded in agreement. "But when your confidence wanes in putting, or anything for that matter, you need to know where to place your concentration so as not to interfere with your potential. The ball and club on a putt became a distraction to you so I just removed the distraction by having you place your attention on the target. Simple, right?"

"I can't argue with that." Tim putted a few more and made almost all of them from three to five feet away. He was amazed at how he could hit the putts solid and square without looking or concentrating on impacting the ball squarely. I was really pleased it worked so well for him, especially because he was the one who introduced me to Joe and made me feel welcome here.

Jake was still swinging away in the bunker. He would walk out and retrieve the balls to try again. Both guys seemed happy. I couldn't believe how good it felt to teach them my technique in a Burlington manner. I felt authentic. When we reached the final tee, and I was busy basking in my success, I hooked it wildly into the left rough. I chuckled to myself. It was the first fairway I'd missed, but I didn't care, and neither did the game of golf. I should still be able to hit the green from there.

Tim and Jake made solid, carefree swings. Their balls landed near each other on the fairway. As we walked I took a left turn and told them I'd meet them on the green. My ball was down a hill, one of the few in South Florida. They couldn't see me from the fairway. I reached my ball and had a blind shot. I was a good 190 yards from the green. The grass was long and I knew I had a flier. I just guessed where the flag was and fired away with a six iron. The ball flew high and arched in a draw pattern onto the green. I assumed it was good by Tim's and Jake's reaction—they clapped as they saw the ball land just a few yards from the hole. I walked back up the hill to join them on their way to the green.

We were satisfied. Jake had his new bunker swing, and Tim had his reverse face spinning the soft wedge shot from grass, as well as the concept of putting while looking at the hole. It was getting pretty dark now, so we finished up and headed to the grill.

The air inside was scented with freshly fried fish and chips, one of my favorites. We found a table in the back of the grill room. Tim and Jake greeted our waitress and in an instant a pitcher of Irish Red was on our table with three frosted mugs. Jake and I ordered the fish and chips. Tim ordered his usual, hot corned beef and cabbage. Jake spoke up as soon as the waitress left. "Well Geoff, I really appreciate the help you gave me today. I had no idea there was such a way to hit a sand shot."

I nodded, "No problem. But I'm concerned about another aspect of your play. We can discuss it sometime."

"No, tell me now. I want to know anything you think would help me with my game."

"Well, Jake, it really doesn't have anything to do with the way you swing the club."

He looked at me curiously. "What does it have to do with?"

"I may be over-stepping my bounds here."

"No, go on. I want to know what you think."

"Well, I am concerned that you're emotionally fragile on the course."

"What do you mean?"

"I mean that you seem totally connected to the good or bad result. That makes you extremely vulnerable to a bad attitude." I paused, wanting to put this in such a way that he would receive it, not reject it. "When you started today, you seemed pissed off. We were kind of walking on eggshells around you, like the other day in the skins game. Nobody is comfortable in that environment. You're robbing your playing partners of their enjoyment and freedom on the course, and you simply don't have that right. Nobody can even give you a compliment for a half-decent shot without you letting them know it wasn't what you wanted or that it wasn't perfect." I kept going. "Actually, I'm a little surprised they haven't abandoned you by now." There, I'd said it. Not politically correct, but correct.

Jake turned a little red and began to rationalize his behavior, just as I would have in the past. "Well, if you hit shots around the green like I do, you'd act that way too."

I paused a minute to think about that. The new authentic me had to admit the truth. "Maybe a week ago, but not anymore. I know exactly how you feel, Jake, and I can tell you from experience you'll never get the most out of your game or your time on the course with that attitude." I could sense that Jake was getting a little irked at me, but I didn't relent. I needed to make the point clear and not retreat. It was his option to accept it or reject it.

I looked at him and continued. "You have a choice about how you respond to your play, good and bad. I guarantee, if you take a look, you'll make the right choice for yourself. You need to disconnect your attitude from your performance."

Tim sat nodding in agreement. He had been waiting a long time for someone to have this talk with Jake, but Jake was so volatile that his friends were afraid to tell him. His behavior was really a form of abuse, and we should never let anyone get away with it.

"Something you could do when you get home is to Google Charles Swindoll and 'attitude.' It's easy to find. Make his ideas your gospel; you'll be amazed at how powerful it will be. It certainly helped me a lot."

Jake took a deep breath. He defensive expression had faded as be began to surrender his tightly clenched old attitude.

I had taken the same chance Joe would have, and it was paying off. I was being true to what I knew was essential for Jake to sustain his move toward better golf and better living. He hadn't thought he needed to change his attitude, only his technique.

Jake blurted out, "OK, I'll do it." We were quiet for a second.

Tim seemed surprised and pleased. He broke the silence. "Teaching seems to come naturally to you, Geoff. I like your creativity and simplicity. For you to get through to this bonehead," he grinned, "that's an accomplishment!"

"Thanks, Tim." Jake was smiling at the truth Tim had just declared. Just like that, things lightened up. Jake had let go of his seriousness. We traded golf stories through the rest of dinner. I had just enjoyed a good day playing, teaching, and now eating and drinking with them, talking golf and life. Jake insisted on paying for our dinner and Tim picked up the beer tab. I tried to contribute, but they would have none of it.

I was exhausted and would need a sound sleep to be ready for my next Burlington lesson. The guys had to go to work the next day. We said our goodbyes and were off. I took the scenic route home. I had the car moving at a snail's pace, taking in the beautiful scene all around, the ocean on my left and the old oaks hovering over the road from both sides. The realization that Joe's magic was working was fulfilling and enriching. I could be at ease when I played, and when I taught.

27

ROBERT: I HATE MY SWING

I awakened to the sound of the wind howling. Salt air filled the room because I'd left the windows open all night. I shut them, then dressed and headed to Lou's for breakfast.

After breakfast I drove to the golf center. The temperature was crisp; there were a few clouds in the sky and lots of wind. Joe had really piqued my curiosity the day before. I arrived with great anticipation and optimism. I wanted to tell Joe about the short game lessons I'd given on the course yesterday. Answers to many of my questions had sifted into place and the bad mood I had carried to Florida was no more than a distant dream.

Robert arrived early for his lesson. Joe had told me what he knew about Robert. He was a serious golfer and had been a low handicapper most of his life. However, he had fallen on bad times golf-wise. After introductions, Burlington asked Robert how it was going.

"Well, life is OK, but my golf game sucks," he chuckled with resignation. Robert gave us a short history of how he had gotten to this point. "I played college golf and then went into the golf business after college. My dad was an excellent player. We've owned and operated golf courses for forty years. But now that I have time to play great courses, I'm very disappointed in my game. My swing feels loose and weak. That's the most discouraging thing, besides the inconsistency—the weakness. I feel like there's no compression in my swing. Everything collapses. The harder I try, the worse I get!" Robert waited for Burlington to react, but Joe was quiet, practically expressionless. When Burlington nodded, Robert continued his complaints.

"I just don't like the way I swing the club. It's very discouraging. I know I lay the club off, and then have a huge loop to get the path in order to find the ball at all. My swing path is way off and I've tried all kinds of ways to fix it, with no success. In fact, a senior golf pro told me recently that it's just the way it goes when a golfer gets older. What it comes down to is, I hate my swing!" Still no response from Joe.

Robert pointedly asked Joe if he thought he could help. There was a long pause. Now that I was familiar with Joe's response time, I didn't get antsy, but I could tell Robert was a little uncomfortable. A few more seconds ticked by before Burlington asked, "Do you believe him, Robert?"

"Believe who?"

"The pro who told you that's just the way it is."

"I don't know. After these past few rounds, I think I'm beginning to."

"Well, then let me see you make a few swings," Burlington said.

Robert obliged and, with a six iron, began hitting shots. The man was obviously athletic, but his swing path was complex. The club started back very straight for a long time, circled around late, and then looped incredibly. As he changed directions, he swooned downward to correct the imbalance. It seemed almost a magic trick the way Robert was able to find the ball and flight it toward the target. He hit a few good shots, but before long, he got frustrated. His shots began to fade and were simply not solid, just as he had told us. Although Robert was frustrated, he seemed satisfied that he had shown Joe exactly what he was talking about.

"Do you see what I mean?" Robert asked, his face twisted. "Do you think you can help me?"

Burlington looked at him and nodded. "I believe so, if you're willing. But the first part of the solution is for you to begin liking your swing. I mean the way you feel physically and emotionally. Even before you hit the ball."

"What?"

"You have a very negative image and feeling about your swing, right?"

"Yeah..."

"And you have identified what you don't like about it?"

"Yes," Robert responded.

"So we need to see why you haven't made the changes. That's why you're here, right? What we need to do first is fundamentally change the image you have of your swing."

"What do we change it to?"

"We change it to something you like, something physically and emotionally appealing to you. When you can trust it, hitting good shots will likely generate a good feeling about your swing. So let's address the feeling you dislike the most. I bet you can tell me which it is."

"Yeah, I want to get rid of the looseness and weakness, and the path too."

"And what is strong, from your perspective?" Joe asked.

Robert paused. Then, "I really don't know." All he seemed to know was that he didn't like what he had.

Burlington pressed him. "If you know what you don't like, then you must have an idea about what you do like or would like."

Robert thought about it for a moment. "I think I need to get my swing to feel as though it tightens up as I swing."

"You mean like a coil?"

"Yes, that's it! I want my backswing to feel like a spring tightening. Like this!" Robert torqued his shoulders and made a swing back.

Joe asked, "Tell me, if your swing felt tight, do you think it would be powerful?"

"Yes."

"Robert, your problem isn't typical. Most folks we see need to loosen up, but you and your swing are a totally different animal." Robert nodded in agreement. "If you felt wound up, do you think that would be better for you psychologically?"

"Yes, absolutely."

"There's one very important thing to do, though, if you want to get this feeling and still have awareness for the club face."

Robert was leaning toward Joe as though he was going to extract the words by force, like a dentist, but Joe didn't seem to mind the proximity. He instructed him, "Take the handle with your left hand and swing it behind you like this." He demonstrated. "That way, you'll tie the backswing pretty tight, which will pull the torso tight, which is the opposite of loose and wobbly. But, more importantly, you will still have club face awareness when you focus on swinging behind you in this manner. And the club face pattern will be fundamentally sound. However, you must do it with your lead hand. Only then will you have club face balance."

I thought about the handle arc from previous lessons; this seemed to be the same thing. Robert looked a little perplexed, so Burlington explained further. "I don't tell people too often what they don't want, but in your case, I need to make an exception. Never try to get the feeling by turning your shoulders independent of swinging the club behind you with your lead hand. Let me give you a little hint about building the simplest fundamental backswing path. The curvature of the swing always occurs when your hands are below your waist and the vertical action always occurs behind you. And one other thing: When it comes to power in the golf shot, it really is a function of the sequential action during the downswing, not the backswing. But I will leave it at that for now. To get you on solid psychological ground we will get rid of your loose feeling of weakness first."

Robert began to swing the handle of the club behind him. It was easy to see the plane and path matching and balancing his physique and the design of the club perfectly. Of course, this was slow motion. The loop and swoon dissolved instantly, too. I wondered if things would change back when Robert picked up speed. Robert looked at Joe and asked, "So, it's like this, but won't I get it too flat?"

Joe shook his head. "Everybody thinks that. But actually it can create exactly the opposite—the more you swing the club behind you early on an arc, the better chance it has to go up vertically behind you later, which would not be flat. And the club will not be laid off—exactly the opposite of what you thought, right?"

The handle getting behind on the backswing.

GB

"Yep."

"Your club was actually low and laid off precisely because you swung the club in too straight a line going back for too long. You thought that swinging in a longer, straighter 'extension,' as they say, would make your swing more upright but the opposite occurred. The club had to go around at some point, right? When the swing path curves around too late, often the weight and momentum of the club flatten the swing, shut the face, and lay off the shaft. And usually this happens for a golfer who has been taught to turn his shoulders as a dominant swing thought on the backswing."

Joe's instruction demonstrated the depth of knowledge. I, like Robert, had thought the opposite would occur. Typically, the way golfers have been trained to think about the golf swing is unhealthy. We really don't know the causes and effects. We have oversimplified the swing and thought that if a golfer swings straighter back, his swing should be upright. Wrong!

Robert's club had to be tremendously rerouted because of it. Joe continued, "I really don't want to continue explaining in this way, Robert, because it won't serve you. I just want you to be able to drop the notion that swinging in a straight line is good for your swing path. The straight line is minimal in a sound orbit, but you have really over-exaggerated it under the false impression that it would have a positive effect on the plane and path of your swing."

Robert still appeared to doubt this; it's hard to give up beliefs that have been embedded for years. Joe saw this, looked Robert straight in the eye, and said, "You know, your best effort got you to this point, Robert. So if I were you, I would begin changing the way I look at, think, and speak about my swing." Joe somehow said all this in utter seriousness, yet with a touch of a grin on his face.

Joe had again taken the puzzle out of a golfer's swing. The way Robert got there seemed paradoxical—until Burlington had explained it. I never thought swinging in a straight line would ultimately make a swing flat—I thought it would surely be vertical. But it could turn into what Robert had as likely as it could be too vertical. Although it seemed the former, laid off and flat was more likely.

Robert was now nodding in agreement with Burlington, finally hooked. Robert began to make more swings. I was glad to see that the complex route of his path seemed permanently dissolved in just a few minutes. It had morphed into a classic swing: a simple circular motion and then, almost without noticing, he would shift downward and forward to support the release of the club head energy into the ball. It was a perfectly synchronized action with little physical or mental effort. Robert practically cracked up at how simple it was once Joe had clarified the swing path principle.

Burlington's skill as a coach shone. Each lesson was different and yet every student ended up in a similar place: more aware of the club's action. In every lesson a wayward golfer grew into feeling secure in the environment Burlington created for them. The atmosphere was friendly, yet there was genuine awareness building all the time. Burlington would challenge them without intimidating them. He simply removed the blocks that we all seem to construct unknowingly, and then when the path of awareness is laid out, it's easy to see what to do. I needed to learn how to build this type of environment with my own students. But I didn't yet know how. With Joe Burlington, it just seemed to happen as a matter of course.

Robert was exclaiming his excitement about hitting shots he hadn't hit in years. "I feel like now I can synchronize my shift into the impact, too!" Robert was grinning from ear to ear when Burlington asked for a time check. I wondered why it mattered this time. Robert looked at his watch. "We've been going about a half hour; do you have to go?"

"No, I was just thinking, you've been here about thirty minutes. Do you think you just received something you didn't have before, or did you just discover something good you've always had, but that's been buried by some false concepts that provided interference rather than awareness?" He smiled. "You see, Robert, if you didn't already have it, I couldn't have put it into you in thirty minutes."

Robert absorbed this. "Yeah, I guess I must have had it. I just didn't know how to tap into it."

"Right," Joe smiled, "you've got it, it's all yours, and it's always available because it comes from within you. Everyone has it! My job is to simply wake you up and lead you to discover your own potential. Now, show me your backswing."

Robert swung the club in a perfect orbit behind him. The club face was slightly open and now the shaft crossed the line. "Good," said Burlington. "Now show me your downswing." Robert shifted downward and forward naturally and the club followed perfectly into the slot. He delivered the club through the impact zone with virtually no resistance. "Great," said Joe. "You're on your way."

Joe was a master at handling different folks and their swing idiosyncrasies. When Robert's lesson ended, Joe filled me in on what was next, but I wanted to know what he considered to be the best path pattern—how the club head travels from beginning to end. "What is the best pattern a golfer can swing, Joe?"

He didn't hesitate. "The club takes on an orbit from behind the ball. If a golfer has well-placed hands and is postured athletically for their particular build, the club will take a course that goes back, around, and up. And it can be completely controlled by the lead hand and arm. That's my preference. It's the simplest pattern that's effective and repeatable. When done this way it's virtually impossible to see the curve in the swing. The average golfer misconstrues this as a straight back pattern, but in reality it's only straight for a short time. If you have to build a swing from the backswing, then suffice to say, back, around, and up. Often golfers will say they just swing it straight back, but again, that's what they may perceive, but we know the club is behind them and in the air."

Feeling versus physics. His philosophy was crystal clear, but I still wanted to see it. "Could you show me?"

As you know, I'm not a fan of developing a swing this way, but I guess you should know for yourself." He stood up to show me the sections of the differing directions the hands travel during the backswing.

"Thanks, Joe. I really needed to see it to understand."

"We've got one more lesson, Geoff, then I have some other things to do. My next student is a good player. I've worked with him little by little for a long time. He should have been here by now. Let's go for a walk with Otter; it shouldn't be long till Bryan arrives.

When we finished walking the dog, Bryan had arrived. Joe introduced me but Bryan wasn't listening, he was apologizing for being late. He had taken I-95 and there had been an accident, trapping him in traffic. Bryan also wanted to videotape the lesson, so he was setting up the camera and all.

Burlington just nodded and motioned for him to go ahead. While Bryan was getting organized, Joe began with a casual question. "What's been happening, Bry?"

The lead hand, arm, and club swing path
sequence of direction: 1, back; 2, around;
and 3, up.

GB

"Oh, I've been playing fairly well, Joe, but I have a few questions that've been bugging me. I'm hoping you can help clear them up." He went straight to the heart of the matter. "You know that for years now I've been following your program of flow, path, and timing."

"Yes," Burlington nodded.

"But my confusion lies in the fact that when I feel I really have it, it doesn't last, at least not long enough. Could you tell me why, if I follow the program, I can't always retain what I've learned or stay on the same level?"

Joe considered the question and after his usual pause, responded. "Bry, as frustrating as this may seem, there is a principle that you must learn to accept."

Bry looked intrigued.

Joe continued. "It's a principle of nature, and golf is no exception. There is impermanence in all things."

"But what can I do about it?" Bryan asked respectfully with a hint of impatience.

"You can do nothing about the principle, but if you think about it, you have been taught to respond in kind to the dynamics of golf and life at any particular moment. You see, the program you've learned takes this principle into consideration. The program only gives you a strategy." Joe continued. "Every moment in our lives is flux."

"But Joe, with all due respect, I felt a couple of weeks ago that I had it!" Bryan proclaimed. "I was so sure about it."

"I'm sorry, Bryan; you never own awareness, it's only on loan to you. We all only pass through the awareness balance, although at times we feel as though we own it. Every aspect of your golf game is a discovery process and continues as long as you work on your swing action and play the game. Learn this principle and you will surely reduce your frustration. You have learned to balance out your swing action through the flow, path, and timing cycle. It deals first with the club and then with your feel. It is imperative that you practice with change in mind. Expect change as the only 'always' you can count on. In fact, embrace it. That's the attitude that will allow you to enjoy the journey more and continue to grow."

Then Joe suggested that Bryan hit a few shots, just to see where he was. Bryan pulled out a mid-iron and began swinging. He had a long, flowing swing and made beautiful contact, which had high energy on the impact. The ball flew very straight, too. He continued to hit a few shots, all very consistent and pretty close to the same results. "Seems to be in good balance today, Bry," Joe told him.

"Yes, it feels pretty good, but I have a question."

"Shoot."

"I've been fiddling around with the idea of feeling connected. I mean, my swing feels firmer, and I feel like I have more control." Joe just nodded. "Anyway, sometimes when I really go for this feeling, I feel a little too mechanical and stiff with my body and the swing. What do you think?"

"I think you should feel whatever you feel. Feel will give you more control. Remember, you're just sensing. It's not fundamental. In fact, it will change day to day."

Bryan rephrased his query. "Well, let me put it this way, Joe. Would you teach someone to feel that in their swing?"

Joe looked surprised and a little dismayed. He replied adamantly. "I really don't teach anyone by my feel. They simply learn to feel based on the accurate physics of their club's action. You're describing your feel for the path or arc through which your hands travel. Being a lanky, flexible supple swinger, 'connected' feels good to you. That's fine. That description is foreign to me, although I understand it. You see, most of the folks I work with have too much tension in their bodies. They're not like you," Burlington said with a wink. "In fact, they would, in most cases, need to feel disconnected—to steal your phrase—to improve their flow and get rid of the physical tightness. However, if being on the prescribed hand arc gives you this feeling, that's fine. Remember, work on the club's action and then describe the feeling."

Again, Joe's program had answered another problem so often associated with golf teaching. There is no way to teach an individual's perception. Rather, Burlington describes the physics and lets his students freely describe what it feels like to them. "The answer to your inconsistency is to balance out your program. At times, you need to work on flow, other times path, and still others on timing. You can't develop a consistent action without balance in your practice. So no one is always going to play the same. The only things you can count on are being ready, accepting and embracing change, and learning to enjoy discovery every day."

"I guess you're right, Joe, but it's so frustrating that things are always changing."

"Then you really need to look at that attitude—that's what needs work, not your swing. There's no fundamental to the way a golfer swings except for his club action. Go to a tour event and watch the swings of the best golfers in the world. Notice how their bodies move during the swing. There is just no way to model them. They're all different. If you try to model them, you'll become confused. In fact, you'll discover their bodies achieve similar results differently. The only close similarity in all these swings is the club's action near the impact zone. Everything else is up for grabs."

"But what about your program?"

"Yes, my program. It says nothing about those things. The only principle in my program is the dynamic action of the club. When you develop a pattern of rhythm, and then a pattern of path and ultimately a pattern of timing, then voila! You have a swing. That's how you arrive with a sound swing."

"But Joe, your swing looks like a classic swing. I like it."

"Thanks, Bry, but I didn't arrive at this point by modeling different body parts and positions on other classic swings. I arrived at it by deftly developing those club patterns. It's a swing, a reliable swing, and my mind knows it." He added that last nugget with perfect timing and effect. Bryan understood. He shook his head and smiled. Always stick to the pattern of the club and accept the flux in golf—and life too.

Bryan shifted gears and asked Joe another question regarding the path pattern and the effect of working solely with the hands. "Joe, you've taught me to pay close attention to my hands for feedback about my swing; can the hand focus get me into trouble like the focus on the shoulders turning can shut the face and flatten the swing too much for some players?"

"Absolutely. If you're not aware of the pattern the hands travel throughout the swing, and you focus on them, you can often create a swing arc that gets very narrow and a club face that's very open. That, in turn, could cause you to lose the natural sequence that occurs from the arc and building momentum in your swing. Even the best focus can send your swing out of balance if you're not aware of the patterns."

"Can you show me what you mean, Joe?"

Without hesitation Burlington pulled a Pathfinder from his bag and placed it on the ground. He bent it into a pattern in which the length was like a virtual wall boundary for the inside path. Then he turned the back curve like an L in the air about five inches above the ground, similar to the configuration he had made for Wally.

"Place your club at the front of the foam and aim according to its direction. Now swing the club under the foam going back in your typical circular pattern and over it toward the impact, without touching the foam," Burlington instructed.

Bryan did just as Joe said. "Wow! That feels wider than I've been swinging, and narrower on the downswing."

"Exactly! You have a great arc for building momentum going back. And then what did you feel going down over the foam?"

"I felt a pretty good shift in my feet and legs to get over it going down."

"That's what I like to hear, Bry; now you're more aware of the club and you're feeling how it influences your whole body. It naturally created a lot of action throughout your body, especially, as you say, in your feet and legs. Now you can modify the degree of it if you wish, but that's essentially the best way I know to get the best arc and angle to strike the ball with high energy toward the target."

"What about the curl? Can that move ever cause a problem?"

"As I just described, Bry, any singular focus could potentially throw off the balance of the whole."

"Even the curl? How so?"

"Well, if you concentrate on the curl too much it could reduce the angle of the club too much as it approaches impact, or vice versa: if you work on angle too much it can reduce the curl. They need to be balanced and worked on in a balanced way."

I was fascinated by this method of creating a balanced swing action. In the past, I would have been all over Bryan to focus on his shoulder turn, his hips, and then his feet and legs, and by the time we finished he probably wouldn't have been able to make contact. I realized this was the power of Joe Burlington's philosophy: If the club is OK, the swing is OK. He didn't have to go into all the effects of sound club action; the whole body's action was the effect. After Burlington and Bryan reviewed the lesson, Bryan went to his wallet. I gave them a little space. As I walked a few yards away, I felt positive energy in my stomach. Dammit, I was getting it! I shook my fist in triumph.

As Bryan hit a few more shots, he told me that he'd gotten a deeper insight into the power of the program and felt he was no longer missing out on the total picture of the path and how to create it.

As Joe turned to go, I fell into step with him. "Geoff, I need to help Bob finish repacking and sealing the lift cylinders on the loader. He'll be here shortly. Feel free to practice!" He strode to his workshop.

I decided to take a stroll around the property to contemplate all I had observed and what was going on in my head. As I turned, I was surprised to see Otter come trotting after me. I guess I'd been adopted. I thought about the day and how pleased I was to be watching Joe's knowledge at work. I also felt good that I was beginning to anticipate how Joe might respond to certain questions. I no longer felt like a complete novice.

After our walk, I left Otter at the pro shop and headed back to the house before dark. I remembered I had leftovers in the fridge and heated them up for supper. I sat down in an easy chair in front of the picture window looking out over the turquoise ocean lightly splashing on the shore. I'd found a worn book by Lee Wulff on fly fishing for Atlantic salmon in Newfoundland. What a sportsman! But a few chapters in, I fell pleasantly asleep.

28

WOO: CAN HE TRUST THE TWIRL?

I'd gotten up early again. This was to be my last day with Joe and I needed to take the time this morning to find him a gift. I took my usual walk down to Lou's to have breakfast. I had been filling Lou in about Joe's lessons since I arrived. I thought it was curious that he had the impression that Joe played golf only as a hobby.

I told Lou of my problem: Joe wouldn't take money, so I needed to find him a gift. Luckily, Lou knew exactly where to go. "Go around the corner just north of Commercial on Federal Highway. There's a fly shop there on the east side of the road. See Dave. He'll have the perfect gift."

I followed Lou's directions and was there in a few minutes. The guy inside was just getting ready to open when I arrived. He waved at me to hang on while he retrieved the key to unlock the door.

"Good morning! Lou sent me down—he told me you could fix me up."

"What do you need?"

"I need a gift for a friend."

"Fly fisherman?"

"Yes, a damn good one."

"Is he from around here?"

"Yes, it's Joe Burlington, the golf pro."

A smile lit up Dave's face. "I know him, and I know exactly what he'd like."

By this time I was accustomed to the fact that practically everyone I met knew Joe in some way or another. "Great!"

"How much do you want to spend?"

"Whatever," I replied.

"Well, I have a very special bonefish rod in the back. It would make a great gift. It even comes with a cedar case." Dave went back and returned with the rod in hand. He began to lift it up and pull it down as if he were casting. "This has really nice action. Joe will love it."

"I'll take it." Dave rang it up and I was off.

I arrived at the golf center in the early afternoon as instructed. Burlington was giving one swing lesson and then a playing lesson after lunch. I checked in at the pro shop and found out he had another maintenance problem besides the work he'd planned to do in the morning. No matter how much Joe seemed to get ahead of the problems at the golf center, there was always some emergency to take care of. He seemed to take it all in stride, though, just accepting it and moving forward on his journey with such grace. I knew I wouldn't be able to respond the same way.

As I peered toward the barn, I could see him walking back and forth from inside the gate to outside near the loader. Bob was there, too. Maybe they hadn't finished the seals from yesterday. I decided to hang out near the pro shop until his lesson arrived. I bought a bucket of balls to warm up before we went out on the course and went over to the practice tee.

I began to hit shots, just feeling the rhythm and direction of my swing, without getting bogged down in the old intricacies I used to employ to get ready. I just felt my swing instead of burying it with concepts. It felt fluid. And I felt like a carefree kid. I didn't know if I would be playing during Joe's lesson on the course, but I wanted to be ready if called upon. I finished the bucket and decided to walk down to the barn. I found Joe and Bob sitting down at their table sipping cold water. They both looked satisfied, as though they had finished a job well done.

Joe introduced Bob and me and then glanced at the clock. "Eddie better get here soon or he'll miss his lesson. We're real tight for time today." He was remembering his playing lesson for the afternoon. Joe and I left Bob in the shop and went around the corner, where he would be conducting the lesson.

Joe looked out toward the main tee. He spied his student coming toward us. Joe looked at my watch and said, "Right on time; you'll love this guy." His nickname is Eddie Woo. He's a commercial pilot, flies for American Airlines. He's peculiar, but a real good guy. He's the type of person who has everything in order. Disorder makes him feel insecure. I imagine that if you went into his closet, all his clothes would be color coded," he laughed. "A great trait for a pilot, but very challenging for developing a golf swing.

"It seems his playing partners have gotten into this interesting habit: His name changes according to how well he's playing. A few months ago he was Ed Woods, playing out of his mind, but recently he has dropped two letters, to Eddie Woo. He had heard that I would be teaching this week and called me just yesterday morning to ask if he could get in a few minutes. He wants to get something straight about his contact. I figured it would be useful for you to see, because his problem is control—and not just control of his golf swing either. He only feels secure when he's in control. He deals in absolutes. He needs to know everything. You know what trouble that can cause when you're trying to develop a golf swing. So here we are again with trust."

Woo approached. "Lama!" he called out. Joe introduced me. Woo shook my hand and went right to his bag. He obviously was not one for small talk. He looked at Joe and said, "I know you don't have much time, and believe it or not I'm close now. I just need to know: How do I strike it square all the time?"

Joe looked back at me and winked. The impermanence principle rose instantly to my mind. I smiled back. We were on the same wavelength now.

Woo demanded, "I need a technique, Lama."

"I have given you one, Woo."

"No Lama, I know you are holding something back. There has got to be a way to hit it square all the time!"

Joe shook his head and chuckled. "Have you worked on the curl?"

"Yes, I love the curl, but what happens after that?"

"In your case, Woo, I would keep rotating."

"Rotating what?"

"Your left hand, wrist, and forearm."

"That seems so out of control."

Joe probed further. "Have you done the 'let go' exercise?"

"Yes, a little. Lama, you are skirting the issue. You hit it square all the time; I know you're doing something I can't figure out." Woo's rapid statements were almost comical. I wondered how Joe would help this guy. I knew that what he was asking for was virtually impossible, but Joe responded with ease.

"Woo, none of us hit it square all of the time. You want absolutes, and there are no absolutes. The golf swing is like life, especially at impact. Everything is an approximation. It's quantum, Woo—the uncertainty principle." As a pilot, Woo knew all about Heisenberg. "You can set up the conditions for striking the ball squarely more often, but there are no absolutes. Until you accept that, I'm afraid you will never end your search for the proper technique. For you to strike it more squarely, you simply need to set up the dynamic environment for release, through our flow and path constants." Burlington always returned to that principle. "Remember how you got consistent in the first place."

Woo shook his head in reluctant semi-agreement.

Joe walked in closer to Woo and said, "I know your problem."

"What are you waiting for? Tell me," Woo demanded like a kid about to get his way.

"Woo, I've given you several keys to balance your swing, right?" Woo gave one quick nod. "The problem is you constantly look in the wrong place for your keys. The answer to your problem lies in the dynamics of your swing, not the various positions you superimpose on it. You've reminded me of a story the real Dalai Lama tells. Let's say you arrive home from a long trip. You've been to ten cities in three days and you're tired. You pull into your garage, get out of your car, and head into the kitchen. But you realize you forgot to get the mail. You turn around, keys in hand, and head to the mailbox. It's stuffed. You slide the key ring around your pinky so you can pull out the wad of mail with both hands. You pull everything out then head back into the house. As you open the door from the garage and step into your kitchen with your hands full, your keys slip from your pinky down into a plant pot. You sort the mail and unpack. When you're finished, you take a nap.

"You awaken still groggy from jet lag, but now you're hungry. You need to go out and get something to eat. You head to the kitchen to get your keys. They are nowhere to be found. The last time you remember having them was when you put them on your pinky at the mailbox. So you search around the mailbox. You look through the flowerbed and run your fingers through the grass. You really look hard but still can't find them. You give up and get your spares.

"The moral to the story? No matter how thoroughly you search outside by the mailbox, you are never gonna find your keys there because they're inside in the plant pot! You must look *inside* to find them." Joe had made it clear earlier in the week that awareness is always an inside job.

Woo looked at Joe with half a smile. He shook his head and chuckled with comprehension. Just like the trout fisherman: You can't catch fish where they're not.

Joe continued. "In my opinion, the answer to your problem is to learn to look in a place that has the possibility of balancing out your swing. It's in the motion, the pace, the timing, the dynamics. And there are no guarantees. Woo, you've been looking in the wrong place for your swing keys!" Joe said with a smile.

"Woo," he continued, "I have described the action before and after impact."

"You mean the curl and twirl." Woo had framed Joe's release of the club head as a spiraling, twirling, whirling action.

Joe smiled. "Yes."

"I can feel and see the before and the after, but what about the middle, the impact?"

"Well, in my opinion, you have to let the middle go. Don't concentrate on the impact, just the before and after; let the angels beat their wings in your favor for the middle. Let the impact go, mentally. I guarantee something good will happen if you do."

I could tell Woo had a hard time accepting Joe's dynamic impact philosophy. At no time during his swing did he want to lose control, or at least his impression of control. He wanted a concrete method that described every muscle and joint action to get the impact. But by now I knew that wasn't going to get him anywhere.

"You mean as the club face approaches the ball, you don't aim it into the ball for a square impact?" he asked

"No, not at all. The club head just passes through square. "If you have the club's two reference points, the before and the after, and you don't interfere, square is the result of those references."

"That's a lot of action. It feels like I have no control when my club spins like that." Woo shook his head, obviously having a difficult time getting comfortable with the concept of dynamism, with the idea that square was the result of fluid action. He wanted to position the club and his body step by step, as though the release was a solid structure.

"Trust me," Joe said. "Solid impact comes from a fluid swing."

Woo with his key before and after impact.

EW2

Woo, like many golfers, thought he had to control the club with a keen eye on the ball and pressure in the hands to make sure he struck it square. He thought he had to impact the ball with tension and pressure to secure squareness. To Joe, control was dynamic: action, lightness, rotation, letting go, energy. Those were the keys.

"Give it a try Woo; forget about being conscious of making square contact and see if you can picture the before and after. Let the club rotate like crazy with this reference before and this one after."

By his practice swings, I could tell Woo was adept at the curl trigger before impact; his problem seemed to be after that. "Lighten your hand pressure so you have a chance," Joe told him.

Woo had continued to clench the club tight for control. "I can't lighten my pressure—how will I control the club?"

Joe seemed to be getting a little impatient. He took Eddie aside and had him make several swings through a Pathfinder so he could concentrate totally on the spiraling action of the club head. They returned and Joe set up several balls. "Just lighten it up and let it go, will you?"

"OK, here goes, but..." Woo made a swing. The club dug deep into the ground before contact. Disgust was instantly pasted on Woo's face.

Joe didn't give Eddie an opening to criticize the fat shot before he interjected, "Good, you did it, just not in balance." Woo had rotated the club like crazy. "Give it another shot." Woo made another swing. It was thin. He had rotated the club again without an acceptable result. "Good," Joe said again. I could see that Woo thought Joe was off base with his compliments. But I noticed Joe never even looked at the ball flight. He focused on Woo's hand action near impact, and it *was* action.

Next, Joe lined up several balls so Woo could continue with no time between swings. I knew the strategy: Don't give him time to doubt, question, or think, only to concentrate on the purpose. Joe was a master at shutting down judgments.

This time Woo curved the ball well to the left. "Good," Joe complimented again. Woo appeared confused, but Joe didn't care about the results, only the action. Woo still hadn't hit one shot solid toward his target, but he kept making swings. Joe encouraged him. "Curl it to the end. Let go with your right hand, finish in the boot." Woo smiled; he knew what Joe was talking about, and complied.

Joe's enthusiasm was infectious, and Woo was no longer trying to perform with a result in mind. He was into the process, feeling his new left-hand, wrist, and forearm action.

Curling to the end with the let-go exercise.

EW2

And then *wham*—a screamer. The ball took off like a rocket, and square as a bear. Woo looked at Joe in disbelief. "I hardly swung! I twirled fast, but I didn't swing fast." Joe smiled at Woo, knowing he was just beginning to scratch the surface of an effortless, powerful release.

Joe next positioned a line of balls ten feet long. Eddie kept whirling the release and the balls flew consistently straight and far. "It's not how hard I swing, it's the twirl!"

"Whatever you say, Woo."

Woo stood there shaking his head. Joe had let him find his way and now he was describing accurately how to strike the ball square and solid. Joe admired the strength and balance of the swing and the ball's flight, then eased back toward me and whispered with an Irish accent, "Isn't she lovely."

That was the strength of his method. And I knew his students could feel his strength and conviction when he taught—it helped them morph into their best authentic selves.

Woo grinned as he let himself go. His release was approaching that of a tour player. He had begun to accept the truth of approximation. He kept practicing, smiling and shaking his head each time he hit the ball. Joe wandered over to pat Otter, who had also witnessed the lesson but without a surprised look on his face. Woo asked me, "How does he do it? He gets me going every time. I need to stick with this; I need to commit to my keys. This is exactly what I needed."

Woo went over and handed Joe a Benji. Joe smiled and said, "Go partner up with Bill, Mr. Woods. You two should be able to take on John and Kate now."

The lesson was one of the best I'd witnessed—and all in about fifteen minutes. Eddie was a skeptic, but Joe didn't give his doubts a chance. He was like a Gatling gun with his instruction. Once he got Woo going, the rapid-fire positive remarks reinforced everything. As Woo was leaving us on his incredible high. Joe, like Columbo, added one more nugget. "Someday, Woo, when we have more time, we will reverse the engines at impact, like one of your landings."

"How so?"

"I will teach you to see yourself from every angle, every point of view— God's view." Woo just shook his head, smiling, and seemed satisfied with today's dose. He waved Joe off good naturedly. I was curious about that comment, but Joe just looked at me with a wink and a smile and said, "Lucky again. Now let's get going."

29

JOHN: THE POWER OF VISUALIZATION

I threw my clubs into the back of the truck, climbed in, and we were off. As we drove north on the turnpike, Joe told me about his next student. "The man I'm going to be working with, John, is a real good-hearted person—very compassionate and non-judgmental—but his confidence is very shaky. He's been asking me to play a round with him for the longest time. His difficulty is taking his best swing and play to the course. I hope you can get something out of this experience, Geoff."

It was a fifteen-minute drive to the course. We parked in the back near the practice range. Joe was a classic trunk slammer—he seemed to have an aversion to locker rooms and clubhouses. We changed our shoes on the tailgate of his truck.

Burlington's friend John was warming up on the practice tee a few yards away. He noticed us and waved for us to put our clubs on the golf cart parked behind him. As I watched John at the end of his warm up, he was striping it directly to his target with a driver. Joe asked me to wait while he greeted John. I realized Joe wasn't going to warm up. They spoke for a few seconds and then approached; Joe introduced us. John shook my hand gently and smiled. He was a diminutive middle-aged guy in good physical shape. His wavy hair had a hint of silver and receded a little under his cap.

John trotted to his cart and hopped in. Burlington took his clubs from my cart and placed them on John's. I would be riding along with them separately to observe. We drove over to the first tee. Burlington took out his driver and put his ball on a wooden peg at the championship markers. After a couple of practice swings, he drove the ball beautifully on a medium trajectory a long way down the middle. So ready and true to form right out of the box. Joe swung as though where the ball ended up was no big deal.

John also made some practice swings. They looked good to me—smooth and with fine shape. John chattered to Burlington while he was swinging, bringing Joe up to date on mutual friends. Both were refreshingly casual. But then their chat stopped and John began what turned out to be a long routine. His face became serious. I could see he had tensed up. He circled the ball tightly as though he was going to ambush it or catch it off guard. He got into his setup, looked down the fairway, and made one last waggle of adjustment.

Just then, a man drove a mower down the far side of the fairway a good distance off. This caused John to halt his routine. He had to start the whole thing again. Burlington waited patiently. John set up to the ball and took careful aim, but then stopped at the ready point again—this time because Burlington said, "Let 'er rip."

If it continued this way, we were never going to get off the first tee! After the third time through the routine, you could hear a pin drop. All of nature seemed to suspend itself for a moment so John could make his swing. Finally he did so, but with an action that did not remotely resemble his practice swing. The ball sailed way to the right. It caught a tree and dropped into the water hazard. John was into his pocket for a mulligan and looked very distressed.

Joe stopped him with a wave. John seemed utterly drained by the emotional energy expended on swinging the driver on the first tee. And this was only the first hole! Here was a golfer who knew what he wanted in a golf swing, but something always happened to interfere. Fear and tension nearly paralyzed him; even his breathing seemed difficult.

John walked slowly off the tee and joined Burlington in the cart. We all just sat there as Burlington began to interview him. "How long has this been going on, John?"

"A long time. Did you see that? I felt like it wasn't even me in my own body."

"I noticed," said Burlington.

"What can I do about it? Is there any hope?"

"There's always hope, big guy, but you're experiencing one of the toughest problems in golf. All golfers face it from time to time. Fear, I mean. John, let me ask you a few questions." There was that trademark pause. "Right before you swing, what are you thinking about?"

"Well, I have lots of thoughts, and then I go blank."

"Give me a concrete example."

"I think about swinging on a good path. I think about closing the face because I would like to draw the ball, and I figure if I get into a routine, I can be more consistent."

"Anything else?"

"Well, I try to swing with a good sense a rhythm."

"Is that all?"

"To be honest, I think of so many things at different times in my sequence that it would be hard for me to list them all."

"OK. Let's begin at the beginning, John. Let me give you a formula a fine musician gives his students." He took out a pad and pen and wrote:

Performance = Your Potential – Your interference

Joe then explained the formula to John using the same musical analogy he'd used to describe it to me. "What this means is, if you have a particular potential, like you see in your practice swing, and if you don't get in your own way either physically or psychologically, your potential and your performance should match each other. Does that make sense?"

"It makes perfect sense, Joe. But how do I go about doing it?"

"Well, first off, we need to clear up the interference."

"I thought that's what my routine would do."

"And you've probably seen it work from time to time. But you can't sustain it, because that's still not confidence—that intangible feeling and belief deep down that everything is OK and is going to work out well, an expectation of success. I've told you before, from the belief comes the action. The belief really does the performing, not your conscious effort. What's happening is that your mind is smart enough to know that the purpose of your routine is to get through the performance. Isn't that precisely the purpose of your routine—to stop the negative self-talk from interfering?" John nodded in agreement. "I believe your doubting mind is a clever fellow. It's as quiet as a mouse until you enter your actual swing with a ball on the first tee of the golf course. It's silent during the practice swing and on the practice tee. But just because it's silent doesn't mean it's not there. Just now it surely let you know that it's within you during your swing with a ball."

John nodded sadly and smiled in agreement.

"Your negative self has an attitude. When your negative self, harbored in your subconscious, figures out that you're playing a trick on it, it's insulted," Burlington said with a smirk. "It doesn't like to be shut out of your modus operandi so it plays a trick back on you. It lies in wait until after your routine is finished and then comes crashing out. You can execute your routine perfectly and try to convince yourself consciously that the simple plodding—step one, step two, etcetera, etcetera—will enable you to cha-cha-cha on the course. But your negative self-belief still has time to show up. Routine is a short-lived fix and can never replace genuine confidence and belief. You need to obliterate the doubt with confidence. It's a daily thing. I think you need to keep working on your belief system, John."

"So I shouldn't use a routine at all?"

"Not to replace confidence. You need to develop genuine confidence. That's the rock to build your game on. It's connected to the belief that you can successfully deliver the club time and again. It's the belief in a successful impact!"

Again, a truth I'd never heard, explained in one sentence.

"How do I do that?" John asked.

"There are many strategies."

As I sat in the cart and listened to this conversation, I noticed one thing this student had going for him, even though he was in a bad state golf-wise: a humble and open attitude. He was disappointed, but not angry or pointing fingers at himself or anyone else. He wanted to begin to solve his problems and was open to suggestions.

"Joe, we've known each other for a long time and I still can't understand why I don't get into the groove and have that confidence. After working with you, I'm OK for a while, then everything seems to go to pieces."

After a short pause during which Joe seemed to contemplate his friend's predicament, he began. "Let's begin with just two strategies that we can couple together to get you out of this funk. The important thing to know is you have to maintain your confidence daily."

"I can't wait," John said with just a trace of sarcasm.

"OK, to begin with, we'll attempt to elevate your confidence through visualization exercises. Go back up to the first tee and with your practice swing, picture the ball's perfect flight. Don't leave until you feel the ball would have flown where you wanted it to go."

John went up to the tee, driver in hand, and made several swings. He appeared satisfied, then began to put a ball on a tee. Joe stopped him in his tracks.

"What are you doing?"

"I'm going to hit one."

"No! Just put a tee in the ground, make a swing, and *visualize* where it goes."

"You mean don't hit a ball?"

"That's right."

I could see John was a little taken aback. "Let me understand you: You do not want me to hit a ball."

"Correct." Joe said.

John made another swing and Joe asked him to visualize where it ended up. He said, "OK, I got it."

As we drove down the fairway to the imaginary ball, I asked Joe, "I thought you needed to let go of the target to get to it."

Joe shook his head and smiled. "Only when the target is the obstacle. You need to find out if the target is attractive and positive, or negative. If it's not a negative and it's not interference, then you use it to your student's advantage. Visualizing the complete flight of the ball to the target could create the best swing too. Every case is different, Geoff; you need to find out what the interference is or what the best mental focus is for each individual." He turned to John. "Now where did you picture your invisible ball ending up, John?"

"I thought it would be back here in the right rough."

"OK, let's go there." We drove to where John said he pictured it landing. Joe asked him, "What club would you use from here?"

"I would swing a six iron since we're at about 160 yards," John offered.

"OK, make some swings. When you get the feeling you want to hit the shot, go ahead and make the swing."

"Without a ball again?"

"That's right," Burlington confirmed. John looked puzzled, but he trusted Joe. He did it again.

"Where did it go when you made that swing?"

"A little short and right again."

"Are you noticing a difference in the feeling of a practice swing and the actual swing?"

"Yes, and I can't figure it out. Why are they so different?"

"Interference, mister," Joe said with humor. "Don't worry, because before the day is out, you may be pleasantly surprised." We drove over to Joe's ball. He looked at the flag, pulled a club from his bag, and punched the ball under the wind directly toward the hole. He indicated it had landed about ten feet from the cup. Burlington smiled. "Lucky again."

Meanwhile John was approaching his third shot. He took a wedge. He was only about fifteen yards from the hole, but had to go over a bunker. He made a few preliminary swings first. The club went deep into the turf near where the impact would have been. John shook his head in disbelief and smiled. He walked into the bunker with his sand wedge to get the imaginary ball out. He made several more swings and then took one last one. This time, he walked near the hole with his putter and swung a few times before his final swing. He looked into the hole and grinned as he walked off the green.

Joe walked up to his putt and stroked it into the hole, completely nonchalant, as though he didn't even read the putt. "Is that all the time you take? You didn't even line it up." I asked him.

"Oh, I did, as I was walking. I didn't see a need to look any further, and, of course, I also got lucky!"

This was interesting. I would bet he hadn't played in a long time and yet he birdied the first hole and thought nothing of it. Right out of the box, he was ready to play. He jumped into the cart and we drove to the next hole, a long par four into the wind again. He had John go first, if you want to call it that—still no ball. John took a few swings and then one last one. He looked down the fairway. Joe asked him, "How was that one?"

"A little better," John replied, "but still to the right. More solid though."

"Good, John—you're beginning to let go."

"I can feel it both inside of me and out." He turned to look Joe in the face and said, "This is very strange, but I like it!"

Burlington got up, took one practice swing, and *wham!* He smashed it down the right side of the fairway.

"Nice shot," I said.

"Thank you," he said. "Almost."

This went on for the next few holes. Joe was basically driving down the fairways and onto the greens. When he missed one, he would just grin, and when he hit what I thought was a perfect shot, he invariably said, "Almost." Meanwhile, John was visualizing every shot and beginning to walk down the fairways and onto the greens in regulation. It was intriguing to watch. I considered that this guy had just paid about a hundred bucks to play this beautifully manicured course and, since the first hole, he hadn't hit a ball.

We came to the tenth hole, a long par four, into the wind again. It seemed that all the holes were into the wind, even though they were going in different directions. John got up first and made his practice swings. Just before he put the peg in the ground to hit his virtual ball, Burlington put a real ball on the tee for him.

"Now you want me to hit one?"

"That's right, John," Joe laughed good-naturedly.

John took a couple more practice swings and *wham!* He sailed one down the fairway a good distance. I couldn't help noticing that instead of looking sapped of energy and wilted, John looked energized. He was beaming and I laughed. It was a joyful golf shot!

John had made no conscious physical changes to his swing, yet through visualizing, in little more than an hour on the course, club in hand, his swing with the ball had completely changed—and matched his practice swing. It was a 'wow' moment for both of us.

Joe was happy too. He got up and hit a big hook into the left water. "Boy, that was a surprise!" he told us. "Concentration. I was so into your success, John, that I got complacent with my own. Oh well...." He teed up another ball and slammed it down the fairway. He said that was it, not an 'almost.'

For the last nine holes, John made all his swings with a ball. He hit them solidly and very much toward the target. I figured he was playing to his potential. I was amazed at the transformation. We finished the round and drove into the shade behind the eighteenth green.

"How do you feel, John?" Burlington asked solicitously.

"Like, let's go play again," John answered. "I can't believe how well I played those last nine holes—five pars and three birdies and one bogey! And I hit all the fairways and greens! I can't remember ever playing this way with such a feeling of confidence! The ball would go where I pictured and my swing would perform just as I'd practiced. I'm so excited, Joe. Thank you so much!"

"John, you had the potential all along. I didn't do anything to your swing. It just emerged when you lifted the bricks of disbelief."

"That's right! I feel a ton of weight has been lifted off my back. I feel light as a feather and energized." John did a happy dance to prove his point.

"Isn't it amazing, the power of visualization? It goes to show you that no matter how much stock you put into perfecting your swing and knowing your technique, it will rarely surface without you feeding your confidence, your trust, and your positive belief that things are going to work out. You must obliterate the doubt, and this is one way to smash it out of your system. It all has to happen in tandem. So can you go to the bank with what you've done here today?"

"Definitely. You've made a believer out of me! I can see that visualization of success and preparing for it by feeling and trusting are the missing tools for playing the game. It seems that combining that with the feeling of the swing is what I needed, more than knowledge of the golf swing," John said.

"You're obviously physically capable of making the swing you want, John. You could feel it in your practice swing, right? But in that instant between practice routine and the actual swing, what was happening? Just going back to the practice tee and not addressing what's happening between your practice swing and your actual swing is not dealing with it. If you keep doing the same things, expecting the results to change, well, that's a little insane. You've spent umpteen years practicing your technique. You needed to spend more time developing your positive belief instead.

"I'll tell you what, let's pretend you never get to practice again." John and I both looked at him with questioning eyes. He laughed again. "I mean working on your swing, fellas. You can't practice that, but you can play every day. Therefore, to practice now means to play. You would need to rely not on your swing technique, but rather on your belief, positive pictures, and your own feeling. You have enough experience in golf to do that. You have enough swing feel. It may surprise you how often you hit good shots that match your practice swings when you believe. Isn't it more fun this way, too?" Burlington smiled and winked, but soon became serious.

"Have you heard the tale of the American POW who was held in solitary confinement for seven years in a tiny underground cell? And the only way he could keep from going crazy was to find something to occupy his mind day in and day out."

"Yeah," I said. "I think it made the email rounds a few years ago." John nodded as well.

"Right. It's been retold in a couple of books too. The story goes that this POW had played golf, but he'd never broken eighty. So he decided to play golf in his head. He figured it would be the perfect activity to take up time and keep his mind off the hopelessness of his situation. Taking about four hours per round, he would mentally play golf on his home track just as if he were physically on the course.

"Many times he played thirty-six holes. He would take his time, imagining every step he took, from tees to greens, even to the point of tying his shoes. He would visualize everything, the hills, the slopes, the sky, the trees, the blades of grass, and especially the swings he made and the shots he hit. It was an incredible experiment in visualization! They say that when the POW was finally released at the end of the war, one of the first things he did when he got home was play a round of golf on his home course. The first round he played, he shot seventy-four, his personal best! Remember, he hadn't physically picked up a club in more than seven years!" Burlington's face lit up from telling this story.

"No one's been able to verify that this story is true, but legends exist because they provide valuable lessons. We just can't underestimate the power of the mind. This man's visualization was so deep and was sustained for so long that his belief system accepted what he created in his mind as reality. When he returned home, it came to pass—the laws of attraction, like a self-fulfilling prophecy! We can all learn from that.

"Of course I'm not suggesting that you go seven years picturing your swing before you play. But maybe you need to do a daily visualizing practice for a few minutes in conjunction with your physical swing practice. When you address the belief system, you can attain your full potential and it emerges like the sun rising over the water every day. The beauty of it is that we can access it through visualization, which comes easy to most of us. We can do it anywhere, at any time. You just got a little dose of it. Kind of neat, eh? From belief comes action."

John was smiling and nodding. He had just seen his potential emerge on those last nine holes and he was eager to go again. As for me, it was proof positive that I needed to adopt a program that involved elevating the belief system along with fundamental swing-feel therapy for my students. I had to find a way to obliterate the negative and to teach my students methods that would help dissolve their fear of failure.

If I'd been instructing John, I know I would have begun adjusting his swing right from the beginning on the first tee. That would have created confusion from the start and it would have turned out to be a bum day for both of us. Now I had a good idea of how to go about getting a swing that seemed to transform instantly from practice to actual. When we had said goodbye, John couldn't hide his enthusiasm to get out on the course to play more holes—a much different scenario than I could have imagined had I been teaching him with my old methods!

30
REFLECTING ON MY FUTURE

Burlington needed to get back to the golf center, but I wanted to know more about strategies for developing confidence. So as we got going on the highway, I asked Joe about it.

"It's difficult for people to understand because a belief doesn't have to be based in logic," he explained. "But those who lack confidence need to begin somewhere. If they have no positive experience, they can't get confidence from their past, right?"

"Right. I'd always questioned why I lose my confidence. It never seemed to be sustainable."

"Yes, that's the most common problem, Geoff. It seems unsustainable because we fail to do preventive maintenance on it, the way we do with our swings or, for that matter, our houses and cars, our health, our relationships or anything else."

Instantly a chord was struck deep in me. Claire. I was taken aback for just a second; had he read my mind again? Did he know I had neglect in me?

But he continued. "It's like taking care of a garden. You can have the best plants in the world, but if don't take care of them, if you don't water them and you let weeds grow, the weeds flourish and your plants are choked out. It's the same with your confidence. All I'm saying is confidence and trust are like any relationship. You need to make a commitment to keep taking care of it. You need to nurture it with visualization, positive mind-talk, sound physical practice, and on-course practice therapies. You need them all.

"We tend to pass over the trust because trust seems so intangible. But we know it's there because it reveals itself on the course every time we swing. We need to do thorough preventive maintenance in our minds."

I pushed thoughts of Claire away and asked, "How much time do you spend each day visualizing success?"

"Picturing success in every situation is my method," he told me.

"Then how often do you use mind-talk to build your belief?"

"I have to work on it daily. Tell yourself a hundred or a thousand times a day for, let's say, a month that your golf swing is great and you're a great golfer. Even if you're not, you will begin to remove doubt. You see, the belief system can change without a physical demonstration of change. You will believe the thing to be true even though your action may not support it yet. 'Act as if.' The belief can precede the experience and then the action has a chance to improve and be sustained. At least with this approach, you won't be in your own way before you begin your practice—that is, when practice is appropriate.

"Then, of course, once you believe, you need to execute the due diligence to support the belief. That's basically the sequence you must incorporate when you start from a negative experience, Geoff. It's exactly how you can pry yourself from a rut. So often we spend time believing that things are not going to work out and then we're surprised when they don't. The starting point is not the physical practice, but rather the mind practice. That gives the physical an opportunity to follow suit."

I could see myself—and I guessed that pretty much all golfers could see themselves—doing things just the way Burlington had described. Every time I had problems in my play, I would just go and hit dozens of balls without addressing my confidence. In fact, I would practice to not get worse and embarrass myself. I could see clearly how backwards, mentally, that type of practicing was. I had never felt ready because even though I practiced hard, I never developed confidence and trust in myself. I had never spent time obliterating the negative and building the positive in my mind. Even if my swing was perfect, I couldn't perform at my best because I only played with half my resources—a body, but no mind, no confidence. If you played football that way, it would be like having five men against eleven.

I was lost in my thoughts as we neared the golf center. It was getting toward dusk, the sun slowly sinking into the horizon. "Geoff, let's go down to the shop. There's one more thing I want to discuss with you. It's the main ingredient for success or fulfillment—my master key. It's what makes life easy and teaching most effective." I nodded eagerly for him to continue. "There's one last quality you must acquire, if you don't already possess it, or should I say, have not let it emerge. One more thing you must do."

I'd been here for days and he's bringing this up now? We went into the shop. He turned on the lights, retrieved the coffee from the morning, and heated it in the microwave. I removed some of his tools from the table to make room and wiped it clean with a shop towel. He poured the hot coffee into fresh cups and we took our seats. He took a slug of coffee and with an uncharacteristically serious look on his face began speaking very slowly and deliberately.

"The final quality you must have is an *agape* love in all your relationships and a special love for yourself, too."

What, I wondered, is *agape* love?

Joe continued, "Everything else worthwhile will come from that. You must care for yourself, and that does not mean being selfish. You could have all the knowledge, all the strategies you have learned this week, and all the experience in the world, but without love, you will never be able to share it the way it needs to be shared. You will not evolve and grow into being your best self without it. This kind of love is essential for you to become a complete coach. You need to be willing to take a good honest look at yourself daily, based on love, and adjust if you need to.

"You know, Geoff, it may be important that you develop *agape* love first, before you resume coaching. You must implement all the strategies you've learned this week, and by being self-caring you can help others help themselves. But it is this *agape* love, where the purpose is supporting another person's quest to be their best, that is central in the end."

I was a bit shocked at his choice of a subject. When I caught up, I realized Burlington was talking about the type of care that serves our needs and then naturally others. I thought I kind of understood that; I felt I had that.

"This caring nourishes your students and you in a whole different way, Geoff." Then again, maybe it was all too deep for me. Burlington picked up on my discomfort. "It feels awkward because it's not the norm to address this aspect of teaching or coaching. But it ought to be. If I didn't love myself, I could not care for you, and the lessons you learned from me would be tainted. They would be filled with how I do things rather than how you need to go about them. *Agape* love allows you, as a teacher, to focus on the student, not on you. How could I help you, or for that matter why would I want to, if I didn't care for you? What I'm getting at is that it's impossible to care for others before you care for yourself," he declared.

I gave him the nod to continue. "This *agape* love is an integral part of communication and a healthy quality in any relationship—especially a teacher-student relationship. This quality will allow you to really enjoy the differences in each of your students and to endure as an instructor. It will create openness in your teaching so you'll be fearless. You'll never be blinded by your success or experience. Forgive me, Geoff, but I feel a need to emphasize this point. It is crucial, so it needs to be indelibly imprinted on your mind, if our time and experiences together are to last."

"OK," I agreed, as I was beginning to get the point.

"You must have real self-caring to teach. It's a simple principle. When you care for yourself, I mean deeply appreciate all your gifts, when you feel real warmth, then you can be at peace. When you're at peace, you have clarity. Then it becomes easy to clearly see the path your students need to take to elevate their awareness and reach their own potentials. A student can feel this caring and begin to trust you and let down their guard so that everything is exposed. Then there's no mask and you get exactly what you see."

He surprised me by pulling a leftover donut from the bag on the table and handing it across to me. It was the last one. I took it, but held it, thinking it belonged to Otter, who didn't care two woofs if it had my fingerprints on it. Burlington resumed his reflection.

"My mother-in-law was that way, Geoff. She was a woman with a deep faith, strength, and endurance. She lived a very simple life, especially after her husband died. She was also a great teacher, teaching by example. She did things in a manner that never imposed anything of herself on anyone. I would say that she lived in a state of grace. You see, a person who is self-caring loves who they are. Their words always come from a good place. These are the people you can trust and they're the people you can learn from the most. They have no need for pretense because they're very secure in who they are and what their purpose is in life." Burlington's voice took on a serene tone when he spoke of his mother-in-law. How unusual, I thought, for a man to admire his mother-in-law so openly. She must have been an amazing woman.

"In the few years I knew my wife's mother," he continued, "I came to understand and love her in a very special way. I had the utmost admiration for her. She was a very spiritual person, too. She said her peace came from a deep faith and from a deep sense of God's love for her. But you see, Geoff, she couldn't have lived the way she did and been the way she was without it being inside her. Everything she did was an outgrowth of what was inside her. She had a deep self-love, true self-caring, and it permeated everything she did. It follows that if you are at peace with yourself, then you will have clarity and really be able to help others, or at least give them an accurate perspective on things."

"So that's how teaching and love go together? You seem to have a totally different perspective on things, Joe, right down to the last drop," I said as I finished my coffee.

"Thank you. The beauty and elegance is in the simplicity of it all, my friend."

I realized that as much as I wanted to, I couldn't copy what I saw in Joe Burlington. I needed to become my best self from within and maybe then I would become the teacher I wanted to be. Better yet, the person I aspired to be.

But Joe wasn't finished. "This love must permeate every fiber of what you teach, Geoff, and it must always be in your communication. You cannot exhibit this quality without it being authentic. It cannot be faked. You cannot buy it, you just must *be* it.

"I have developed strong feelings about communication and the direction it's going in our culture. They say we communicate better now than ever before. But it is very superficial. Take e-mail and text messages. They're instant, but often like Morse code—not complete and rarely with any emotion. We have high-speed communication, but it has become less and less soulful. We have gotten so far away from communicating on a deep level. We rarely take time to find out what's really happening in the lives of those we deal with. We hardly write good letters anymore or take the time to really put something down that comes from our hearts. Letters are becoming a lost art form." I felt the weight of my cell phone in my pocket and thought about how I used it.

"Students of golf have become that way too with the new technological advances. That was my point earlier about the direction instruction has gone—more information, but less ability to play and enjoy by feeling. As a teacher, it's important for you to find out your students' thoughts and feelings. You need to know what's going through their minds because those things manifest themselves in their swings. If you see the inside clearly, then you have a good shot at adjusting the physics.

"That's why, when you asked me about the most important aspect of teaching, I knew right away what it was to me: listen and observe. Pay attention and do it in a loving way," he advised. "Your best teaching must come from the heart. You must love the discovery actions of your subject. You need to love your students and communicate that to them. It really helps the process.

"That reminds me, Geoff. I have something I'd like you to read."

"Of course," I said.

"It's a letter from the Civil War era. I think it might get my point across better than anything I could say."

He went to his standup toolbox and rummaged through an upper drawer. "Here it is." He pulled out a creased sheet of paper. "This letter was written at the beginning of the Civil War. It's an unbelievable communication from the heart. I copied it down from that Civil War series on PBS a few years ago.[11] It was written by a soldier from Smithfield, Rhode Island, a major in the second Rhode Island Volunteers. He was on the front lines at the first battle of Bull Run in Virginia. His name was Sullivan Ballou. He handed the page to me. "Wait, let me get my instrument and I'll play a tune to go with it." He got his fiddle from a cupboard and pulled it from its case. As he chinned the violin and adjusted his bow, he said, "This way you'll get the full effect."

This was getting a little too far out for me, but by now, I was kind of used to it. There we were, two grown men in a workshop, Burlington playing the fiddle and me reading a letter written over 150 years ago. And this was a lesson in teaching golf. If the other pros could see me now, they'd think we both were crazy. But by now I trusted Joe and knew better than to doubt his judgment. If he thought this would help me get more in touch, I was willing to go along.

He began to play and I put on my reading glasses and began to read aloud. His fiddle had a deep tone and the sound echoed off the walls and concrete floor of the barn. Burlington played softly, beautifully, and slowly at first. The music was exquisite, but seemed very sad. As I read I could tell the letter obviously came right from the bottom of the soldier's heart, yet my own heart was not in it; I was uncomfortable.

Joe stopped playing. "You're not listening to yourself read. You're going to miss the meaning. Slow down; hear yourself. Speak softly from your heart, Geoff."

So I started over, much slower, and the words began to take on new meaning. It felt as if this soldier was right there with us. I could feel my throat begin to tighten. There was so much love in this letter, and regret, too. This soldier knew he would never lay eyes on his wife and children again. It made me think of Claire.

I could picture Sullivan Ballou trying to write under the dim light of a candle on a dark, muggy summer evening. He had managed to pour all he was feeling into this letter. My voice began to crack as I continued to read. I couldn't remember ever feeling this way while I read something.

July the 14th, 1861, Washington, D.C.

Dear Sarah,

The indications are very strong that we shall move in a few days, perhaps tomorrow. And lest I should not be able to write you again I feel compelled to write a few lines that may fall under your eye when I am no more.

I have no misgivings about or lack of confidence in the cause in which I am engaged, and my courage does not halt or falter. I know how American civilization now leans upon the triumph of the government. And how great a debt we owe to those who went before us through the blood and suffering of the revolution. And I am willing, perfectly willing, to lay down all my joys in this life to help maintain this government and to pay that debt.

Sarah, my love for you is deathless; it seems to bind me with mighty cables that nothing but omnipotence can break and yet my love of country comes over me like a strong wind and bears me irresistibly with all those chains to the battlefield. The memories of all the blissful moments I have enjoyed with you come crowding over me and I feel most deeply grateful to God and you, that I have enjoyed them for so long, and how hard it is for me to give them up and burn to ashes the hopes, the future years when, God willing, we might still have lived and loved together, and see our boys grown up to honorable manhood around us.

If I do not return, my dear Sarah, never forget how much I loved you, nor that when my last breath escapes me on the battlefield, it will whisper your name.

Forgive my many faults and the many pains I have caused you. How thoughtless, how foolish I have sometimes been. But oh, Sarah, if the dead can come back to this earth and flit unseen around those they love, I shall always be with you on the brightest day and the darkest night always, always, and when the soft breeze spans your cheek it shall be my breath, or cool air your throbbing temple it shall be my spirit passing by.

Sarah, do not mourn me dead, think I am gone, and wait for me, for we shall meet again.

Joe stopped playing a few seconds after I finished reading the letter. We sat quietly for a few moments.

I now knew what I had to do to reach Claire. I would finish the letter I had started. The music and the letter had captured me. It was as if Joe had planned it all along. I didn't know what to say. Of course, Burlington was perfectly content to say nothing. I took a deep breath, "That was beautiful."

"Thank you."

"How long have you been playing?"

"I've been studying for years, but I'm just now learning to play music," he replied.

"What do you mean?"

"I mean with feeling from within, from the heart. Exactly how you will learn to teach golf, Geoff, if you open yourself up. How would it feel if you could get that deep during a golf lesson?"

"I don't know. It would probably take a lot out of me."

"Yes, but it would give you the feeling that your time was well spent, and the student would feel that way too. They would really know you cared. That's very important. And it only takes a few minutes to do...."

"However, I don't love my students the way Sullivan Ballou loved his wife..."

"Of course not, but you want badly for them to know you care. It's the depth that counts, right?"

"Yes, it is, but it's still just a golf lesson."

"Ah, that is where we differ. Yes, it is a golf lesson. But it is also your life and their lives and we need to get the most out of every moment. For the lesson to be memorable and lasting, the experience needs to be deep."

"How do I achieve that?"

"Well, look at what we just did. Will you ever forget this moment, you reading and me playing? You need to be creative and figure it out for yourself. The feeling you got inside, if I read you right, was very deep. You need to find your way," he said quietly.

"No, I won't forget this time..." I was choking up, to my great surprise.

Joe continued. "There were a lot of different types of love in that letter—the love of spouse, children, and country. It's timeless, isn't it? All you need to do is figure it out." Then Joe slapped his knee, breaking the solemnness, and said, "Well, that's it. You have the strategies, the confidence in yourself, and everything you need until we meet again. That is, unless you have more questions for me?"

Of course I had more questions, but I was speechless and just let out a big sigh. He noticed my pause but didn't say anything. I was really affected, but felt drained, physically and emotionally. This lesson was exactly what I needed, the last piece of the puzzle. I felt I could go on and help myself and progress on solid fundamental ground. More, I felt ready for life, ready for life with Claire.

If she would only give me a second chance.

As he was putting his fiddle back into its case, Joe said, "You know, it's late. You want to get something to eat?"

"I don't want to intrude."

"No intrusion; I'm alone tonight. I know a place in Deerfield that has great seafood."

"Sure, I'd love that, but I feel a little grungy. Do I have time to take a shower?"

"Of course. I need to get cleaned up too. Let's meet there at 7:30. The place is called the Whale's Rib."

"I'll find it on my GPS." "Great. We can talk about anything else you may have on your mind over supper."

31
DINNER

I felt privleged to be having dinner with Joe. As I drove north, the sun was setting out my left window in a kaleidoscope of soft colors. Purples, yellows, and pinks were strewn across the scattered clouds on the horizon. I was beginning to appreciate all that was going on around me in a new way. In the past, such a sunset would have escaped me.

The restaurant was a hole in the wall. Some may have called it rustic; to me it seemed more worn out, like the hotel in Flamingo. Old nets and fishing gear were hung to the walls. The lighting was dim and the patrons were working-class locals, for sure. It was noisy and crowded. Joe had beaten me there. He had snared a booth toward the back. I wormed my way through the tight tables to his corner. Joe had already ordered himself an Irish Red. He caught the waitress's eye and a beer landed in front of me almost instantly as I took my seat opposite Joe. It was good, full-bodied beer with a nice head in a frosted mug.

"How did you know?" I asked.

"Just guessed," Burlington said.

"My dad used to brew beer just like this. It always brings back memories." We lifted our glasses together over the thickly varnished table.

Joe made a toast. "Cheers," he said, "and a long and healthy life."

"What a day we had. I can't tell you how satisfying..."

"Yes, it was great," he said. "I forgot how much fun golf can be, and John's great breakthrough makes it all worthwhile, eh?"

The waitress returned to our table to take our order. I hadn't even looked at the menu, so I looked at Joe for suggestions. He took the cue. "How about some fresh cod and chips and a little salad?"

"I guess you want the special, Joe?" the waitress asked with a wry smile. "It seems to me you'll never get out of this cod rut."

"Yeah, well, when I find something good, I stick with it. I prefer to call it a good groove." The waitress smiled, shook her head and was off.

I collected my thoughts about all Joe's lessons before I spoke. The thought that kept ringing in my mind was how quickly he developed a rapport with his students. I wanted to know how I could do that. Besides the level of trust he established in each lesson, this whole business of being able to see oneself while swinging intrigued me. I had been taught that the one reason to have a swing coach was because you *couldn't* see yourself. So I asked Joe about the 'seeing oneself' trick. "How does it work? I mean, how can it be taught?"

He took a swallow of beer before he began. "It goes back to what I've been getting at since our first day together and, for that matter, what I tried to do at that seminar. We all need to evaluate ourselves continuously to really keep evolving and progressing, right?" His voice hushed and it was hard to hear him in the noisy room. I leaned into the center of the table. I needed to hear and understand every word.

"The beginning of the lesson for a teacher of this method is silence. The teacher must have the wisdom not to superimpose his beliefs on the students. He must let them make the trip to awareness, only showing them the openings. Let them decide whether they want to enter a new and different place within themselves. At this point, the only activity of the teacher is to get to know the students. Students will pick up on this and begin to feel safe. That is the beginning of trust; letting go can follow. Even defensive students will be disarmed and the teacher will have no masks to sort through. It really makes the experience rewarding for all.

"You, my friend, must become an expert at listening and hearing. It is the listening that allows me to make good choices. You should say nothing at first. Allow students to learn to listen to themselves, which is ultimately the goal, right? You could begin by mirroring back to them exactly what they said to you so they can hear for themselves what they have said. This way they usually won't become defensive, which is to everyone's advantage.

"The spaces between the notes are an integral part of music," he said. "In conversation, the spaces between your remarks are as important as the words themselves. That's what I call absorption time—time for the transformation within the student to take place." He lifted his beer again.

"Remember when you asked me for a roadmap?[12] An sage once said, throw away the map; teach in a manner that allows enough freedom, creativity, and awareness for the students' sense of direction to become needle sharp. That way, when they really get going, they can travel without a map. They will never be lost. That's another reason why golf should never be reduced to analysis alone. In fact, that's why I so strongly object to video. It's so easy to misuse, and it lends itself to reducing the necessity of the students to develop their feel keenly. The lessons need to embody the actions of the students and their responses. And time is essential for it all to take place."

I felt like a bobble-head doll, nodding in agreement. But I returned to my original question. "How do you teach someone to see themselves?" Burlington swallowed the last of his brew. With a satisfied look on his face, he took a big breath and exhaled. Only then did he begin to speak.

"Let me tell you of an experiment I tried with a young student of mine. He's a good illustration of learning to see yourself as you swing. One summer long ago, young Al came down from Canada to work with me. He was a great student, a total pleasure to be with. We did everything together. We worked, we played, we practiced, we ate. To tell you the truth, I don't remember a moment during his stay that was not just right. He became a good friend of my wife, too." Joe paused while the waitress set down heaping plates of food.

"One day we were working on his swing path. I had described all kinds of ways for him to improve, but he still struggled. He was having trouble translating what I was saying into swing improvement. And he was hard to read because he wanted my advice to work so badly that he wouldn't tell me what he couldn't understand. But this day he finally blurted out, 'I just can't see it!' I was a little shocked, but really it was exactly the feedback I needed to help him move forward. A light clicked on.

"I told him to wait a minute while I ran down to the barn. I soon returned to the tee with the old Ford loader and asked Al to get into the bucket. With no hesitation he hopped in and knelt down. I slowly lifted him about fifteen feet in the air. Then I engaged the parking brake and got down. I grabbed my driver and attached an orange streamer to create a four-foot trail behind the club as it swung. I set up to the target and began swinging directly beneath him." Joe paused to let me absorb the picture.

I looked up at Al during my swing and saw understanding come to his face. He could now clearly see not only the orbit of the club travel but also the relationship of the swing path, the target, the ball, and me. Changing his point of view had shown what words and other demonstrations had failed to make clear.

"For Al to see things differently, I'd needed to make an indelible impression in a different way. Next I asked him to close his eyes and see if he could picture the pattern. And he could. When I brought Al back down from the loader bucket, he picked up his driver, anxious to show me what he'd learned from his new perspective. He'd gotten it! Next, I asked him to close his eyes again and hit a shot, feeling his swing form the picture he had in his mind. I needed him to elevate his reliance on his proprioceptors rather than his physical eye." Joe gave me one of his winks to remind me of the keystone science behind his method.

"I wanted Al to truly sense what was going on out of his sight and at a speed his physical eye couldn't pick up. I knew if he could use his sense of feel, his mind's eye first, he would have three tools to work with to elevate his awareness for his swing pattern. There was no way he could go wrong with that much redundancy. We all have beautiful awareness backup systems operating all the time, and they can be forced into action by shutting down the physical eye. Proprioception is inextricably linked to feel. It is an amazing tool to develop in any athletic endeavor. The proprioceptors are what send feedback to the brain, so we must find strategies that put them into action."

"You mean, muscle memory?"

"That's right."

I switched the dialogue back to Al. "Did it stay with him for the long haul?"

"It did. He began making swings at first with just fair contact. I would reinforce his feel development by asking him to continue feeling the swing and picturing it with his eyes closed. His brain accepted his ability to swing using his proprioception as the sole awareness tool. And Al marveled at the incredible accuracy of his swing feel for tee shots."

"Did you do anything else with Al?"

"I asked him to open his eyes and pretend they were closed when making a swing. He thought that was strange! It was a whole different mindset. Changing his point of view did the trick. Since then, Al has been able to picture his swing as though he were directly above himself.

"We practiced seeing from every viewpoint. I would move all around and ask, 'Can you see yourself now?' Finally he had all the views clearly in his head, and what an advantage he has had since! Video could never take the place of this technique. Video can be helpful, if used judiciously, but most often it's not. What could be better than having your own video going on inside your head whenever you want it? Now, Al could see from inside what was going on outside." Joe caught the waitress's eye with a small wave.

"So a golfer needs to be able to see himself. We always have this view available to us, we just need to access it, and you as an instructor need to use your creativity to show your students how to do that. We can all have twenty-twenty inner vision, in golf and in life, but we need to know how to focus our sight," he declared. The waitress set down another pair of beers.

Just then a dark-haired woman passed very close to our table. I lost my focus for a second and from nowhere Claire came to mind, catching me off guard. I was so ready now to turn my sights to her! Now that I was looking at us from the outside, I desperately wanted to get back in. I was visualizing us together on the beach outside the Pedersens' when Joe cleared his throat, probably noticing that I was somewhere else.

Burlington chuckled as he reminisced about his time with Al. "I would wait for Al to respond and he would wait for me, so we had these sort of silent standoffs. Then we would both burst out laughing. I wanted him to realize it was all in him, the change, I mean. And my purpose in teaching him, as with you or anyone else, is for me to become obsolete. Change most often needs to take place over time. Perfectionists, for example, in this culture don't really allow time for change and tend to view learning as an event rather than a process." I could see myself again as a young perfectionist and understood that that was a handicap and not something to be proud of.

"That idea tends to place a lot of pressure on them and they end up frustrated. They act as though the process is something they shouldn't have to deal with. Of course, that's a fatal flaw because it sets them up to give up. Then they come back for another lesson, and then give up again, and the cycle never ends. A waste of valuable time! Remember the point I was getting at during the seminar in New Orleans?"

"Yeah, Joe, those guys were such jerks," I said.

"That's not what I'm talking about. I really don't hold it against them. Their real problem was their unwillingness to be open. Those folks refused to let new ideas in or accept any point of view but their own. They've been taught to follow a set of rules that form a solid belief structure in their minds. Those beliefs are the foundation for the way they perceive things. This naturally tends to limit growth. Creativity is stifled and there can be no progress. This gap between perception and reality is obscured by unwillingness to take another look. My approach doesn't fit into that belief system, which limits the parameters of their life experiences and what they will accept as truth. So their teaching is sadly compromised by these rules."

"Doesn't it make you angry," I whispered. "How can their closed attitudes not affect you?"

But Joe got onto another tangent, not paying attention to my response. "There is plasticity to the wiring in the brain, though. It's a rather new discovery in neuroscience. It opposes the 'can't teach an old dog new tricks' mentality: You can if the dog is willing! Willingness allows that plasticity to come alive. Our minds can blaze new trails down the neurological ski slope at virtually any time in our lives. You can build a new belief system. That makes life exciting, doesn't it? And new experiences allow new pathways to form in our brains, allowing us to constantly evolve for the better. This doesn't only happen in golf, it happens in life too, don't you agree?" I nodded. "Anyway, that's what I think."

"I still don't get how you can be so detached from the way you were treated in New Orleans. They didn't give you a chance to even introduce your ways..."

He waved his hands, "Geoff, it's no use getting caught up in that. But you're right, detachment requires a lot of practice." He added, "I don't take myself too seriously. I'm constantly laughing at myself; there's so much to learn and most of it is about ourselves!" He paused to chuckle. "Only when we step outside ourselves can we have some inkling of what's really going on. This is why I attempt each day to start with a beginner's mind. I understand professional dancers do it all the time when they begin rehearsing a new piece. They begin by first learning to walk again, the most fundamental way to begin. They're able to learn something from that starting point every day, often something that in the past escaped their attention—all because they begin from the beginning. It only takes a few minutes.

"Think about it, Geoff, and you'll understand why I was met with such resistance at the seminar. My remarks were so contrary to what that audience had perceived as traditional and acceptable. I was probably viewed as a golf heretic. They were uncomfortable with what I said because of their fear, and their reaction was typical of anyone feeling this way—very insecure. They discredited and labeled me. But I'm used to it; it really didn't bother me, except for the disappointment I felt for them."

Through the night we drank another beer accompanied by more of the all-you-can-eat battered cod. The dinner was delicious; Joe had made a good choice. And our conversation had covered a lot of ground. But it was now getting late and the room had gone quiet. There were only a couple of diners left and the wait staff had begun cleaning up.

I made a commitment to myself. I was determined that I would begin each day anew. Joe called the waitress over to see if it was too late for some coffee. She smiled and insisted the staff would be cleaning up for some time yet. "Have whatever you want Joe," she told him. "I know how you feel about our apple crisp." I glanced at Joe and could see he was succumbing. We had caught the warm aroma when the waitress had delivered a piece to a nearby table.

So over coffee and pie our conversation began anew. "Joe, what do you think about these world-class players who insist that they don't want to rely on timing?"

"I believe they're operating under the false impression that timing is something bad—some sort of complicated recovery system that only comes into play when the swing shape or speed gets out of whack. Timing is actually critical in a golf swing, just as it is in life itself. It's as critical a fundamental as there is, as you can imagine from the very precise hand and wrist action I've taught you, the cup and curl, and so on. No, in my opinion underestimating the value of timing is a grave error. This could really mislead the novice golfer attempting to improve the club face and angle awareness in the impact zone," he told me with a sorry shake of his head.

"I just don't understand how these great golfers can be so far off the facts as explained by you. Why don't more of them come around to your way of thinking?" I must have looked visibly confused. It seemed to me that Burlington's program should be as popular as it was successful, and I didn't understand why it wasn't.

"We could go on and on about their perceptions, but when something has been drummed into your head so firmly, it's difficult to change. Let's leave it at that. What I have imparted to you these few days is diametrically opposed to many of their views."

There was a pause in the conversation. I hesitated, because my next thought had taken me by surprise. But I jumped in. "Would you mind if I asked you for some advice, not on golf, but on a personal level? About my relationship, or lack thereof, with my former fiancée?" As usual, he said nothing at first, which allowed me to open the floodgates. I told him how he had opened my eyes not only in golf, but about life in general. I poured out descriptions of the great times Claire and I had enjoyed together, and then our recent troubles. I told him how I wanted to rekindle the relationship. I told him of my phone messages to Claire and my fear that she was spent of our relationship and that there was nothing left in her tank. I explained to him how my not being ready to make a decision had appeared as a lack of commitment. And on and on. When I finished, the moment was awkward until he broke his silence.

"Do you have a photo?"

"Of course." I went into my wallet, pulled out the picture, and handed it to him. It wasn't typical, almost a profile. She wasn't exactly smiling either, but it was my favorite. It showed her in a pensive mood. Joe studied the picture. He remained silent, apparently digesting my story. He seemed to be looking into the picture, not just at it. My mind began its insecure dance, wondering if I'd overstepped my bounds. I sat there inwardly reprimanding myself for taking such a bold step.

"Has she responded to your messages?"

"Not so far, no. That's what concerns me. No returned calls, no nothin'." I looked at him. "Who am I kidding? It's over."

"I don't know Geoff; it's hard to say. But she may surprise you. Looking at this picture, I feel an energy—it's unmistakable. It rings loud and clear for those who can sense it. From your description of Claire, I would say she is in touch. That's about all I can tell you." I was frustrated and uncomfortable just talking about it.

So I changed the subject and with ease he went with me. "Joe, something you said has struck a chord in me since the seminar. What did you mean when you told the pro, 'one should be careful how one defines success.' How do you define success?"

"In my mind, Geoff, the Lama had it right. Actually, philosophers have been practicing success down through the ages, just not this culture's brand of it." He paused as usual, looked down at the table, and slowly defined it in a manner that a five-year-old could understand. "It's simple, really. Success only has to do with relationships. It's very tightly woven there. To be successful, all you need to do is reduce suffering and increase joy, in every encounter.[13] Think about it: It's what we've been working on this whole time, because it all boils down to this. All you can be is your best self, and from day to day, be better than your previous self. That is your competition. That is all you can really control. After that, you have to let the chips fall where they may. Be true to yourself and, like Baryshnikov used to say, just be better than your previous self."

Joe's voice intruded into my thoughts. "Listen." He drank down the last drop of decaf. "It's getting late; let's meet again tomorrow morning for a few minutes and you can give Otter a proper farewell. I do have a few maintenance things to do, but why don't you come over for a bit before you head to the airport."

We got up from the table slowly and stretched. We had been there a long time. I took care of the bill. Joe thanked me and we walked out to our cars. As I opened the car door, I called over. "Joe, one more thing; I almost forgot." I took the cedar box from the front seat and handed it to him. "Here, this is for you."

"What's this?"

"It's a life box," I kidded. "You have given me new life." It was pretty dark where we were standing, so we moved under one of the parking lot lights.

As he opened the box a smile came over his face and he shook his head. "You needn't have done this, Geoff."

"I know, but I felt like it."

"An original Orvis bamboo fly rod. Nice!" I hoped this gave him some understanding of my appreciation. He unraveled the cloth case and one by one put the four pieces of the rod together. He took the rod in his left hand and lifted it as though he were going to cast. He beamed appreciation. "This is perfect, Geoff. Thank you."

"I knew you would put it to good use and appreciate it."

"That I will, laddie."

"Besides, it makes up for the rod I damaged on our fishing trip."

"It's better than that one." Joe seemed elated at the gift and that made me happy, too.

I told him I would indeed come by for a few minutes in the morning.

32
MY LAST NIGHT

I reflected on what had happened today and, for that matter, the past few days—especially this evening. Change was happening inside me. I could feel it bubbling up. It was a little unsettling, but it was positive. Joe Burlington was my example. Just being himself, never trying. As I had been told I would, I was learning naturally without really being aware of it. It felt unforced.

I drove along the A1A, the two-lane road built in the early 1940s that runs adjacent to the ocean along the whole east coast. The speed limit is very low and you can really appreciate the view of the ocean. I drove a little north and found a beautiful untouched stretch of beach with no condos or homes. I parked on the side of the road and made my way through the dunes to the water. I felt a need to stop for a moment, soak it all in, and count my blessings. Being in the midst of nature at its best only enhanced the deep sense of everything fitting into place.

I began to walk. It was dark and the moon was almost full. A few of the bright stars hanging in the sky still shone faintly. A glorious night! The ocean was calm and the splash of the waves touching my feet was in perfect rhythm. The tide was going out. I could feel a gentle breeze on my face coming off the ocean, and I experienced a special calmness, an assuredness that I didn't recall feeling very often, except when I was very young.

I wondered what Joe was thinking when he extracted tangible meaning from Claire's photo. She wasn't into surprises. No, this time his instincts were a bit off track. Even so, I wanted to believe, and my imagination leapt to dreams of making love with Claire on this very beach. And to the many good things I had absorbed these past few days. I was feeling them very deeply. I would have a whole new set of tools to work with when I left this place. I walked on and on along the shore, realizing this visit with Joe Burlington was no accident.

I was feeling that intangible confidence he'd spoken about. I thought about all the different situations I'd observed and been a part of from the beginning: the maintenance, mower repairs, and irrigation fixes; the fly fishing; the golf without a ball; and all the different ways Burlington had taught his students—and me. I still wondered how he could have so many interests and yet apparently be highly skilled in all of them.

I felt energized in a different way, as if I could move steadily forward and not ever run out of gas—like a steady barge on a river, or a freighter on the ocean. This new confidence was different. I used to be like a speedboat that ran fast—and then ran out of gas. Confidence would wane and I'd be running on fumes, then I'd stop altogether. This new slow and steady move in the right direction gave me the assurance that this growing feeling was not just a temporary success. I felt I could improve and sustain it, as though I had the strategies that would support me through whatever situation might arise. I knew then that I'd never have chronic golf problems again.

I returned to my car and headed back to my place. I had certainly gotten a lot more than I ever dreamed possible. Maybe I could come back too—that was in the back of my mind; perhaps another trip in a few months. Maybe even with Claire. My newfound confidence extended to her. I thought maybe if I could speak with her face to face, I could win her back.

I began to think through the next few hours and everything I needed to do before I left. Maybe I would leave one last message for Claire, hoping she wouldn't just press 'delete.' I needed to clean up at the B&B, but there wasn't really much to do, as I'd used little more than my bed and the kitchen. I'd pack my bags tonight so I could meet with Joe and say goodbye to Otter first thing. After that, I would go to the airport straight away. It was back to the cold; winter was still in full gear at home. I dreaded it, mostly because I would have to wait weeks to put this new program to use. That's life. But thank God I had a program now so I could look forward to this season. I just hoped somehow I could use the interim time to show Claire I was ready for commitment.

As I approached the Pedersens' I noticed a light on in my room. I was sure I'd turned them all off and locked the door before I left. I pulled into the drive and went to the front door. It was unlocked. I began to feel nervous. I went back to the car and got an iron from my golf bag, just in case. I walked into the house, trying to adjust my eyes to the darkened room. It didn't seem as though anything was out of place. I made a pass through the whole downstairs. Nothing.

I began to cautiously tiptoe up the stairs with my heart in my throat and my club over my shoulder, cocked and ready. I moved down the hall, and as I peered through the half-open door to my room, I saw that my reading light was dimly shining.

And then shock, relief, and finally disbelief poured over me. I lowered my club and breathed. Still in her jacket, Claire sat on the side of the bed reading the unfinished letter I had left on the small bedside table.

I froze again. I didn't know what to do. I wanted to know what was going through her mind. How did she feel about my letter? She sensed someone and turned. She looked beautiful. I still didn't move. I saw a tear rolling slowly down her cheek. Involuntarily I moved into clear view and she took a startled breath; I had scared her for an instant.

She let go of the letter and ran to me. Without a word, she clenched me in a hug. Our bodies melded together as I returned her embrace. The emotions were overwhelming. I tried to tell her what the letter meant; she looked up at me and gently placed her finger over my lips. She didn't need an explanation. We released. She wiped the tears away and said, "I've missed you, love." I was still unable to speak clearly. I just shook my head, but realized she knew the depth of my feelings. A flash of Joe passed through my mind. How did he know she would know?

After coming back to reality, I asked Clair if she wanted a glass of wine, coffee, or anything. "Wine," she nodded.

"Good. I have a couple of nice bottles of red downstairs for gifts to take back home. I'll be right back."

"No, you go downstairs. I need a few minutes to freshen up. I'll be down shortly."

I literally leapt down the stairs to the kitchen. I found glasses in the cupboard, uncorked one of the cabernets, and poured the deep red wine. I went into the living room with only the lights from the kitchen filtering through, placed the glasses on the coffee table and sat on the love seat, wondering and waiting. I took a deep breath. I was consumed by the thoughts firing through my mind. 'Take it easy,' I counseled myself.

I took a slow sip of wine, letting my taste buds absorb the flavor, hoping the wine would take effect and calm me down. But I didn't know if I should be calm. If I was going to be excited this is the excitement I preferred. The wine was full bodied and dry, just as Claire liked. A few more minutes passed, then I heard the creek of the old staircase. In the darkness I could just make out her outline as she stepped down the stairs barefoot in a lace-trimmed black slip, cut just above the knees. She came over and gave me a soft kiss. I handed her the glass and we toasted. I was still in the clouds.

"Geoff, I'm sure you know that coming down here goes against all my professional training. But something strong told me to come and I followed my intuition." She paused, smiled, then moved closer and caressed my unshaven cheek. "I can't tell you how many times my mind questioned this trip. But then I thought, sometimes in life, things aren't black and white. As much as I loved you, I really didn't understand you fully." I sat there silent. She continued, "Then I began listening closely to your messages. I realized that in making this trip you had made the right choice for yourself. Ultimately it may be the best choice for us as well. It's difficult to know. You know I rarely make exceptions. But now, you are my one big exception."

At that moment I felt total contentment welling up in me. It was something in a relationship that I don't think I had felt much, if ever, in my life. I felt known. When I thought about it, most of my friends didn't really know me. My siblings didn't know me, my parents really didn't know me. I knew they loved me, but they didn't *know* me. But now Claire did, and so did Joe Burlington. What else could I hope for? That was more than my share, a blessing of abundance. I felt I knew her too. I knew every curve in her face, her beautiful face, her voluptuous body, her loving heart, her pragmatic mind, and her strong sense of justice in this world.

She continued to explain her reentry into my life. "I didn't mean to barge in on you but when you left those messages about the changes taking place in you, good memories came rushing back. My feelings were so strong I knew I needed to come. I called the Pedersens and went and picked up a key. My plan was to surprise you." She looked sideways at me with a little curve of a smile.

"That you did."

"And then when I was about to closet my jacket, I saw your letter to me. I realized in an instant I had made the right decision. I could just feel a change in you. Whatever was happening to you was beginning to reveal itself, and it was a good change. I could tell it was authentic."

"You know, you sound like Joe."

"Really? I want to meet him."

"You will, tomorrow. I need to make one more trip over."

"Geoff, before, I was looking at our relationship as though you were the only one who needed to change, but in truth, we both needed some transforming. I think you found the right help in your guy." I nodded in agreement. We both took a deep breath and a long sip of wine.

I looked into her eyes and said, "I'm so glad you came. I didn't know if you would be willing to try for us again." She looked at me with consoling eyes and reached over and touched my shoulder to reassure me.

It was very late now. I motioned for us to go upstairs. I took a few minutes to take a quick shower while she readied the room and opened the windows to let in some fresh ocean air. When I returned, she had lit a candle and turned out the lights and there was soft easy listening on the clock radio. She was waiting for me in bed. I slid in next to her and realized I had forgotten how soft her skin was.

Before dawn I awakened to the sound of the waves slapping in rhythm against the dunes. I quietly went downstairs and made coffee. I came back to bed and lay there just enjoying my coffee and watching Claire sleep. It was a beautiful and peaceful sight. I felt content all over again.

Claire was a slow riser, but the smell of coffee always got her going. She yawned, stretched her arms, and opened her eyes. I kissed her good morning softly. "Have some coffee," I pointed to the cup I had placed on the table next to her. She loved her first cup of coffee.

After she'd taken a few sips, I looked at the clock and said, "I don't mean to rush you, but we haven't much time if we're gonna have breakfast and meet Joe before we catch our flight. She smiled back at me and didn't seem to register the time constraints the flight posed on our morning. "How about while you get dressed, I get everything closed up and packed in the car. We'll go down to Lou's, have breakfast, and I can tell you all about Joe Burlington."

Claire was able to get into high gear after that first cup of coffee. It was only a few minutes later—record time!—when she came down the stairs with her overnight bag and a suitcase. I couldn't imagine why she'd brought so much luggage. "Ready?"

She nodded. We locked up and took a brisk stroll down to Lou's. As we approached, the familiar smell of coffee, freshly baked bread and bacon filled the air.

We entered the diner and Lou greeted the two of us. He had a hard time hiding his surprise as a smile spread over his whole face. He came out from behind the counter to greet us. Claire gave him a hug and I shook his hand and gave him a half-hug. I could tell he was happy that Claire was with me. Seeing us together seemed to make his day. We took a booth in the back and ordered our usual. We were both in a state of mind not unlike that of a couple after the first night of their honeymoon.

"Tell me about your guy."

"What guy?" I smiled mischievously.

"Come on, Geoff," she said with playful eyes, "Joe!"

"OK, OK. Where shall I begin? You already know about the summit and what happened in New Orleans." She nodded. "And how I came to find him here in South Florida. So let me begin with the day I arrived at his golf center. You know how sometimes you can be overwhelmed by celebrities that seem larger than life? I mean, their persona. They have the looks, all the attributes, and the manner that go with being important in our culture. Well, Joe is *not* that guy! He is, at first, totally underwhelming. At least that's the first impression I got. He seems to be a regular guy who happens to be pretty good at teaching golf, but as you spend time with him, you realize your first impression was extremely shallow." I began to tell her about my adventure.

Claire sat captivated. "I could tell something was going on with you..."

I stopped her. "Claire, you were right all along. I needed to change. I knew it, I just didn't know how to go about it. I needed someone besides you to help me. I needed more than golf lessons, and guess what? I got more than golf lessons. I want to tell you everything but it's such a blur it's hard to describe."

"I can only describe Joe's golf center as a hole-in-the-wall range; it's here in Pompano Beach. To be honest, if you'd taken a look at the place you would have questioned it too. When I arrived something told me to get the hell out of there, but another voice followed and told me to stay. I listened; what did I have to lose?" I began to tell her of each day, describing everything that happened as it passed through my mind, as best I could remember. But mostly she wanted to know about Burlington and how he was able to get through to me.

"Actually, he didn't get through to me at all." She looked puzzled. "But he did show me how to get through to myself." She smiled and chuckled. "Claire, I don't know if I can adequately describe to you, or for that matter to anyone, what has happened to me these past few days—what it feels like to experience the gradual changes taking place within me. During this journey I believe I have moved toward some measure of enlightenment within myself, us, my golf game—in truth, life itself. The awareness I'm experiencing now isn't what I thought I was looking for or what I expected. But I like it. And now I know exactly what I need, and what's more, how to nurture it. Burlington made that infinitely clear. He shared things with me that I simply couldn't put into words."

"How so?"

"I can feel that elusive confidence that seemed so distant before and never lasted. I notice things in a different way." Her eyes livened as she seemed to picture what I was saying. I thought of Burlington and his technique; I still had a hard time categorizing him and it. He simply did not fit into any category. He wasn't a golf pro per se, he wasn't a guru, he wasn't like anyone I had experienced before. And now I was a totally different person. How could I explain all this to Claire? I just said, "Now I find myself coming from a wholly different perspective."

"Tell me more."

I paused, took a slug from my coffee cup, and tried to think of what to tell her next. "Well, for one, he predicted that you might surprise me."

She shook her head. "How would he know that? I decided to come here just yesterday; I didn't even know if I would go through with it until I fastened my seatbelt on the plane!"

"I only showed him a picture of you and described our relationship just last night. I don't know how he knew, he just did." We both just stared at each other in amazement for a moment before I continued.

"Let me tell you about his golf lessons. When he gives a lesson, there's none of the new technology that I use, no video, position models, and the like. His approach has no relation to the modern mechanistic golf world we know. When he begins a lesson, his first order of business is not about golf at all. He begins by finding out about his student's personality and experience. He establishes a rapport. Then he inquires about their golf problems from their perspective. Claire, it was nothing like how I used to conduct lessons! It's just him and his experience relating to a student—everything coming from within them and then within him.

"And he has a way with language. Words take on different meanings when arranged in his manner of speaking, and they seem to be exactly what his students need. He always seems to know what to say. It was like magic. Or...not magic, it was more mystical than magical. That's the word, he was like a mystic."

"A mystic?" Claire leaned in, intrigued.

"He has a timeless, mystical knowledge. I felt everything he did was done through an intuitive source deep within him and beyond reason." I had a flash of insight. Now realizing even more what Joe was about, I leaned in to tell Claire. "That's why, at first, his behavior and language seemed so strange and cryptic. He just comes from a totally different source than I was accustomed to. And there's no separation between how he lives life and teaches or plays golf. There is cohesion and connectedness. He relates golf and life to physics, believe it or not, in particular the aspect of that science that tells us all things are connected."

It was all pouring out of me now like water over a dam—I couldn't stop the flow. "And he made a big point about perspective, too, that attitude plays the major role in life and it doesn't matter what you do or where you are. Joe believes that what matters is who you are with and how you relate! Relationships are key, and I saw him demonstrating that a special love needs to permeate all encounters. He kept reminding me to recognize the holistic nature in all things." Poor Claire couldn't get a word in.

"To make his point about the physics of the golf swing he used a foam Pathfinder he designed and a tee as a pointer in a special glove. His philosophy for developing a swing was completely foreign to me. He kept emphasizing, 'Don't teach the individual parts; the whole creates the parts.'"

Claire's eyes encouraged me to explain more. "You develop the whole swing, and then the parts of a swing—the body's action—are a result of the student picturing, feeling, and knowing the complete action of the club. This way he can make it simple and not conflict anyone. Claire, he has turned the learning process upside down, or should I say right side up. He says there needs to be a paradigm shift. But he didn't just shift the paradigm, he flipped it.

"Do you know how I know that what he teaches is the truth? Because everyone got it, and no one was confused! Claire, I received an indelible imprint in my mind. Right now as I am telling you, as we sit here, I see even more clearly the purpose of everything that happened during the week." I shook my head and chuckled, looking downward and now smiling inside. "Anyway, after a few hours I was getting hooked. His message was clear. And it's a good message, Claire, it has a heart."

I reached across the table for her hand. "I want badly to live what he preached—no, he never preached, he expressed, laid it all out there and gave everyone a choice. I liked the freedom in his message." Her eyes showed me we had really connected on a different level this time.

I let go of her hand, took one last sip of my lukewarm coffee, and said, "We better go. We need to get there soon. No telling what he will be into." She drank down her last sip of coffee. I paid the bill, tipped the waitress, and we bid Lou farewell.

I drove faster than normal. We arrived at the golf center in record time. We parked and walked up the ramp into the clubhouse. Jimmy greeted us with a smile and winked at me when he saw Claire. "Want me to call Joe on the squawk box?"

"No, that's quite all right, we'll just head down there if that's OK."

Jimmy nodded. "Sure!"

We walked behind the main tee to the barn. Otter was there under his pine tree snoozing away. He raised his head as we approached, gazed up at us, and gave us a pitiful brown-eyed look. Claire bent down to scratch him under his chin and around his ears. He lifted his paw when she stood. I couldn't tell if he was thanking her or asking for more. We walked over to the open doors of the barn and I called for Joe. There was no way he could hear me with the compressor bellowing. The air-hose was stretched a good twenty feet across the floor onto the other side of the shop. I followed it to a pair of moccasins sticking out from under the Kubota carry-all. I chuckled to myself and thought, well, she's gonna get the whole enchilada.

The compressor shut down and the place fell silent. "Joe?"

From down under we heard "Geoff, good, good, I'm glad you came. Could you hand me the grease gun on the table? Use a towel to pick it up." Claire stood in the doorway with a puzzled smile. I went over to the table with a shop towel and got the grease gun for him. I handed it down to his outstretched hand. I still couldn't see his face. "Thank you. I'll be done in a second."

Claire still hadn't followed me in. I knew what was going through her mind. Leaves had blown in from the yard. Everything was about, there were tools laid out on the tables and floor. She was beginning to get my drift about the place, just as I had a week or so ago. Two more minutes passed, then Joe crawled out from under the machine. He was a bit dirty and sweat was dripping from his brow. "Good morning," he said as he wiped his hands. We were facing away from Claire and he hadn't noticed her yet.

"I have someone who would like to meet you." We turned and as he caught sight of Claire a smile spread over his face. Claire came in. I was proud of the way she looked. She was wearing a dark green golf shirt that complemented her Irish brown eyes. She extended her hand to Joe. "Good morning, Mr. Burlington."

He didn't seem surprised. "You must be Claire."

"Yes." She beamed as warmth radiated from him, as it had a week ago.

He nodded. "Yes, very, very nice to meet you. So you got his message. I'm glad. It seems you two are on the same page now."

She smiled and said, "Yes."

"That's good, real good. I have had a wonderful week with your man. He has rejuvenated me." I was pleasantly surprised by his description of our week. I thought I was the one who was rejuvenated.

"Really?" she said.

Then Joe remarked, "I understand you're heading back to the cold north today."

"Ah no, not really," she said. "That was Geoff's original plan but..."

I interrupted. "Honey, actually, really, he's right, and we don't have much time if we're gonna make our flight."

Claire looked at me with an impish grin. "I have one more surprise. We don't have a flight today."

"But the tickets..."

"Geoff darling, I've arranged it all. I had my friend Sandy set us up on Silver Seas Cruises for a week in the Caribbean. We do have a lot of catching up to do, don't you think?"

"Of course, of course." Joe nodded in agreement.

I looked at Claire. "You *are* full of surprises! It's all arranged, then?" She nodded. "OK, I'm there," I shrugged. Then I turned to Joe. "I don't know what to say except thank you."

As he looked at me, his eyes radiated deep warmth and connectedness. "Geoff, remember, it was always in there." He pointed to my heart. "I just helped you draw it out. You have all it takes. Now go and do what you were born to do." He looked at Claire. "You've got a good man here; he really loves you."

"I know," she said.

"Take good care of each other, it's well worth the effort." His words and the fact that we had to leave caused my eyes to well up. I leaned into him and gave him a farewell shake with my right hand and a goodbye hug with my left. He returned the hug and patted me on the back as he whispered "Geoff, you have your wings; carry on."

Joe walked us out the gate. Claire reached up to give him a kiss on the cheek and whispered, "Thank you."

Both of us were reluctant to leave. We walked away hand in hand, then paused for just a moment to glance back. Joe was kneeling down stroking Otter's chest. He looked out toward us to give one last wave. It struck me at that moment that Joe had given us the keys to our future. We turned and walked away together...into the next moment of our lives.

NOTES

1 Fritjof Capra, *The Tao of Physics* (Shambhala Publications, 1975).

2 Serendip. "Proprioception: How and Why?" by Shannon Lee, 2008. http://serendip.brynmawr.edu/exchange/node/1699.

3 "Proprioception: How and Why?"

4 S.J. Anthony Demello, *One Minute Wisdom* (Doubleday Dell Publishing Group, 1986).

5 Betty Edwards, *Drawing on the Artist Within* (Simon and Schuster, 1986).

6

I whispered, 'I am too young,'
And then, 'I am old enough';
Wherefore I threw a penny
To find out if I might love.
'Go and love, go and love, young man,
If the lady be young and fair.'
Ah, penny, brown penny, brown penny,
I am looped in the loops of her hair.

O love is the crooked thing,
There is nobody wise enough
To find out all that is in it,
For he would be thinking of love
Till the stars had run away
And the shadows had eaten the moon.
Ah, penny, brown penny, brown penny,
One cannot begin too soon.

7 Barry Green with W. Timothy Gallwey, *The Inner Game of Music* (Doubleday, 1986).

8 Demello, *One Minute Wisdom*.

9 Ahrandati Roy, *The God of Small Things* (Random House, 1997).

10 Wayne Dyer, *The Power of Intention* (Hay House, 2010).

11 Ken Burns, *The Civil War*, Episode 1, "The Cause" (PBS, 1990).

12 Tom Morris, *True Success* (GP Putnam's Sons, 1994).

13 His Holiness the Dalai Lama and Howard C. Cutler, *The Art of Happiness: A Handbook for Living* (Riverhead Books, 1998).

PHOTOS AND SKETCHES

GB   Gary Battersby

TC2   Tom Christensen, Jr.

TC3   Thomas Christensen III

KT   Kate Tappert

FT   Freddie Tichner

EW   Elliott Wexelman

JW   Jennifer Wood

EW2   Ed Wortzman

Order more copies of

The Golf Mystic

Email completed form to garobattersby@gmail.com,
or mail to 3909 Indian River Dr., Cocoa, FL 32927

Name _____

Address _____

City _____ State/Province _____

Zip/Postal Code _____ Phone _____

Email _____

Ship to (if different from above):

Name _____

Address _____

City _____ State/Province _____

Zip/Postal Code _____ Phone _____

Quantity ordered _____ × $24.95* = _____

*plus applicable taxes. Books ship free the same day orders are received and typically arrive within 2 to 5 days.

Credit Card type: Visa _____ MasterCard _____

Credit Card # _____ Expiry _____

Name on card _____

Signature _____

Order more copies of

The Golf Mystic

Email completed form to garobattersby@gmail.com,
or mail to 3909 Indian River Dr., Cocoa, FL 32927

Name _____

Address _____

City _____ State/Province _____

Zip/Postal Code _____ Phone _____

Email _____

Ship to (if different from above):

Name _____

Address _____

City _____ State/Province _____

Zip/Postal Code _____ Phone _____

Quantity ordered _____ × $24.95* = _____

*plus applicable taxes. Books ship free the same day orders are received and
typically arrive within 2 to 5 days.

Credit Card type: Visa _____ MasterCard _____

Credit Card # _____ Expiry _____

Name on card _____

Signature _____

ABOUT THE AUTHOR

Gary Battersby fell in love with the game of golf and the art of teaching the swing at the early age of nine. Initially, he caddied and worked on maintenance crews, in bag rooms, and on driving ranges in the Midwest region of the United States. By age fourteen he was teaching club champions and beginners alike who recognized his golfing talent and gift for communication.

Just after college, Gary was invited to work with his longtime friend and Hall of Fame teacher Bob Toski. Since 1982 they have conducted clinics together in America and Japan. In 1989, they developed the first Golf Learning Center in America at their South Florida location. The Toski Battersby Golf Learning Center has been consistently ranked by *Golf Digest* as a top 10 teaching facility. Gary has also developed the highly successful PathfinderPlus system of self-coaching.

Gary has many other interests. He has had a special love for music since he was young, playing the violin and performing music ranging from bluegrass to classical in ensembles and community orchestras. Gary; his wife, Ali; and two dogs, Luke and Samme, divide their time between their home in Boca Raton, Florida, and their farm in the mountains of northwestern North Carolina.

CPSIA information can be obtained at www.ICGtesting.com
Printed in the USA
BVOW09s1140060515

399178BV00004B/88/P